SINISTER URGE

SINISTER URGE

THE LIFE AND TIMES OF ROB ZOMBIE

JOEL McIVER

Backbeat Books

An Imprint of Hal Leonard Corporation

Published in 2015 by Backbeat Books
An Imprint of Hal Leonard Corporation
7777 West Bluemound Road
Milwaukee, WI 53213

Trade Book Division Editorial Offices
33 Plymouth St., Montclair, NJ 07042

Book design by Tom Seabrook

Printed in the United States of America

Library of Congress Cataloging-in-Publication Data is available upon request.

ISBN 978-1-61713-616-0

www.backbeatbooks.com

This book is dedicated to
Jeff Hanneman of Slayer

Contents

FOREWORD

Rob Zombie is who I want to be when I grow up—a heavy metal musician who makes scary movies. Like Zombie, I'm a horror-movie fanatic, and I love writing horror and making metal music. Zombie's done all that and more. His many remarkable achievements both impress and entertain across the worlds of music, movies, animation, art, and elsewhere.

As a kid who once said he always "wanted to be Alice Cooper, Steven Spielberg, Bela Lugosi, and Stan Lee," Rob has become all of his heroes in one unique and original package. A multi-platinum-selling musician, film director, screenwriter, and film producer, Zombie has come a long way since being a kid from Massachusetts who released his band's first album on their own record label.

Sometime in the 1990s, I first caught Rob when he made an appearance on MTV's *Headbangers Ball*, when it was hosted by Riki Rachtman. He was drawing and painting all this rad horror artwork on the *Headbangers Ball* set. I loved the art he was making, and not long after that episode, I discovered White Zombie's heavy groove and horror-and-sex imagery.

Since then, Rob has gone solo and continued to crank out albums, movies, and cartoons. I'm convinced that there's nothing that Rob can't do: his creativity has no bounds. Moreover, he holds horror in his heart and puts on the sickest live concert, with the sickest production you'll ever see. I know, because I've been fortunate enough to see it all, from backstage and the front row.

Rob Zombie inspires me, and this book will inspire you, dear reader. His story, in the hands of Joel McIver, is a genuine win—an extremely compelling and fun ride which you'll find is definitely worth the price of admission.

Jeremy Wagner
2015

Author and musician Jeremy Wagner has written lyrics and music for several albums with his acclaimed death metal band Broken Hope. He has published fiction through St. Martin's Press and Perseus Books. Wagner's novel *The Armageddon Chord* received a Hiram Award; it was a finalist for Emerging Novelists' Novel of the Year, was recommended for a Bram Stoker Award for First Novel, and was reviewed in *Publisher's Weekly* and *Rolling Stone*.

INTRODUCTION

"Nobody knows anything about me, which is kind of good. I keep it that way. Everybody thinks that they know everything, but they don't know anything, and that's the way to be."—*Rob Zombie to Aquarian Weekly, 2012*

He's right, of course. No one really knows anything about Rob Zombie.

That's because Rob Zombie is, in spirit if not technically so, a concept rather than a man. "Rob Zombie," the label, can be applied to a universe of music, films, and visuals that ranges from the surreal to the terrifying and back again.

Rob Zombie the man is Robert Cummings, a kid from Massachusetts who has spent his first half-century absorbing and then reproducing a garish combination of horror, theater, and performance art. That's the person this book aims to portray. I'm looking at the big picture, too, so if you want tour itineraries, awards lists, album reviews, guitar models, and so on, go visit the internet. That's what it's for. I want to know what the hell Rob Zombie's art means.

This book doesn't dig into Rob's personal life, other than when it's necessary to do so in order to discuss his artistry. It doesn't seek to reveal his secrets or expose juicy stories. Frankly, there's enough juice in what this unique artist does on a professional basis. What this book does do is take a long and appreciative look at the work he's done over the last three decades and place it in context. Where does a man like Rob Zombie fit into the world in 2015? What is it about his dark, compelling art that reaches out to so many people, and what does that say about us?

Whether you appreciate Rob for his music, his films, or—as I have strived to summarize—his overall aesthetic vision, you'll enjoy this curious tale. At the end of it, you may not have learned much about the man's private life, because that is not the purpose of this book, but you'll have gained a new perspective on what his worldview means for all of us. Rob is a modern everyman: a Goethe for the modern world. The fact that he chooses to express his talents through the medium of horror makes his story even more compelling.

You will note that I've titled each chapter after a 1970s horror movie. In each case, the title is relevant to the content. I flatter myself that the man himself would appreciate this touch.

Joel McIver
2015

SINISTER URGE

ONE

It's Alive!

(1965-84)

It's funny to think how life reflects art, just as much as the other way round.

Robert Bartleh Cummings, later Rob Zombie, the most renowned horror auteur of his generation, began his life as part of that horror-movie staple: the all-American family. The kind of family that you see at the start of all the best slasher films, whose contented daily routines occupy the opening scenes and set up the first act for some carnage courtesy of a demonic villain like Freddy Krueger or Jason Voorhees . . . or Michael Myers, star of this story a few chapters down the line.

Zombie, as we'll refer to him from this point on even though he remained Rob Cummings for another twenty years or so, was born on January 12, 1965, in the town of Haverhill in Massachusetts, the son of Robert, a furniture upholsterer, and Louise, a housewife. His younger brother Michael arrived in 1968. In an interview with the *Boston Globe*, the boys' mother recalled them as being quiet, well-behaved fellows who enjoyed painting, drawing, science fiction, and cheesy TV programs—in particular *Star Trek*. "They were big Trekkie fans," said Louise, who drove her sons to *Star Trek* conventions in Philadelphia and New York. "They were so much alike."

Later, when the elder and younger Cummings had morphed into the Devil's own progeny as Rob Zombie and Spider One, Louise remembered the boys' relatively sedate upbringing and chuckled, "I'm tired of people saying, 'What do they do for Thanksgiving, eat out of skulls?' I used to kid people and tell them I was Satan's mother. But now I don't tell so many people."

Haverhill doesn't sound like much fun, to hear the Cummings brothers talk about it. "It's full of cemeteries. It's boring. When you're a kid, you don't realize it. It's only when you go back that you realize how bad it is," huffed the elder sibling. "You walk down the streets at night, and no one's around. You could do anything you wanted, and no one would notice."

Education didn't go down too well either, apart from the occasional creative endeavor. It wasn't that the Cummings kids weren't clever or artistic: Zombie eventually did well enough to join the National Honor Society, the organization for hardworking and/ or dominant students that has chapters in many American schools. But in essence he was bored, rebellious, and irritated by social conventions, even becoming a vegetarian in his teens after watching a TV documentary about slaughterhouses. (Assuming this occurred at some point in the late 1970s or early '80s, you'll agree that he was some way ahead of the trend.)

When I interviewed him in 2011, Zombie explained, "I thought school was incredibly boring and I hated it. I couldn't sit still; I couldn't focus. I would always stay up really late at night because I wanted to watch movies on TV, so I would fall asleep in school all the time. I was dead on my feet all day long."

It's a familiar story. Frustrated with the tedium of school, our man looked elsewhere for fulfillment, and found it—luckily for him—just at a point when the golden age of American rock was in its pomp. "The time period that I discovered music," he told the writer Henry Northmore some years later, "everything was just huge. As a young, young kid, the first music I ever discovered was Alice Cooper, KISS, Queen, Blue Öyster Cult. Everything was larger than life, so it was just burnt into my brain that bands were larger than life, they weren't just regular guys playing music. That's just the way that I saw things, and I guess that never left me."

Right from the starting blocks, Zombie was looking for something out of the ordinary—a sound, and a look, that wasn't just normal. Remember, this was the 1970s, and while rock could be extreme, most of the biggest bands on the radio and TV looked pretty much like your dad. Beards, moustaches, long hair some of the time . . . but most of the time, rockers looked like accountants. Take a look at Kansas, Styx, REO Speedwagon, Boston, and indeed any of the bigger stadium bands. There's not much excitement there.

Still, live music came early to Zombie. At the age of five or six, he attended a Tiny Tim concert at Haverhill's Veterans of Foreign Wars Hall. But while he recognized "Tip-Toe Thru' the Tulips with Me," Tiny Tim's big hit from 1968, the young Zombie found the overall experience overwhelming. As he later put it, his brain simply couldn't handle it.

Zombie's other source of cultural inspiration as he grew up a bored teenager in Haverhill was the movies. Again, as with rock music, the era in which he matured was the perfect hothouse environment for anyone interested in something a little more extreme than the everyday stuff consumed by everyone else. The first movie to make a big impression on him was *King Kong*, which seemed to echo the larger-than-life, over-the-top feel of much of the rock music of the time.

In fact, the visual and aural arts blended into one for this dissatisfied kid. If it looked and sounded good, it worked for Zombie—and movies, TV, and music were all one rich stock of information. In fact, much of the music he loved came via the small screen. He loved the Monkees before he had ever heard of the Beatles, and the Banana Splits before Led Zeppelin.

An enthusiastic artist from an early age, Zombie spent endless hours drawing and painting, inspired by the imagery poured into his brain by cinema, TV, and LP sleeves—the last of which, as anyone over thirty will tell you, were true works of art in the pre-digital era. Books, too, played their part, in particular a certain true-crime classic from 1974. His mother owned a copy of *Helter Skelter*, Vincent Bugliosi and Curt Gentry's account of the Charles Manson murders, and although the more graphic images inside were censored, he wanted nothing more than to see them. This may be simply the all-encompassing interest of the average kid at work, of course, rather than anything more sinister.

Was Zombie a contented child, looking back? If you talk to him now, as I have a couple of times as a journalist, he seems very relaxed about life and his place in it—and he certainly doesn't regard his upbringing as a miserable one. He was just bored out of his mind, unable to find satisfaction in any endeavor. As a child, he would enter drawing contests at the local public library, and would often win, but he would never be satisfied with the results himself. This alarmed his teachers, as he recalled in an interview with *Rolling Stone*. "I would always get really mad whenever anybody told me something was good—nothing was ever good enough for me."

Crucially, though, the sense of wonder the young Zombie experienced when he saw a crazy TV show or a blockbuster film, or read a lurid comic book or novel, never left him, and it continues to inform his adult work to the present day. How many of us can make a similar claim? Zombie's recall is passionate when he's asked—as he frequently still is—what it was about his childhood that made his future activities so lurid in nature.

"I rcmcmbcr as a kid going to see everything from *Halloween* to *Jaws*, and I literally walked in, I didn't know anything," he told moviefreak.com in 2007. "I assumed that there was a shark in the movie, but I wasn't even sure. *Close Encounters*, *Raiders of the Lost Ark*—I had no idea what any of those [were about] . . . even *Star Wars*! I remember going to see *Star Wars*—I didn't have a fucking clue what it was. I knew it was, like, a science-fiction movie, but that was it. And then you just sit there, and you're just blown away."

"I love the movies of the '70s, the fashion, the look, the feel," he added. "And, I think it's probably because, at that point, I was at the right age to just be bombarded by it. I just remember, as a kid, every movie I went to, at that time period, just seemed mind-blowing. You could see *Jaws* [one day]; the next weekend you'd see *Close Encounters*, then you'd see *The Godfather* and *Taxi Driver*."

It wasn't all great cinema back then, of course. As in every decade, a small amount of all art in the 1970s was amazing in quality, a similar amount was terrible, and a vast swathe in between those two extremes was just average. But there was something, a difficult-to-define quality about the best films of the era that made them special, and not in the same way that the best '60s or '80s films excelled.

"What sets that decade apart for me is that those movies were made in a time where the director was key," mused Zombie. "The director was the god on set with the vision. And I think as the '80s crept in, it became more about actors and gimmicks and studios, you know. I still think the '70s was the last great time where films were being made for the sake of the film and not for the sake of the money. Even though, of course, people were always trying to make money, it seemed like art was still important."

Later, Zombie became known for his work as a horror-film director, but it's important to establish at this early stage that films famous for their gory content alone were not his primary interest. Movies in which violence was an underlying theme were much more to his taste. "Gory horror movies don't rank on the [list of] movies that I like," he explained in an interview with Carlo Cavagna at AboutFilm.com. "Good horror movies are great, but I just like good movies. I don't just watch Grade-Z garbage. That just bores me to death. So, some of my favorite movies, growing up [were] *Bonnie and Clyde*, or even a movie like *Charly*, the Cliff Robertson film, because the use of the split screens and the camera work really affected me, as a kid."

Camera work affecting a teenager? That might be seen as precocious, or just an exaggeration through rose-tinted lenses, but in fact it does seem that the mechanics of filmmaking—in other words the cinematography, the translation of the screenplay, and the actual scene-framing moves—made an impact on the teenage Zombie. His fellow director Quentin Tarantino has made a similar claim about his own youthful experiences with movies. In the case of both men, it makes sense: each expresses a deep-seated reverence toward 1970s cinema, technologically primitive though it certainly was.

Zombie would later recall that it was in the early '70s that he really became fanatical with film. Every time he turned on the TV, it seemed, a classic, game-changing, or otherwise great movie would be about to start, be it *The Great Escape* or *Willy Wonka and the Chocolate Factory*, *Frankenstein* or *The Wizard of Oz*. The '70s was the heyday of great cinema, as far as Zombie is concerned, and in hindsight it's difficult to disagree. After all, what does the current decade have to offer in comparison? *Frozen*? Please . . .

Life at the movies for Zombie and his brother occasionally blurred into reality. Their parents worked at traveling carnivals for some time during their kids' youth, which makes sense, given the vast circus of artistic creativity that emerged from the Zombie mind in later years. Of course, it sounds improbable: perhaps a bit too convenient a story for a writer chronicling Rob Zombie's history. But no, it's all true.

Carnivals (or circuses, if you prefer) are not entirely wholesome places to be. In fact, they can be terrifying and amusing at the same time. We've all seen horror films where the evil clowns leer into the camera and the fairground organ music is loud and atonal. The screams of laughter from the rollercoaster might as well be screams of fear— and that's before you even enter the ghost train or house of horrors.

"It's not the nicest world," Zombie agreed, when interviewed by *LA Weekly*. "As a kid, you get exposed to the crazier underworld of the carnival. Me and my brother, when we were very little, we'd be inside the haunted house playing all day. So, already, what people are paying money to be scared [of], we're just playing in because it's fun. We saw the inner workings behind the machines. So, yeah, I guess it was my first aesthetic glimpse at something that could be considered showbusiness on some level."

These places can be violent, too. In 1977, a riot broke out at a carnival where the Cummings family was working. Tents were set on fire by angry punters who felt they had been ripped off in some way. "Everybody's pulling out guns, and you could hear guns going off," Zombie recalled. "I remember this one guy we knew, he was telling us where to go, and some guy just ran up to him and hit him in the face with a hammer—just busted his face wide open. My parents packed up real quick, and we took off. I think at that moment, they were like, 'Okay, new plan!'" So ended Zombie's potential future career as a carnival worker, although obvious echoes of that path resound in the work he ultimately went on to do.

What does all this do to a kid's social standing? After all, being obsessed with films and rock music only make you cool to a certain degree, and even then, school kids were and are not blessed with tolerance for the geeky habits of others. "Rob and I didn't get along with too many people," said his brother Michael. "Some mornings we had to fight our way onto the school bus." No surprise there.

In fact, Zombie was the polar opposite of the sports-mad jock, although he worked his way out of that situation in due course. A temporary solution was to dig ever deeper into the screen, whether cinematic or televisual. Even back in elementary school, Zombie was a TV addict, memorizing an entire week's broadcast schedule and watching up to eight hours of programming a day.

What were the Cummings parents doing? Other things, clearly. When I asked him if his folks pressured him to do well at school, Zombie replied, "Not so much, no. Ha ha! I did graduate high school, though, because in my last couple of years I figured out an incredible scam. Essentially I shouldn't have graduated, but I realized that if I signed up for many, many art classes, I could get my grades up enough to graduate. Basically, I went to school, signed in, and then left and did other stuff all day long. I just made sure that all my artwork got turned in. I got straight 'A' grades in art and I got perfect grades for attendance, although I was never there. Nobody was paying attention, so I got away with it."

What this general lack of interest in a regular education gave Zombie was an interest in things that were different or unorthodox, and ultimately surreal. As he told *Rolling Stone*, culture in general was more mysterious back when he was younger. Had he been told that Gene Simmons or Alice Cooper was from Mars, he would have been delighted. He was greatly impressed by *Willy Wonka and the Chocolate Factory*, too, not least because he thought the film was a true story. By the time he was old enough to know otherwise, he was disappointed.

An early visit to Disneyland was another formative experience. Determined to inhabit this fantasy zone forever, he told his parents that he would never work. Not for the teenage Zombie the daily grind that most people face, although, in fairness, a lot of teenagers spout rebellious stuff along the same lines. What is more compelling is his apparently inexorable attraction toward all that is dark in life. The films played their part, of course, especially the horror movies that proliferated in the 1970s. As he later explained to the A.V. Club, he had a feeling when watching those movies that the plot was unlikely to turn out well for anyone. Zombie attributed this to directors such as Wes Craven and Tobe Hooper, both of whom were products of the Vietnam era. Movies directed by younger filmmakers, even the auteurs among them, were just not likely to have the same impact, because the mindset behind them was much less rooted in a grim reality.

On multiple occasions, Zombie has admitted that the frightening side of any art was what attracted him most, certainly in the younger years under discussion here. "I guess I need some heavy psychoanalysis," he later said, presumably with some flippancy, "but I don't know . . . just ever since I was a little kid, that's what I found exciting. If there was a horror movie on TV or a baseball game, I wouldn't even consider [which one] I was going to watch, and I don't know why. It wasn't because I thought it was cooler, or that it made me cooler. It's kind of funny, when you watch little kids, how they just instinctively gravitate toward certain things, and I don't know why. It makes no sense."

To his credit, unlike many other rock stars of his ilk, Zombie makes no attempt to mythologize his background as an explanation for his interest in darkness. After all, in today's social media–driven world, he could claim that he'd been brought up by a pack of werewolves and people would believe it. Instead, when asked, he simply states that he has no idea why he likes the grim stuff. This point needs to be labored because it's the linchpin of this book for anyone seeking to understand the source of Zombie's creativity.

We've talked a lot about Zombie's love of movies, and we've mentioned his interest in rock music, but the former appeared to outweigh the latter until he left home. Perhaps this was because the idea of actually making music, or even playing it for pleasure, wasn't prevalent in the Cummings household.

"I didn't know anyone who played an instrument, or even owned one," he remembered. "No one in my family even seemed to like music that much. I discovered music through watching the television, because most of the shows had a musical theme—like *The Monkees*, or cartoons like *The Groovy Ghoulies* or *The Archies*. It didn't matter what the goofy characters were, they always had a rock band."

TV also led Zombie to an appreciation of country music. The popular country-themed show *Hee Haw* is cited by many musicians as influential in the 1970s; hosted by singers Buck Owens and Roy Clark, it featured variety acts of varying degrees of C&W-ness.

"I always loved Buck Owens because that was the one thing I remember as a kid," Zombie recalled. "I don't ever remember my dad liking anything—not just music, anything. But he seemed to love Buck Owens [and] *Hee Haw*. . . . so yes, somehow *Hee Haw* was very influential in my life."

He also liked soul and funk music, as he explained to writer Joe Daly. "I like music that has a groove. Any kind of music. Hard rock music has always had a groove. I mean, Led Zeppelin is the grooviest fucking band ever. That's something that sort of just went away from hard rock, and I have always loved it. A lot of times, bands get scared of it, I think, because I'll see a band and they'll lock into a groove and it's so heavy and the fans are going crazy and then they shift gears and go into some kind of blast beat, and you can see the crowd kind of stop. I'm thinking, 'Dude, you had 'em! You were fucking going off! What the fuck? Calm the fuck down, you had the crowd fucking raging.' But they get scared. I dunno if they do, but it seems that way, anyway."

Among the first records Zombie remembers buying, as a kid in the early '70s, were Billy Preston's "Space Race" and the Jackson 5's "Dancing Machine." Of the latter group he told Daly, "When you watch them play that live, when they were young—insane." Elton

John was another favorite. "'Bennie and the Jets'—that was pretty groovy. I really liked Eddie Kendricks. He was great. I'm searching my mind now for all the 7-inches I had as a little kid, because I was always leaning toward stuff that was funky. Oh, the Stylistics. I had a bunch of music from the Stylistics. Earth, Wind, and Fire were pretty funky. Parliament."

Zombie put his varied taste down to the spirit of AM radio in the early '70s. "They just played everything together. You listen to KISS and Alice Cooper, then you listen to ABBA. I didn't care. I liked everything . . . if you're like, 'I only listen to metal, I only play metal and I only like metal,' then you're going dry with influences."

All this music rubbed off on Zombie, and before long he began to consider the idea of making some himself. "At some point I got a guitar," he said. "Then I did what so many people do: you find a couple of other guys with instruments and you start a band. I picked bass and my other friend picked drums. My high-school band went nowhere because we all got sick of each other."

Perhaps the reality of being in a band didn't quite match up with Zombie's inner concept of what a band should be like—big, brash, and vivid. Anyone who has jammed in a dusty rehearsal room knows that the dimensions of any group soon shrink down to the size of the least accomplished player, and this was undoubtedly made worse by Zombie's love of epic productions by the likes of KISS and Alice Cooper.

"I just thought everything was like that," he explained to writer Steven Rosen. "Like, oh, if you have a band, it's this giant crazy thing. [It's] hard to erase that from your mind . . . I mean, people want to see a fucking show and they want to be entertained. Maybe with other forms of music it's different, but with rock music and metal, that's the way it is. In my mind, that's the way it is, and that's what I've always stayed true to."

Where would anyone go to form a band like that? The answer came once the former geeky kid had become a rebellious teenager—and, finally, a free man. Graduating from his despised Haverhill High School in 1983, thanks to the cunning arts scam he mentioned earlier, Zombie wasted no time in getting the hell out of Massachusetts. At eighteen years old, he moved to New York City, then as now the essential cultural hub for anyone living east of Chicago, where he took up a place at Parsons School of Design.

His ambitions at this point were keen, if not as clearly expressed as they would be in later life. For now, all he wanted to do was get clear of Haverhill.

"When I was a kid, there were all these things I wanted to do," he recalled. "I wanted to make movies, I wanted to be in a band, I wanted to have an amusement park. You just have all these crazy ideas. You just want to do all these things, and the first thing that happens in life is everybody starts telling you why none of that will ever be possible. I never bought into that idea. I always thought, 'Why can't I do everything? Why do I have to pick one and just be happy with it?'"

On his first day in New York City, Zombie witnessed a murder. As he later recalled, "I was up in my room and I heard screaming, so I looked out of the window and saw someone being killed. Day one, and I was already involved in a murder case."

To paraphrase Zombie's beloved *Wizard of Oz*—you're not in Massachusetts any more, Rob.

TWO

HOUSE OF DARK SHADOWS

(1985–92)

Looking back at the almost indescribably fatiguing years that followed his move to New York City, Rob Zombie had an interesting take on the nature of deprivation.

"When I got to NYC, I lived so far below the poverty line, because I didn't give in and get a job at 7-Eleven," he said. "I think you can thrive in misery. Great things come out of being hungry and cold. Once you're pampered, you get lazy. I still don't do anything to pamper myself. . . . You have to have almost psychotic drive, because you're going to have years of failure. My advice: don't quit!"

Not that any of this positivity was evident in his early years in New York. Working as a bike messenger while attending Parsons School of Design—an occupation he later described as the worst job ever, one that kept him in shape but was otherwise devoid of advantages—Zombie began frequenting the legendary (and now closed) club CBGB in the East Village. A few exceptions aside, however, he wasn't impressed with what he saw. In fact, he would later state that, after a couple of years of going to shows at the venue, he couldn't believe how bad the bands he saw there were.

Zombie soon took refuge in the cinema, usually choosing to see films of the grittier persuasion. Asked by the excellent horror film site EatMyBrains.com about his favorite horror movies, he admitted that they were all "pretty typical," nominating *Dawn of the Dead* as a favorite and recalling that, at the time, he thought that it was as extreme as movies could get. However, on watching the truly mind-blowing *Cannibal Holocaust* in a low-rent movie theater on 42nd Street in New York, he swiftly changed his mind.

Let's reiterate, however, that gore for its own sake did not inspire Zombie as much as subtlety and emotion. "It's always about the characters," he insisted. "It's not about the blood and the guts and the gore, because that doesn't do anything for anybody." *Jaws*, for example, "could have been just some movie about a big shark, but the characters, the three characters on the ship, with Robert Shaw and Roy Scheider and Richard Dreyfuss . . . [they] were just so incredible and so believable that you were so swept up in their journey [and] you felt like you were on that boat. So, any tiny little thing was terrifying . . . the characters are what's compelling, not the violence or anything like that."

Within a year of moving to the big city, Zombie met Shauna Reynolds, who later adopted the stage name Sean Yseult. A fellow student at Parsons, Yseult had caught his attention in the school cafeteria, and he had asked her out via a friend. In 1985, the two came up with the idea of a band called White Zombie, after the 1932 horror film of the same name.

Yseult kindly provided an interview for this book. "I moved up to New York from North Carolina when I was eighteen," she recalled, "and I was asked to be in a hardcore band called Anti-Warfare. They were very short-lived—I don't know if they even played a show! I'd only been up there for a month or two when I met them, and they asked me if I'd play bass with them. I'd grown up playing piano and violin, and I figured the bass had four strings so it couldn't be too different from the violin. I said, 'If I can get a bass, I'll do it.' I don't think any people grow up thinking, 'One day I'm going to be a bass player!' People usually want to be lead singers or guitarists.

"I knew a band from Raleigh, North Carolina, called Stillborn Christians. Their bass player sold me his bass, a Global, for fifty dollars, and I took it back to New York. It didn't even have a case, so I carried it on the plane. Anti-Warfare asked me to learn 'I Don't Wanna Go Down to the Basement' by the Ramones, so I did. It wasn't rocket science compared to the violin and the piano. It was an easy instrument for me to pick up. I certainly don't consider myself an incredible bass player, but I can play anything that I want to play, and I can pick up songs by ear and play them."

Although Yseult was playing the Farfisa organ in a punk band named Life at that point, she was happy to switch instruments. "I met Rob, and at that point I had a guitar, which I was going to try to learn. We both wanted to start a band, so we started one together. We started dating and he was like, 'It's gonna take you too long to play guitar: we need a really good guitarist. You play bass!' Ha-ha! I was like, 'Okay!' I think bass players are generally the most accommodating person in the band: bands need a bass player, and somebody's got to do it. We just want to help out!"

Life's guitarist, Paul "Ena" Kostabi, and a drummer, Peter Landau, were also recruited to play alongside Zombie and Yseult in the new band.

Landau also recalled his brief stay in White Zombie for this book. "I went to Parsons School of Design with Sean," he began. "Like most art schools, everybody there was either starting a band or in a band already. I hadn't played any instruments before I got there, but some friends of mine needed a drummer and I said, 'Sure, I can do that!' I couldn't do it very well, but I did it well enough for my first band, which then broke up.

"Then Sean said, 'My boyfriend and I are doing a band, do you want to play with us?' Sean and I were both into the same kind of music, like Flipper and stuff like that, so I said sure, and that's how I met Rob. He was a big comic-book guy, and he was into horror movies, and so was I, so I got along really well with him. Paul Kostabi, who was playing guitar at the time, was a nice guy too.

"We would practice in this dingy little studio on the Lower East Side, but I never really committed to White Zombie, because the singer from my first band—who was also my girlfriend—and I were trying to get another band together, called Da Willys. No one outside New York has heard of us, but we were on some compilation called *Hard and Heavy* on a video magazine back in the mid-'80s. We were just a kind of drunken blues-punk band. I liked the White Zombie guys, but I thought they were too metal! What the hell, I was just a kid . . ."

Asked what kind of person Rob Zombie was in 1985, Landau explained, "Rob was really driven, and really focused: he had a great work ethic and he wasn't really into drugs and alcohol, like everybody else was back then. He knew what he wanted: he basically told me the drumbeats, like he would tell everybody their musical parts. He would hum them to us. He had a real musical vision."

Original songs came together slowly, with the quartet bashing out riffs in a run-down practice room and using cheap equipment in the manner of student bands since time immemorial. None of them were over-burdened with experience when it came to making music, with Kostabi and Yseult not even bothering to tune to E, as is standard. As a result, the guitarist and bassist simply tuned to one another, meaning that songs in any given practice session would meander up and down between keys.

"In the early White Zombie days," Yseult recalled, "when we were pressing our own 7-inch singles and playing in the basement, neither me nor the guitarist had a tuner, so our strings would get looser and looser because we'd just tune to each other. When we went out on tour, people would say, 'My God! What do you guys tune to?' and we'd say, 'Each other!' We had no idea. Who knows what the hell we were tuned to? That helped to accidentally create our sound."

Asked how the songs coalesced in the early days, she explained, "I wrote a lot of the riffs, so I played a lot of the guitar lines on the bass. When I wrote, I was thinking more like a guitar player. Rob rarely wrote riffs but he would orchestrate the songs. I'd say, 'I've got this riff,' and he would say, 'That's good,' or 'That sucks, let's do something else.' The guitarist and I would take him what we'd written, and we'd piece the songs together with Rob. Lyrics were always written in the studio."

Take a listen to White Zombie's first EP, a self-released effort that came out in November 1985 on the band's own label, Silent Explosion. It's fair to say that this ultimately successful band came from humble beginnings. It's called *Gods on Voodoo Moon* and is occasionally referred to as a single rather than an EP, although the difference barely matters this many years later. "Gentleman

Junkie," "King of Souls," "Tales from the Scarecrow Man," "Cat's Eye Resurrection," "Black Friday," and "Dead or Alive" are the songs, delivered chaotically and in lo-fi quality by Zombie (who was calling himself Rob Straker at this stage) and his band—but not without musical skill. What stands out most on listening to these songs is the air of rebellious nihilism that infuses them, largely because of Zombie's yelled, atonal vocals and the barely-in-tune riffs beneath them.

Zombie wasn't exactly setting out to make pop music, it seems. His primary motivation in setting up a band in the first place was simply to show the cozy New York art-rock scene that surrounded him that he could do it—that and to have some fun, since his studies at Parsons weren't generally to his taste.

"My main influence in starting to make music was the fact that I was going to a lot of awful shows, paying money to see bands that were incredibly horrible," he explained. "It had an any-idiot-can-do-this vibe to it, you know? I mean, I wasn't hating everything I saw, but I wanted to make music that I would really enjoy. To just entertain myself, basically."

In addition, Zombie and his band knew that a memorable stage show was essential. In his specific case, you only need to look back at his formative influences to see where that came from. At the time, glam-rock along the lines of Twisted Sister was popular, but the bands concerned still lacked the dynamism he was hoping for. As for art-rock—or "noise-rock," as the music was often labeled—those groups offered no performance energy at all, yet expect the audience to cheer their every move.

It's interesting to consider with hindsight that a line was drawn between "alternative music" (as no one called art-rock and post-punk in the 1980s) and heavy metal, when the latter was clearly the more extroverted in terms of stage production. To clarify, metal at the time was not the multi-stranded genre it is today. In 1985, you essentially had "old" metal bands like Black Sabbath, Motörhead, and Judas Priest; rock bands like Van Halen, who more or less slipped into the metal category; newish bona-fide metal bands like Iron Maiden; and a whole lot of L.A.–style glam-influenced nonsense, from Bon Jovi to Mötley Crüe on down. The really exciting stuff was the new wave of thrash metal from Oakland and the Bay Area, primarily courtesy of Metallica and Exodus, although the odd Los Angeles band such as Slayer was beginning to make a major impact by '85.

None of this really resembled the music that White Zombie were putting out, however, and there was no concrete reason why they should emulate any of these other bands. They were students of fine art, after all, with a broader appreciation of music than, say, the relatively simple British biker-metal that was influencing the Bay Area thrashers at the time. Punk was more White Zombie's thing, and indeed the songs on *Gods on Voodoo Moon* do sound as if they've been bashed out by a bunch of unruly garage kids.

"We were never a straight-ahead band," Zombie mused, two decades later, when I asked him how White Zombie fit in back in the early days. "Even when we were in the art-rock scene, we were metal, because we all had long hair and we liked to head-bang and jump around, which none of those bands did. Then, when we moved into the metal scene we were too weird, because we had beards and dreadlocks and because of the way we dressed. We got gigs opening for other bands like Danzig and Anthrax and Megadeth, and the crowds were looking at us like, 'What the fuck is this?'

"Almost all the metal bands had the Metallica look—skinny

black jeans and whatever—and we looked like a bunch of freaks, so we never really fit in. And then when grunge hit, we were too metal to be grunge and not alternative enough to be alternative! We had to forge our own scene, but I kinda liked it in a way, because I never wanted to be pigeonholed."

A mere 300 vinyl copies of *Gods on Voodoo Moon* were pressed, the majority of which were never sold. Why? Because no one gave a damn about White Zombie—but also because Zombie himself didn't rate it highly and made little effort to sell it. The band members were a bunch of students whose sound could be heard from dozens of other acts in New York at the time. They also never played live, which meant that the EP didn't have an outlet and that music fans had no chance to hear the songs.

This clearly had to change, but first came a slight reshuffle in the band. As drummer Landau recalled, "I don't think Rob was very happy with the first single. We recorded it in Brooklyn or Queens, took some photos in a photo booth, and Rob put together the single. I was happy to help out, but my other band, Da Willys was taking off, so I left. It was all casual: White Zombie needed me; I helped them out, then moved on. They had their direction and I had mine."

While the split was amicable ("When I moved to California about ten years ago," Landau added, "I bumped into him and we've stayed in touch. He's still the same guy"), a drummer was required, and one was found in the form of a high-school student called Ivan de Prume, whom Yseult knew from her previous band, Life. Kostabi also departed and was replaced by Tim Jeffs, whom Zombie knew from the Parsons School of Design.

Jeffs was a mellow guy who simply wanted to jam and have some laughs, as he revealed some years later. "I just wanted to play for fun, in a band, [so] when Rob asked me to join White Zombie I said yes right away. I guess you could call it a hobby. It was so easy for me. Rob already had a drummer and a bassist, so all I had to do was show up with my guitar and I was in. We all got along really well. For me it was a hobby that included getting paid a little money after the shows."

It's interesting to note that Rob was already the prime mover behind the actual business and image of the band, even if the music came mostly from the other three. He was also never a user of substances. Jeffs explained that the band members were all drug free during his tenure; Zombie rarely even drank beer. Furthermore, he took the organization of the band very seriously, plunging into it with full commitment and creating the look and the marketing, designing the record covers, naming all the songs, and even coming up with the record label's name.

The new lineup finally played their first live show on April 28, 1986, at CBGB. Onstage, the group were energetic, if not quite the live behemoth they would later become. Jeffs recalled that later shows occasionally involved the inadvertent destruction of equipment, although it's unlikely that any deliberate, all-out smashing of gear took place. White Zombie was a band that looked and sounded like rock 'n' roll outlaws . . . but, in reality, business was beginning to take precedence.

Now starting to build a profile, White Zombie released a two-track single, "Pig Heaven" / "Slaughter the Grey," in May 1986. Although the quality of the recording was better, thanks to the facilities at 6/8 Studios on Houston St and Bleecker Street, and Zombie's vocals appeared at a less obnoxious level than they had been on *Gods on Voodoo Moon*, the single failed to attract many listeners. What was a band to do?

23

Giving up appeared not to be an option, although that was aided no doubt by a slight change in Rob Zombie's commercial fortunes. Moving on from his glittering career as a bike courier, he swung himself a role—albeit a lowly one—in the TV industry, as a production assistant on the CBS kid's show *Pee-wee's Playhouse*. For those who don't remember it, *Pee-wee's Playhouse* was a mildly amusing variety show aimed at pre-teens and hosted by the entertainer Paul "Pee-wee Herman" Reubens, a curious fellow who later endured a series of unpleasant public revelations and legal cases related to his private life.

"I worked on the first season," said Zombie, in an interview with filmmaker Mick Garris. "I was working at this place called Broadcast Arts, which made TV commercials. They were known for being the funky, hip new place: they did Twizzlers commercials and things like that, and then one day they said, 'We're going to do this thing with Pee-wee Herman.' It's funny, because no one there seemed to know who Pee-wee Herman was."

"It was a cool job to have," he told *Westword*. "It was everything from delivering stuff to doing little crap work around the set. I don't even know if I was a PA. Whatever is just below a PA. I'm not even sure it counts as below a PA, but that was my job. Lowest rung on the ladder. It was cool, and I liked it." Besides Herman, the cast included sometime *Saturday Night Live* comedian Phil Hartman, while William Marshall, who played the 1972 exploitation character Blacula in the film of the same name, was the King of Cartoons. "There were all kinds of people I really liked on the show. So it was pretty exciting."

◆

By 1987, Jeffs had been replaced in White Zombie by a guitarist called Tom Guay, nicknamed Tom Five, apparently because he had the ability to sound like five guitarists at the same time. He was clearly a musician of more serious caliber than his predecessors. A third EP, this time a bona-fide mini-album called *Psycho-Head Blowout*, was released in May. Check out the cover: you'll see Rob Zombie dressed like a cross between Captain Jack Sparrow from the *Pirates of the Caribbean* film franchise and an old man from the north of England. That cardigan is hilarious.

The music, however, is a little more serious. Thanks to Tom Five's prowess as a guitar player, the songs are both tighter and heavier. Zombie's voice is a little lower than the eldritch shriek that marred the previous White Zombie releases, while the Yseult/de Prume rhythm section is locked tight and placed high in the mix. In other words, this is a body of work that stands up (relatively) well to constructive criticism, close to three decades after its release.

Life was still a struggle for White Zombie at this point. Noise-rock, art-rock; whatever you wanted to call it, it was a useful niche for the band to occupy in the late 1980s, but bigger fish moved in that particular pond, namely Sonic Youth, whose records from the era outclassed and outperformed anything that Rob Zombie and his crew had released to date. The problem was simply that he and his band didn't really fit into any of the categories so beloved by music writers. The "Riot Grrrl" scene might have welcomed them in a few years later, thanks to the presence of Sean Yseult; grunge might have opened its arms to them in the early 1990s. Alternative rock as we came to understand it around 1992 was still a crucial four or five years off in the future.

"We were a bunch of people who could only play our instruments a bit," said Zombie, "and like any band, the members would change every five minutes. That's just the way it goes. We were always serious, but it took a couple of years until anyone even remotely gave a shit at all, and I mean on a really tiny level. There was a New York scene that White Zombie got connected to . . . it was cool, we felt like we had a tiny home, at CBGBs anyway."

A turning point—the first of many in White Zombie's career—came in August 1987 with the recording of the band's first full-length album, *Soul-Crusher*. Released in November on Silent Explosion, but—crucially—picked up by the Caroline label for reissue the following year, the album marked the first time that large numbers of people began paying attention to White Zombie.

Soul-Crusher was engineered and produced by Wharton Tiers at Fun City Studios, and this, too, is a crucial point. Tiers, known for his work with Sonic Youth and fellow art-rockers Pussy Galore, gave the band-members much-needed direction when it came to the sound and performance of the tracks. Although the music is still some way from the evolved modern metal that would typify the next two White Zombie albums, the crunch of the guitars and the improved precision of the vocal point clearly to the path ahead.

The album begins with "Ratmouth," a sneering punk-rock dash through primal, staccato riffs, before "Shack of Hate," a powerful track with layers of chaotic guitar and vocal. Tom Five's playing, involving several often-dissonant strata of sound, keeps the overall feel messy, even if the rhythm section remains fairly professional. After this opening one-two, "Drowning the Colossus" drags the listener into slowed-down doom metal territory, while "Crow III" is pure groove of the kind that Kyuss and other desert-rockers of their ilk would make famous in the same decade. "Die Zombie Die" is less compelling, based on a hollow bass riff from Yseult and too much whined vocalizing, but "Skin" is more focused, offering synchronized heaviness to complement Zombie's still uncomfortably nasal vocal performance.

It's a fairly heavy album up to this point, with the only hint of the noise roots that had plagued the band evident in some of the more extravagant guitar overdubs. "Truck on Fire" and "Future Shock" offer up a barrage of low-down, stomach-churning bass, while "Scum Kill" builds from a garage-rock intro to a moderately gripping clutch of guitar lines that present a more coherent whole than can be found elsewhere on the album. Finally there's "Diamond Ass," perhaps the best song on *Soul-Crusher*, based as it is upon a doom-laden descending riff and screams rather than the usual irritating wail.

Is *Soul-Crusher* a heavy metal record? At least partly. Those riffs are too heavy to avoid the classification. The old noise-rock label may have been unjustified anyway, as Zombie explained in *Creem Presents: Thrash Metal*, not long after the album was released.

"We just got called a noise band because we had such shitty equipment," he protested. "It was like playing through cheap stereo speakers. It's so funny, because in New York, no one will admit they're a noise band, even those who know they are. But when you get outta the city, everyone's dying to be called a noise band. They all think it's this really swingin' scene."

The album's influence ran deep for an indie release. None other than Kurt Cobain of Nirvana included "Ratmouth" in a list of his favorite songs in his diary, published posthumously in 2002 as *Journals*. The press gave it a cautious thumbs-up for the most part, especially in the United Kingdom, where the weekly music magazines were keenly attuned to American rock of the alternative persuasion:

it was this focus that led them to give Nirvana so much attention in the early 1990s.

One notable review came from the UK's *Melody Maker*, for whom David Stubbs wrote, "[White Zombie's] hallmark is a rather neat, hollowed out psychedelic guitar noise that cuts diagonal swaths through the thrashscape like the wind rushing through a kitchen. I'm reminded once again that if White Zombie were British, they would be writing overrated football chants for the edification of journalists of other music papers, before being consigned to obscurity after a three-week rock life of urinating for the benefit of paparazzi photographers and chasing bimbos 'round ligs. . . . But there is still a pocket of soiled but unspoiled air in America where a certain kind of thrash moronicism can sustain its good name. This is more Jackson Pollock than vomit stain, and let's have more."

Tom Five was replaced by John Ricci after the release of *Soul-Crusher*, but not even another lineup change could derail White Zombie now. After all, no less a personage than Iggy Pop had mentioned the album as one of his favorites of 1988 in the "Readers and Critics Poll" for *Rolling Stone* that year. More live dates followed when the musicians could get time off work, which for Yseult and Zombie meant graphic design at the cheesier end of the magazine publishing industry.

Yseult takes up the story. "I'd been in school for photography and design, and I'd been working three jobs at the same time to get by. I worked in a Xerox store, where we did photo reproduction. I would sneak a lot of record artwork and flyers in there and get it done for free. But when I graduated I went out and took the first job I was offered, because I had purple and black dreadlocks and

I didn't think anyone was going to hire me! So I walked into this place and it was a nice design studio, and the woman liked my portfolio. Then she said, 'This is all really good, but this is what we do here,' and she leaned down and picked up a huge stack of porno mags and dropped them in front of me. I started laughing and she said, 'You're not offended?' and I said, 'No, I guess not,' and I got the job.

"This was before computers, so I'd spend all day on these huge matte boards, drawing key lines and laying out type and drawing boxes for photos. The only thing that was kinda gross was that I'd have to look at the photos for half a second to see if they were portrait or landscape shaped, so I'd know how to lay them out. It was definitely not my thing, man: I'm so not into porn! But it was a job, and my boss was super cool. It started off a little above minimum wage, but then she kept giving me pretty good raises, so I was doing all right and I could pay the rent. And it was all soft-core stuff: I don't think I could have handled it if it was hardcore. There was a magazine called *Velvet*, I think, and another one called *Cinema Blue*, which had pictures in it of actresses taking their shirts off in films. They were the kind of stupid celebrity magazines which they had before the internet.

"The funniest part is that, after I'd done what I did, which was key line the photos, she needed somebody to tape the photos up on the wall, project the photos, and sketch the image on there by tracing the photo. She hired Rob to do that, and he did a great job. He did googly eyes on them and it was hilarious. That was really funny. I've always been really quiet about that job because it was a bit embarrassing! But it was a good studio, we had lots of laughs there."

Zombie laughed when I asked if he was required to utilize any serious art skills on the porno magazines. "Nah, I just had to make sure everything was straight," he said. "Nobody was really concerned with it looking pleasing, I just had to make sure that the spread-pussy shots didn't end up where the staples were. It was a great job, because I made good money. That was the last job I ever had!"

◆

Things were finally beginning to move for White Zombie. Caroline Records had requested another album, which arrived in February 1989 in the form of *Make Them Die Slowly*. Listen to this brief (less than forty minutes in duration), seven-track album today and it becomes rapidly obvious how near to a full-scale conversion to metal this former noise-rock group had undergone. The riffs are chugging and palm-muted, Metallica style, rather than strummed or groovy as before; Zombie has finally reduced the pitch of his voice to a bark from the yelps of before; and new guitarist John Ricci plays with economy and precision rather than layering track upon track in the manner of his predecessor, Tom Five. There's even a dive-bombing guitar here and there—a clear nod in the direction of the heavy metal shred style that had been so antipathetic to White Zombie's previous approach.

Note that *Make Them Die Slowly* marks the first occasion on which the name "Rob Zombie" appears on an album sleeve, meaning that we can now refer to him that way without any conflict with Cummings or Straker. People had called him Rob Zombie for so long, he said, it simply became who he was. That may sound slightly naïve, coming from a performer who was so aware of the importance of a stage image, but you can understand Zombie's point. Think of all the musicians whose names have been conflated with those of their bands: Alice Cooper, Marilyn Manson, even Dani Davey of Cradle of Filth (rechristened "Dani Filth" by the metal press).

Asked if there was a conflict between Rob Zombie the rock star and Robert Cummings the artist, the singer referenced a serious precedent, namely Alice Cooper, whose stage and private identities did not clash. Conflict did occur elsewhere, however. The *Make Them Die Slowly* album was recorded not once but three times in 1988, according to Sean Yseult, who disliked the experience. "I've tried to erase that out of my mind," she said. "We made it once, it sounded good, Rob hated it. We made it again, the songs getting more and more uptight and overwritten, and got interrupted halfway through."

Lo and behold, who should intervene but the veteran—perhaps "cult" would be a better word—musician, producer, and all-round alternative arts guru Bill Laswell, who contacted Caroline Records with an interest in working with White Zombie. His version was the one that made it to record stores and, although it sounds a bit tinny, in terms of songwriting it's a step forward. "Demonspeed," the opening cut, feels economical in its arrangement compared with the more jam-based early stuff, especially when a tempo change occurs halfway through. "Disaster Blaster" is more doomy and less of a tribute to radio metal, its slow, sludgy riff marching along satisfyingly while Zombie delivers a vocal that finally approaches a naturally low range.

"Murderworld" and "Revenge" are less gripping, sidling along in a largely forgettable manner before "Acid Flesh," with its Motörhead-style drums and a fast-picked guitar line that points directly in the direction of Heavy Metal with a capital *H* and *M*. "Power Hungry" is more metal-by-numbers, boasting double kick drums from Ivan de Prume that are more enthusiastic than expert, while "Godslayer" rounds off *Make Them Die Slowly* with a reasonably convincing stab at sinister, atmospheric rock.

Band life still wasn't easy at this point. Money was always a problem, and balancing work hours with the demands of being in an ever-growing band was becoming a nightmarish juggling act. While the relationship between Zombie and Yseult might reasonably have been expected to suffer under these conditions, in fact it held steady for quite a while.

"It wasn't weird, because we didn't know anything else," the latter recalled. "I'd never been in a band before, and neither had Rob, so it seemed normal. We were together 24/7, because he had a job where I worked, so we'd get up, got to work, then we'd go eat, and then we'd take the subway to practice and then we'd come home and start all over again! We practiced every night. The whole thing seemed very normal. It worked fine."

Immediately after the album sessions, John Ricci quit White Zombie as a result of carpal tunnel syndrome curtailing his guitar-playing activities. His place was taken by Jay Yuenger, a musician who had grown up on the Chicago hardcore scene. His band, Rights of the Accused, had released an EP as far back as 1983 and played live with bands such as Minor Threat, Flipper, and Discharge. He was a man with much to offer the Zombie cause, then, although initially he had been obliged to work hard on his guitar skills to keep up.

Yuenger joined White Zombie just before the release of *Make Them Die Slowly*, during what he later referred to as bizarre circumstances. John Ricci, his predecessor, had only been in the band for about six months, quitting after recording the new album. The first recording had been executed with Wharton Tiers at Baby Monster studios before Bill Laswell persuaded Caroline Records that he should take over. At this point, Ricci left and Zombie met Yuenger in a branch of Tower Records, leading to his recruitment into the band.

Life was still refusing to improve for White Zombie. As Yseult recalls in her 2010 book *I'm in the Band* (the title a reference to how often stagehands would refuse to believe a woman could be a heavy metal musician), the Lower East Side apartment in which she and Zombie lived had no heating or air-conditioning, but it did come with plenty of rats and cockroaches. Puddles of water and rat droppings were everywhere, not to mention the occasional hobo who would squat down for a dump on the staircase, which was also where the hookers operated. Bagels costing twenty-five cents, coffee at fifty cents and slices of pizza for a mighty seventy-five cents formed their staple diet. This situation grew even worse when White Zombie embarked on a series of European tour dates in '89, where, as Yseult recalled, a coffee cost $3.50—against each band member's daily allowance of $3.

Looking back, Zombie told writer Steven Rosen, "Well, we were kind of outcasts. We were definitely in our own world. I mean, I didn't even know what was going on in the world. We know we were like living on the Lower East Side. Everything the band appeared to be, was exactly what it was, nothing was fake. We were all living in the Lower East Side. Everybody was flat broke; no one had any money. You know sometimes we would eat the free Hare Krishna food in the parks, that they would feed to homeless people to survive . . . it was like a band of bums."

When Rosen asked him if other bands made an impact on Zombie, he laughed and replied, "I didn't even have a television, I don't know what was going on in the world. You could mention the #1 record to me, and I would have no idea who it was . . . we were so far off the map. It was like our whole existence was Lower East Side, CBGBs, that world. That's what came out of totally not comprehending what was going on, which is a good thing, I mean, it was what let the band become the band that it was going to be, because we put no restrictions on it, because we weren't even aware that there were restrictions. You know, we didn't know how things are supposed to be done, and we didn't give a shit, basically."

Still, the band had found an audience at last, and they stepped up their game accordingly, actively seeking a major-label deal in order to lift themselves out of the indie territory they'd occupied—and in which they'd only made a measly amount of progress—since 1985. This finally came after the release of an EP, *God of Thunder*, later in 1989, produced by a friend called Daniel Rey.

The *God of Thunder* EP featured a photo of White Zombie plus an unidentified goon in KISS singer Gene Simmons's makeup. It emerged that Rob Zombie had dreamed up the idea of irritating Simmons—famously protective of any KISS trademark—to the point where legal action would bring White Zombie some much-needed publicity. In the event, nothing happened, but Simmons was certainly aware of it, and he didn't forget about it. Almost two decades later, he ran into Zombie backstage at the inaugural VH1 Rock Honors event, at which KISS were among the bands celebrated, and reminded him of the photograph. "I thought it was funny that after all those years that he could even remember that we did that," Zombie told Rosen. "I don't even remember that we did that!"

White Zombie went on to play shows after the release of *God of Thunder*, one of which impressed Geffen Records A&R executive Michael Alago, who had become well-known after signing Metallica to Geffen four years previously. In 1990, Alago arranged for Geffen to fund a White Zombie demo, produced by J. G. Thirlwell, the maverick Australian musician behind many projects but best known for albums released under variations of the Foetus name. This led directly to the offer of a deal by Geffen.

Pretty much every major record company had turned White Zombie down before this happened, remembered Zombie. He was in talks with RCA at the time, who had recently signed the bands Raging Slab and Circus of Power, both of whom were friends with White Zombie. Geffen was where really wanted to be, however, simply because its roster was among the cooler artists lists in metal at the time.

It emerged much later that J. G. Thirlwell had been keen to produce White Zombie's album and not just the demo, but for reasons that remain unclear, this never happened. Speaking to Phil Freeman at the *Wire*, Thirlwell put much of this down to miscommunication. "I know I could have [got] a much better performance out of Rob. I think I was more in tune with it, with what they were doing, you know. But they were pretty amazing when they started out. We became friends and then Geffen started sniffing around, so we did a lot of pre-production and finally we recorded the demos in Rhode Island and mixed them down here in Long Island City. They . . . turned out great. I should have done that album. I'll notch that up to stupid mistakes."

Whatever those mistakes were, they led directly to White Zombie making their major-label debut album with Andy Wallace as the producer. Then an up-and-coming rock and metal console-tweaker, Wallace had engineered and mixed a whole slew of important albums, from the Cult to Sepultura, including the small matter of Nirvana's *Nevermind*, probably the 1990s' most culturally significant album. However, he had only operated as the lead producer on three albums to date, by the Front, Slayer, and the Rollins Band, and he was champing at the bit to see what he could do with White Zombie, an act whose imagery and use of electronic elements made them rather different to the bands he had worked with before. The sessions took place in May 1991 at 3-2-1 Studios in New York City and resulted in an album that represented a genuine turning point: *La Sexorcisto: Devil Music, Volume 1.*

Before the album's release, on March 17, 1992, White Zombie continued to play live. Asked by *In Your Eye* how the recent European and American tours had been set up, Yuenger explained that the band had used a low-level Dutch touring company called Paper Clip. The shows were as frenetic as ever, according to the late Gidget Gein (real name Brad Stewart), then the bass player for the band Marilyn Manson, who were new on the scene time and appeared as White Zombie's opening act. A couple of songs into a show in Tampa, Florida, Gein jumped up and hit his head on a monitor at the front of the stage.

"I was bangin' my head and swingin' my hair around and blood was flying everywhere," Gein recalled, seemingly in one breath, "and the people in the crowd all thought it was part of the show or whatever . . . my sound guy was trying to grab me to get me offstage and he looked at my head and told me I had to get offstage, but I was like, 'No, no, no, I've gotta play,' so I played like the whole show and afterwards I passed out from massive blood loss."

La Sexorcisto arrived just as heavy metal was changing its public face, rapidly and permanently. For at least five years before this sea change, glam and thrash had divided the metal scene pretty much equally, in America anyway: you could be on one side or the other, but not both, and perhaps people were sick of this state of affairs.

In 1991 and '92, three seminal metal albums were released, beginning with Metallica's "Black Album," their eponymous fifth record. Nirvana also released their second album, *Nevermind*, and the Red Hot Chili Peppers issued their fifth, *Blood Sugar Sex Magik*. Heavy enough to appeal to head-bangers, melodic enough to attract non-metal fans and catchy enough so that the postman could whistle them on his way up your garden path, the songs on these two game-changing records completely redefined the shape of heavy music.

The Chilis' brand of clean-cut, funk-laden rock had been on its way for a while, now we come to think of it. In their early days, RHCP were a ferocious band, delivering amped-up, punk-influenced funk in L.A. clubs and crossing over to the metal scene with ease. Competitors with a broadly similar sound, notably Faith No More but also lesser-known acts such as Living Colour, Infectious Grooves, and 24-7 Spyz, had been assisting in the rise of funk-metal, but when the Chilis recruited über-producer Rick Rubin to tweak the faders on *Blood Sugar Sex Magik*, millions of new fans came their way faster than you could say, "Nice royalty check, Anthony."

Then there was Pantera. Although groove was clearly in the hearts of Phil Anselmo and his merry Texan men, their early influences included Megadeth and Slayer, and you could hear this in the songs "Rise" and "Fucking Hostile" from the band's classic 1992 album *Vulgar Display of Power*. A couple of years later, Machine Head emerged with *Burn My Eyes*, also a groove-metal album but one with the occasional fast beat—specifically in the pulverizing "Blood for Blood"—to quicken thrashers' pulse rates. Both bands continued in this direction into the mid-'90s, with Pantera delivering the amazing "Strength Beyond Strength" on 1994's *Far Beyond Driven* and Machine Head thrashing it up on "Struck a Nerve" on *The More Things Change . . .* three years after that.

The "Black Album" had been so huge that the songwriters in pretty much every other thrash metal band around decided to try and bite off a chunk of Metallica's mainstream success for themselves. Megadeth, Testament, and Anthrax all slowed their songs' tempos right down, leaving old-school fans feeling not a little betrayed. The sole exception to this unwelcome rule—certainly among bands operating at any significant commercial level—was Slayer, who deserve enormous recognition for one simple thing: they didn't slow their songs down. Their 1994 album *Divine Intervention* may have sounded a bit wonky, thanks to the various producers who tinkered with it, but the songs were brutal, evil, and above all fast.

The general tendency, though, was for the thrash metal bands of yore to attempt a radio-friendly direction or, failing that, to simply split up. Exodus, Forbidden, Vio-Lence, Flotsam And Jetsam, Sodom, Dark Angel, Destruction, Nuclear Assault, Onslaught, Death Angel, and a bunch of other bands either vanished or were reduced to a shadow of their former selves. Kreator went goth. Sepultura went groove. Thrash metal was, to put it bluntly, yesterday's news.

The bigger picture, now that we're looking back at this era with the benefit of twenty years' hindsight, is that heavy metal was simply repositioning itself. Traumatic as it felt at the time, thrash metal was not going anywhere: it just downsized for a while, replaced superficially by other forms of heavy music. By 1994, Korn had arrived, bringing their down-tuned groove sound to the masses and selling truckloads of CDs in doing so. Chugging, solid riffs replaced fast crunchy ones in the affections of a new, younger generation of metal kids and lo, the nu-metal sound was born.

Once nu-metal had taken a foothold, it was tenacious. Korn went multi-platinum while thrash fans sulked. Coal Chamber followed. Deftones arrived. Limp Bizkit emerged. When Slipknot smashed their way into the charts in 1999, the war of nu-metal versus thrash metal was so definitively decided in favor of the boiler suits and masks that the very word "thrash" seemed laughably old-hat.

You can see where White Zombie fit in. Not a metal band for their first few releases but very much one by the time the turning point came, they gauged the moment perfectly, slipped seamlessly into the chaos—and never looked back.

◆

These were the good times; the myth of the major-label deal had come home to roost. But while White Zombie may or may not have been poised for stardom, at this point the band members were still flat broke. Of course, the deal was still a great thing to have, as Yuenger later noted. "We were interested in signing to a major so that we could have some source of income, and . . . to know that your records are in stores. You'd be amazed at the number of times we'd go into a town and people would go, 'Well, I came to see you because you're from New York City, but I never heard one of your records. I can't find 'em.' That was especially true in Europe. There were whole countries like that. We'd play Yugoslavia and the kids only came because they knew we were this metal-type band from New York City."

Being relatively new to White Zombie and yet witnessing the band go through their biggest change yet, Yuenger must have found the period from 1991 to '92 a surreal experience. He had a career behind him of sorts, something that the rest of the band lacked (aside from Yseult, who had gained her fine arts degree from Parsons after the others dropped out). His prospects were scarcely optimistic, after all.

"Even though we were signed to a major label, we were still broke and touring in a van and playing clubs to basically nobody," Zombie sighed, in an interview with the author. "It wasn't until we had a hit with *La Sexorcisto* that we felt like we were a success. Before that, no one gave a shit: that album changed everything, almost overnight."

Asked to sum up the defining points of White Zombie's career, he observed, "When you start a band, you're just hoping to find any four people you can get in a room and [play] with. You're not worried about anything other than that. It seemed like the band finally solidified into the unit that it was on the *Soul-Crusher* record—that was the pinnacle of what we were doing at that moment in time. And then it changed again, and solidified into what it was with *Sexorcisto*. That's what I thought. The band really had two different lives. *Soul-Crusher* was as far as we could take [that] sort of New York underground insanity, and *Sexorcisto* was the beginning of taking White Zombie out to the world's face. That's really what was obvious to me."

For now, White Zombie needed to relocate to survive. The bills were just too high in New York City. Sean Yseult was the one who came up with a solution. "When we finally got signed to Geffen," she recalled, "we didn't get serious advances from them: it all went toward making the record. We did have a little per diem so we could eat during the making of the record, but we had to quit our jobs for six weeks to go in and record with Andy Wallace. We'd left to go on tour before that, which was cool because our boss was okay with that—but this time she warned us that this time was the last time, so we couldn't go back to our jobs afterward.

"We were pretty much broke, so our A&R guy, Michael Alago, got Geffen to give us $5,000. Now, five grand in NYC between four people doesn't go far. I went to L.A. to visit our friend Daniel Rey, who had produced the *God of Thunder* EP. It was much cheaper out there, and also our label was there too, so—long story short—I convinced the band that we needed to move out to L.A. if we were going to make this $5,000 last. We packed up the van like the Beverly Hillbillies and piled in and drove all the way across the country to L.A. It was the best thing we ever did, because we found out later that they were going to drop us, because Michael quit Geffen and went back to Elektra, where he had signed Metallica. If we hadn't moved to L.A. and become friends with everyone at the label, they would have dropped us.

"So we got an apartment for under $1,000 a month. Rob and I both had a little money saved from our job, but not much, and Jay was working at Wacko, a cool art gallery kind of place. Ivan was a man-with-a-van kind of guy, he did moving jobs, and Rob and I just got by on the pennies we'd saved for a few more months until the record came out. Then we put everything in storage, because we couldn't even afford to keep one apartment between the four of us. We made it through, but we were at Geffen every day, working on the packaging and the promo and publicity. We finally got on the road and we stayed there for two and a half years straight, until we could afford to not be on the road!"

Why do bands stay on tour for so long? One: the money. Two: because it means you don't have to get a normal job. Three, and most crucial of all: because promoters and/or venue owners ask you to come and play. Why do they ask you to come and play in their clubs? Because they know people will buy tickets to see you play and then spend money on food and beer. Why do people do that? Because your music is good—and that, finally, is what happened with White Zombie. *La Sexorcisto* was a full-evolved album of accessible rock/metal tunes with an interesting electronic edge and a fascination with the darker side of life that a lot of music fans of a certain taste and demographic liked.

A whole stack of sampled dialogue and sound effects from various sources litter the album's fourteen tracks, some chilling, most cheesy, all fairly amusing. The first song, "Welcome to Planet Motherfucker / Psychoholic Slag," begins with a barrage of explosive background noise and ambient destruction, before lines from the 1965 film *Faster, Pussycat! Kill! Kill!* (a movie whose entire aesthetic reflects that of White Zombie) appear, as well as dialogue from *The Mummy* (1932) and the legendary 1978 zombie flick *Dawn of the Dead*. By comparison with White Zombie's earlier material, the music is the straightest heavy metal imaginable. The bass—treble-heavy in the way that later became a trademark on Pantera's early albums—underpins a simple guitar groove overlaid with Rob Zombie's roared vocals, themselves the most obvious sign of evolution in the White Zombie sound.

"Knuckle Duster (Radio 1-A)," the second track, is twenty-four seconds of radio-style interference and mixed dialogue that leads into White Zombie's first bona-fide hit, "Thunder Kiss '65," which was released as a single and became a medium-sized success on the US Mainstream Rock chart, making #14 on its third release. The song also received a Grammy nomination for "Best Metal Performance" of 1993, a startling development for a band who—until comparatively recently—had been making resolutely uncommercial music.

Asked how the samples became a signature part of White Zombie's sound, Zombie explained, "It was just something I always wanted to do. I didn't even know how you'd do it, almost. I mean, we were doing stuff in such a primitive way, like miking a tape recorder and playing a tape; we were so green. We didn't even have equipment; when we got our equipment to play shows, we would steal stuff. I remember breaking into a club, stealing amplifiers. We didn't have anything, no money.

"The only person I was really aware of who is doing that sort of thing was Jim Thirlwell with the Foetus records. We were friends with him, and he actually produced the first demo. So I guess he was the only person I knew of doing that type of thing. I'm sure there were other people, but I was not really aware of them . . . Ministry maybe. I didn't even know who Ministry were at that point. I remember somebody mentioned them, I thought I remembered them as being this English disco band back then. I didn't know who they were. It wasn't until like [Ministry's breakthrough album] *Psalm 69* that someone played it for me. I remember people saying, oh it's really heavy . . . I knew the few things I liked, and kind of ignored everything else. I like the Cramps, I like Van Halen, I like Black Sabbath, I like Alice Cooper, I like the Birthday Party. I like these sorts of things, and other things, I just was oblivious to. I had my box of like ten cassettes, and that's what I listened to, when I was riding my bike, delivering packages."

Looking back at these innocent times, Zombie remarked, "We were young musicians just learning how to do everything, how to play, and how to be in a band. But, that was sort of the beauty of it anyway. You don't know the rules, so you unknowingly end up breaking all the rules." For Zombie, playing live has always held far more appeal than recording, which he found "kind of a drag." How an audience responded to a song would also have a big impact on that song's future. "When they really like a song, it makes it great. So 'Thunder Kiss' was always a great song for me. It was our real breakthrough and it was our most normal song—a song that a normal person might enjoy!"

None other than Iggy Pop provides spoken-word narration on "Black Sunshine" alongside yet more lines nabbed from *Faster, Pussycat! Kill! Kill!* A truly modern-sounding metal song with clicky, dexterous bass parts in perfect unison from Yseult and Yuenger, the song powers neatly along with "MTV rotation" written all over it. Look no further than this song for evidence of what happens when the magic combination of "up-and-coming band," "commercial metal producer," and "major-label recording budget" occurs.

"Soul-Crusher," the song that had attracted Geffen A&R exec Michael Alago to White Zombie in the first place, nods partly toward to the thrash metal sound with its fast-picked guitar intro but soon settles into a mid-tempo plod. Fortunately, the second half improves after a tempo change, with a groove riff cutting in that makes the song stand out from the rest of the heavy metal pack of 1992.

"Meanwhile, behind the façade of this innocent-looking bookstore . . . " is the audio sample that kicks off "Cosmic Monsters Inc.," taken from a 1966 episode of the vintage *Batman* TV series, then still of cult appeal before the modern film franchise took hold of the mainstream. The song itself is not particularly memorable, although the super-tight synchronized playing of the band deserves kudos. Another hint at the Zombie ethos comes with the line "They come from the bowels of hell," taken from perhaps the most camp film of all time, *Plan 9 from Outer Space* (1959).

"Spiderbaby (Yeah-Yeah-Yeah)"—named after the 1968 film *Spider Baby* but laden with horror samples from *Hellbound: Hellraiser II* (1988), *The Omen* (1976), and *The Exorcist* (1973)— is unremarkable until a drastic change in its midsection. A creepy, atmospheric gathering of gently plucked, atonal chords and layers of wailing guitar take the song in an unexpected direction, to the composers' credit. Most notable is the spooky call to prayer in Arabic, taken from *The Exorcist* and obviously intended to evoke that film's otherworldly sense of unease.

"I Am Legend," yet another reference to vintage kitsch culture in the form of the 1954 dystopia novel of the same name (brief plot summary: the last man on earth fights off demonic zombies) begins with a subtle and welcome ballad-style intro. Clearly not one-trick ponies, White Zombie create here an emotional sonic landscape that contrasts starkly with the storm of riffage that follows. Another brief collage of radio static and movie dialogue titled "Knuckle Duster (Radio 2-B)" comes next, before "Thrust!," a radio-friendly groove-metal tune. With its slick chorus and bass-heavy bottom end, it's made for commercial exploitation. Yuenger's expert, Jimi Hendrix–indebted shredding in the latter half is all the more remarkable given his claims of being unable to play lead guitar a couple of years before.

After "One Big Crunch," a repeated line of "Only parts of the corpse have been removed" by some emotionless voice actor, we're into "Grindhouse (a Go-Go)," a doomy song with more focus on heaviness than groove. If it's average rather than compelling, the next song, "Starface," has more substance. Loaded with dialogue from *Star Trek*, the 1979 horror flick *Phantasm*, and other sources of more or less universal cheesiness, the song offers the best showcase yet of the band's musicianship on *La Sexorcisto*. Finally, the album signs off with the six-minute "Warp Asylum," a restrained, almost reflective assemblage of riffs and percussive vocals.

Listen to *La Sexorcisto* in one sitting and the impressions it leaves are many and disparate. Firstly, the number of movie references leads you to wonder whether Rob Zombie simply wanted to be a film director, using music as an early stepping-stone to that end. Secondly, why did a generation respond so willingly to the frankly comedic levels of retro culture ladled all over the album? Were we really so backward-looking in 1992 that anything from the 1970s or earlier seemed attractive? Whatever the case, the public loved *La Sexorcisto*, sending it to #26 on the *Billboard* 200 and all the way to #2 on the Heatseekers chart.

This album marks the point at which White Zombie went from nobodies to somebodies—and fairly significant somebodies at that. Rob Zombie commented a few years back that the band had gone through two major shifts, first with *Soul-Crusher* and then with *La Sexorcisto*, which marked "the beginning of taking White Zombie out to the world." But make no mistake: this is far from the perfect album. *La Sexorcisto* is a stepping-stone between the early White Zombie material, which ranged in an unfocused manner from the interestingly eccentric to the frankly unlistenable, and the much more commanding releases that followed. In the tradition of 1992, the sound was fairly lightweight and thin, although this would have been to do with the light, sparse mix rather than the musicians' intentions or performances.

An obvious comparison is Pantera, the Texan metal group who had undergone a broadly comparable change in style in 1990, two years before *La Sexorcisto*: like White Zombie, they had scored a major-label deal and, in the hands of a capable producer (Terry Date, shortly to work with White Zombie), had issued a slick but lightweight-sounding album, *Cowboys from Hell*—a much slimmer, less impactful body of songs than the albums to follow. In this White Zombie were also like Pantera, but let's not get ahead of ourselves.

◆

Three years of hard slog followed before a new album appeared. Still, the group's deliberate, newfound dedication to the heavy metal sound was destined to pay off in spades. As Zombie recalled, "It wasn't until around 1989 that we were like, 'Ah, we're gonna try and get on some of these metal shows, just because this whole New York art scene thing is just a dead end.'" It was at this point that White Zombie started playing club shows with bands like Suicidal Tendencies and Slayer. "That was really bizarre because we weren't metal at all, and we had all this crummy equipment that sounded like crap—and these bands had like 900 Marshall stacks and sounded powerhouse!"

So why did the rock audiences in a dozen countries warm to White Zombie with such alacrity? Perhaps because of the power of the stage show. Not every song in the WZ catalogue was a winner, after all, so the live performances needed to transmit sufficient energy to the crowds to get them animated and on message. This happened, slowly but surely, throughout the territories in which the band moved. Rob Zombie would stalk the stage, making expansive movements with his hands and spinning around while headbanging: Yuenger and Yseult (surely White Zombie are the only band ever to have incorporated two members with *Y* surnames, apart from AC/DC?) would mosh with the best of them. The production, of course, helped things along nicely, pyro blasts, TV screens, dry ice, and all.

Be under no illusions: the arrival of professional management also helped White Zombie to find their audience. Writer Marc Weidenbaum, one of the few journalists to get access to Zombie's private quarters in the early days of his rise to fame, has a unique perspective on this. Writing in *Pulse!*, he noted how, while acts such as Frank Zappa and KISS had offered "specific visual manifestations" of their music onstage and on record, "few could claim the kind of essential—and, most importantly, self-produced—visual/musical affinity that Rob has achieved with White Zombie. The band's growing legion of fans thrill to the garish, horny, cartoon images that coalesce into a splendiferous, toxic-green visual aura around each White Zombie single, album and tour." And all this, Weidenbaum added, was the work not of a hired hand in a record company art department, but of Zombie himself. "The fact remains: no band playing songs for the masses these days is as all-consumingly visual as White Zombie."

Weidenbaum went on to illuminate the close-knit world that had built up around White Zombie, an act he described as "a small family . . . attracting a growing network of family friends." Drawing together the network's various strands, he explained how Andy Gould and Walter O'Brien, White Zombie's managers, were "associates at Concrete Management, the primary artist-management company for metal bands," which also hosted an annual Concrete Foundation Forum, "the most important convention in the metal industry." Concrete Marketing's Bob Chiappardi had recently overseen *Nativity in Black*, a Black Sabbath tribute album for which Zombie contributed a version of "Children of the Grave," while Gould's girlfriend "owns the video production company that produced the 'More Human Than Human' video" and *Astro-Creep* producer Terry Date had also worked recently with Prong, "another Gould/O'Brien client."

Still, problems were legion for White Zombie in the wake of *La*

Sexorcisto. First there was the slight issue of clearing the samples used, which—in classic rookie style—no one had really considered before the album was recorded. "Geffen's an L.A. label," recalled Yuenger. "They have a little office in New York, but it's really a satellite office. We only really had contact with this one guy from Geffen in New York. We said, 'We like to sample things, we like to use samples in our music.' He said, 'Sure, go ahead, we'll sort it out later.' So we just sampled all this stuff like crazy. Next thing we know, we're in L.A. having a meeting with these really, really sharp music industry lawyers, who are like, 'Where'd you get this sample? Where'd you get that one? What's that one from?'

"You do things in the studio, you have fun, you get some thrift-store fifty-cent record and sample something off that, and the record's on some label that doesn't exist any more. The person who's saying whatever you're sampling is dead. You think, 'Oh cool, this is neat, this sounds cool.' Next thing you know, you have a lawyer telling you, 'Well, since we can't find the company and we can't find the guy, we have to find the guy's family to get permission to clear this sample.' That's the kind of thing that really puts a damper on fun. Actually there was a version of *La Sexorcisto*, a white-label advance copy, that went out with a couple of samples on it that were not on the album. Then they made a new version."

US and overseas dates populated the whole of 1993 and most of 1994 in response to the wave of public interest in *La Sexorcisto*, which ultimately sold two million copies and went double platinum. There was a musical zeitgeist in the early 1990s into which *La Sexorcisto* seemed to fit, and for the newly successful musicians, this was a steep learning curve. Merchandise was—and remains—a major income stream for any rock band, and in White Zombie's case, a lot of kids wanted to buy one of their T-shirts. The demand was too much for the band to handle, complicated by the fact that Zombie continued to design all the band's products, even while surrounded by the chaos of the tour dates. Ultimately, the band had to recruit professionals to assist—the price of success, right?

In September 1992, White Zombie traveled to Europe for two months of shows opening for Danzig, including three dates in England, five in Holland, six in Germany, and three in Scandinavia. The following month they powered through the same countries again, as well as debuting in Switzerland, France, and Italy. An American jaunt followed, still in support of Danzig but now with desert-rockers Kyuss opening the show. This lineup—mighty by anyone's standards—swept through Washington, Oregon, California, Nevada, Arizona, Texas, Oklahoma, Missouri, Wisconsin, Illinois, Michigan, Ohio, Pennsylvania, New York, Maryland, Connecticut, Massachusetts, and Virginia. That's a lot of road miles, especially when you're hurting for money and still some way from comfortable travel and accommodation options.

At least White Zombie had some corporate muscle behind them now. Only the personalities of the band members could stop the group's progress now. But that would never happen . . . would it?

THREE

THE BROTHERHOOD OF SATAN

(1993-95)

Be careful what you wish for. In the case of White Zombie—now actual rock stars within a year or so of the release of *La Sexorcisto; Devil Music, Volume 1* in 1992—success came with its own near-fatal pressures.

The post-*Sexorcisto* tour regime was brutal, although Rob Zombie, Jay Yuenger, Sean Yseult, and Ivan de Prume were all in their early-to-late twenties at the time and resilient enough to take most of the relentless everyday strain of bus to hotel to venue to hotel to bus . . . and repeat. The nightly show itself was a spectacle, as a visit to YouTube will show, although it didn't really hold a candle to gigs from later years, when real money was ploughed into the production. Zombie bestrode the stage in a variety of unusual headwear, dreadlocks swinging everywhere, while the other three musicians head-banged like possessed people.

A slight setback occurred in 1993, when Ivan de Prume was replaced by a new drummer, Phil Buerstatte—presumably due to differences of opinion, judging by the muted responses given by both sides—but this didn't slow White Zombie down a jot. By this point, "Thunder Kiss '65" had made an impact as a single, with the accompanying video—a cheap but effective performance effort adorned with some visual FX—making unexpected headway. After the video was included in an episode of the puerile but amusing MTV show *Beavis and Butt-Head*, gaining those moronic fictional characters' approval, the song became a significant boost to White Zombie's profile. In fact, the band rapidly tired of answering questions about *Beavis and Butt-Head*, and the singer would sometimes yell from the stage words to the effect of, "Who needs the cartoon Beavis and Butt-Head? I can see a million real Beavis and Butt-Heads right in front of me!"

A whole swathe of new metal bands now emerged, superficially different in many ways but all united in that they were moving away from the old, 1980s metal template. Hip-hop beats were a motivator for some, electronic elements for others. In every case, the old coiffed manes, pink guitars, and spandex was on its way out. The new wave, dubbed nu-metal by some industry goon, was quite the fashionable thing between 1994—when the Bakersfield quintet Korn's first album appeared—and 2000, when the movement peaked.

So who were the progenitors of this sound, or at least the rap and rock element of it? The first successful example of a rap-metal tune came in September 1986, when Run-DMC and Aerosmith collaborated on a reworked version of the latter's classic "Walk This Way" and topped the singles charts worldwide. Five months later came the Beastie Boys, who released a raft of singles including the influential "(You Gotta) Fight for Your Right (to Party)," which featured guitar by Kerry King of Slayer. This was followed by rapper Tone Loc, whose February 1989 hit "Wild Thing" contained a simple guitar riff under Loc's famously laconic rap. Soon after this came Faith No More's "Epic" in February 1990, and "Bring the Noise" by Chuck D. and Anthrax in July 1991. The rap-metal floodgates subsequently opened to allow dozens of rapping rockers out of the woodwork, and a movement was born.

In terms of fully fledged rapping over metal riffs, much of the movement's essential impetus can be ascribed to Rage Against the Machine. This Los Angeles band's involvement in the nu-metal sound absolutely has to be deconstructed if we're to understand where White Zombie found themselves in the wake of *La Sexorcisto*. They never rapped—although Rob Zombie's delivery shared some of that style's rhythmic qualities—but they sailed very close to the nu-metal style in several other ways.

The following may not make for happy reading if you're a fan of thrash metal or hardcore, as nu-metal is now practically the most unfashionable music ever invented, but bear with me for a minute. Looking back, the nu-metal movement came and went with such speed, and its image was so driven by fashion, that even at its peak there was massed resistance against it, let alone after it began to decline. Interviewers liked nothing better than to needle Rage Against the Machine front man Zack de la Rocha and the other Rage members about their responsibility, or otherwise, for the rise of the nu-metal sound. The singer usually diverted such accusations.

"To say that Rage Against the Machine were primarily responsible for that sound is a little misleading," he told *Rock Sound*, rather snootily, "and a little ignorant of musical history in the States. There were so many bands fusing hip-hop and punk rock, for instance,

Michael Franti in San Francisco or Anthrax and Public Enemy, or KRS-One rhyming over an AC/DC remix, there's a very clear history. What makes us unique within the convergence of that music is the fact that we did it with live instrumentation, and that we drew upon the lessons that Bob Marley and Public Enemy and the Clash passed on in terms of seeing music as a weapon."

A related but less prominent subgenre was funk-metal, a slightly clumsy term applied in the late 1980s to any rock band whose bass player used a slapping style. The best-known funk-metal acts were the Red Hot Chili Peppers (who later achieved global success with a more pop-oriented approach) and Living Colour (an impossibly talented group of players who were just too far ahead of their time to keep it together for long). Other funk-metallers ranged from the credible, such as Infectious Grooves (a side-project of hardcore punks Suicidal Tendencies), to the relatively obscure, such as the Dan Reed Network.

When these new styles joined forces with the new Seattle rock sound, grunge, against traditional metal bands, even mainstream rock acts were unable to sustain much impetus. For a metal band to survive, it had to be diverse (Faith No More, Primus), too big to touch (Metallica, Iron Maiden), or too small to count (the legions of black and death metal bands). Even apparent untouchables such as Motörhead and Mötley Crüe only survived by the skin of their teeth.

Grunge was an unusual movement in recent rock music, in hindsight. Sure, there were some great songs from that scene (as no one really liked to call it). The flagship band, Nirvana, wouldn't have reached such stratospheric heights without melodies that people could sing in large numbers, and the fact that lesser groups such as Alice in Chains, Soundgarden, and Mudhoney utilized metal, punk, and classic-rock elements in their songwriting meant that an international fan base more or less had to accrue.

Where the grunge movement did stand in opposition to White Zombie was in its philosophy, a sometimes defeatist ideology based on the idea of uselessness and protest. This was reflected in many of the bands' onstage performances, which were often less than dynamic. Of course, this didn't resonate with Rob Zombie and his band, who took their live cues from the great shock-rock performers of the 1970s and before.

In 1994, when White Zombie were recording their next album, they tuned their guitars lower than the standard A440 pitch, simply because riffs sound heavier that way. Within three or four years, newer alternative metal bands such as Fear Factory, Godsmack, Korn, and System of a Down were taking this new sound right into the upper reaches of the charts—looking different, singing differently, tuning their guitars low, rapping and emoting about personal trauma or political commentary. Marilyn Manson also came into the public eye, like White Zombie with a horror-show version of metal.

Within a few years this ripple effect spread as far even as thrash metal stalwarts Slayer, whose 1998 album *Diabolus in Musica* was heavily influenced by the new sound. By then—although we're looking ahead some years now—the bands now most closely associated with nu-metal were on their first album (Limp Bizkit, Coal Chamber) or just about to break into the public eye (Slipknot, Linkin Park), after which point the battle for supremacy would be all over, won in nu-metal's favor, until approximately 2002.

Why did nu-metal bands achieve such prominence? After the initial wave at least, it was because the record industry came up with ways to exploit the sound for their own commercial purposes. Years later, Rage Against the Machine's primary motivator, Tom Morello, gave the whole evolution of 1990s rock a revealing perspective when he said that alternative music, as it was labeled at the start of the decade, had consumed its own creators when it became part and parcel of mainstream entertainment.

"In some ways it [success] screwed them up," Morello told Gibson.com. As far as he was concerned, almost all of the key bands of the era—Nirvana and Nine Inch Nails, Tool and Smashing Pumpkins, Rage and Jane's Addiction—had one thing in common: a love of underground music and punk rock. Then, all of a sudden, they were playing in huge venues and seeing their videos air on MTV alongside the latest Backstreet Boys single. And that, as far as Morello was concerned, created "a sort of 'arena rock' personal crisis." This, he continued, would explain why bands like Tool or Nine Inch Nails were prone to disappearing for years between albums. "There was none of that thing of putting out an album every six months to try to capitalize on momentum, and try and become the biggest band in the world. These bands were all vexed, and afraid of being seen in the same light as the bands they disparaged, or the bands their heroes had disparaged."

Once that slackening of motivation had occurred, Morello said, it was only a matter of time before the record industry suits came up with the idea of rent-a-clone "alternative" bands. "Inside every cigar-smoke-filled record-label boardroom in the country, executives were saying, 'If only we had a Rage Against the Machine that sang about girls, and would show up for video shoots,'" Morello added. But when those bands did appear, they lacked the substance of a true Rage or Nirvana. "There were the nu-metal bands, the Pearl Jam wannabe bands—bands that sold millions of records, but who had nothing like the talent of the groups they were trying to emulate."

I'm not saying that White Zombie were a nu-metal band, because they clearly weren't. But like Fear Factory, Nine Inch Nails, and Marilyn Manson, they infused all sorts of influences into their own brand of metal—from industrial to electronic to plain weird—that made them excellent running mates for the nu-metal bands whose rose alongside them. This is the environment that White Zombie inhabit in this chapter, and the one that follows.

◆

Exposure for White Zombie was now coming thick and fast. A boost to their profile came with a brief scene in the 1994 film *Airheads*, the tale of a bumbling heavy metal band in the great early-'90s *Singles / California Man* tradition. As was usually the case in such trifling movies—a similar case being Cannibal Corpse's cameo in *Ace Ventura: Pet Detective* the same year—White Zombie were filmed performing a song, "Feed the Gods," in the background of the main action. They also contributed the song to the soundtrack. In another scene, Yseult and Yuenger are seen playing their instruments on a version of the hardcore band Reagan Youth's song "Degenerated."

Looking back at *Airheads*, Zombie snickered, "It was kind of fun to see how wasteful and stupid they are with movies. It's what you always wonder about with movies: why do they suck, and why do they cost so much? Once I got involved with it, it was kind of obvious: there's too many people, and no one wants to be responsible for a decision that could backfire. They just shovel money out the window as fast as possible. . . . most of the people who hold those positions aren't really fans of music or films, they're just business people making a product."

The *Airheads* appearance meshed neatly with regular interviews on MTV—the obvious channel for the band in an era when the kids liked their metal vivid, irritating to the older generation and just slightly tinged with taboo. Album number five was booked for recording at NRG Studios in late 1994 with Terry Date, who like his predecessor Andy Wallace was known for the heaviness he could coax out of guitars and the presence with which he imbued any rhythm section.

A downside came when Zombie and Yseult split up around this time, but the parting—initiated by the latter—was "amicable," she said, and the band was in no danger of splitting because of it. Perhaps more stressfully, Buerstatte—who had developed a serious drug habit, and who as Zombie later put it had "done some bad things to the band"—was fired, to be replaced by a seasoned drummer, John Tempesta, who had played in the veteran thrash metal bands Exodus and Testament.

The change in drummer was inevitable, as Yuenger noted some years later. "Our first drummer, Ivan de Prume, left us in the middle of an intensive tour, and we got this interim drummer who was very compulsive and had substance abuse issues," he recalled. "We had this giant show in L.A., and the drummer disappeared beforehand and went on a bender. He was totally fucked up, showed up five minutes before show time. So, we play this show knowing we're firing him immediately afterward. The problem, though, was there were all these record company people backstage . . . we had to stand around smiling for a while, pretending everything was totally cool."

In October 1994, an album of Black Sabbath covers entitled

Nativity in Black was scheduled to be released by Sony, featuring songs from White Zombie, Biohazard, Sepultura, Faith No More, and other mid-'90s metal acts. Of the tribute album, Sabbath guitarist Tony Iommi—the Godfather of Heavy Metal—reasoned, "I'm very honored that bands have actually done tributes to us and mentioned Sabbath as their influence. It's great, I feel a great achievement inside because many years ago, twenty-four years ago even, when we'd only been going a couple of years, and we were doing interviews in England, they were saying, 'What are you thinking? You must be finished by now!'—trying to wrap us up after a couple of years! We didn't think this was going to go on. And now here we are, twenty-odd years later." (It must have been an interesting experience for Rob Zombie himself when tribute albums to *his* bands started appearing within a matter of years.)

The making of the new White Zombie album, ultimately released on April 11, 1995, as the exhausting-to-type *Astro-Creep: 2000—Songs of Love, Destruction, and Other Synthetic Delusions of the Electric Head*, was a rather different process than that of making *La Sexorcisto*. For starters, White Zombie had a much bigger budget to work with, allowing them more studio time to get the music right. This was matched by a rise in the musicians' creative ambitions: this time, the songs had to be right from the word go.

To enable this, serious effort was devoted to pre-production, with many long hours spent in rehearsal studios, the crude results of which were recorded onto a boom box. "Sean and I would bring in things that we'd worked on at home, but a lot of times those riffs would get twisted around over the course of a day," Jay Yuenger told the Australian writer Joe Matera many years later. Throughout these many hours of playing, thinking, arguing, and playing some more, Zombie himself would sit in a corner, reading the newspaper, until something he heard caught his attention. "I guess you could call it editing," Yuenger added. There had been some talk of adding electronic components and samples to the mix, but no real specifics given. "We tried to make the songs as good as possible and as played by a live rock band. It was really difficult because Rob never wrote or sang anything until he got into the recording studio, so the tunes never seemed like anything more than collections of riffs."

It was a relief for all the band members to have serious budget behind them this time. "It was pretty amazing to be in a situation where everything lines up: there's a big budget, you're at one of the best studios in the world, you've got a producer who's done some of your favorite records, and you're being encouraged to be as creative as possible. We all worked very hard, and it was very rewarding. I was absolutely dead set on doing everything as well as humanly possible. I was totally unwilling to settle for anything guitar-wise that I was 100 percent unhappy with, and I knew that with the position we were in, I could work on the tracks until I thought they were done."

Terry Date, who was hired to mix as well as produce the album, had a marathon task ahead of him. In a time before Pro Tools, when infinite numbers of tracks were not possible, if you needed more than a studio's standard twenty-four tracks for each instrument or vocal, you needed to physically connect more than one recording console, with the concomitant headache at setup and mix-down stages.

"It was a seventy-two-track recording, forty-eight analogue and twenty-four digital!" laughed Yuenger. "You have like five vocal tracks and then you have eight guitar tracks, and then a dozen drum tracks, and then you have to save tracks for the sampling that you bring in and out. We had two studios, one [where] we were working on the guitar parts, in the other the samples, so the tapes were going back and forth all the time. It took close to six weeks to complete the recording and production of the album. It was cool to have much time to spend: with the first Geffen record we only cared about completing the album as fast as possible and getting the hell out of the studio to tour . . . I seem to remember three twenty-four-track tape machines chained together, if you can imagine. Remember, you couldn't make an album with a computer yet, so all the loops and sounds were on tape.

"Terry nearly had a nervous breakdown trying to mix all that stuff, and he told me years later that he was certain that he'd ruined the album, which was funny since he did such a good job on it. . . . Terry's not so much an artistic producer, as far as helping arrange your songs or the vibe or whatever, but he's incredibly technical, which turned out to be a real positive for the album, which was big on ideas that were very new then such as samples, layered sounds and extreme EQ-ing. And also being pretty small on, you know, beautiful melodies."

When *Astro-Creep* came out in April 1995, it was immediately apparent that White Zombie had followed a similar path to Pantera. The sheer presence of the guitars on *Astro-Creep* dwarfs those on *La Sexorcisto*, while John Tempesta's background in heavy-hitting thrash metal bands paid off in spades. Terry Date had worked the same magic that he had with Pantera's own second major-label album—*Vulgar Display of Power*, released in 1992—and had created a massive sound for the three musicians in White Zombie. Rob Zombie himself was now singing at a comfortably low range for the music, squeezing fewer words into the verses and allowing the musical arrangements to stamp an impression on the listener.

"Electric Head Pt. 1 (The Agony)" opens *Astro-Creep* in uncompromising style. The palm muting on the guitars is pure Metallica-style chug, with few of the strummed open chords that had given so many White Zombie songs a rock feel in the past. Tuned down to C-sharp, the guitar and bass make a formidable combination—one to which Rob Zombie has more or less adhered in subsequent years. "Super-Charger Heaven" continues the aural assault, but leavened with an anthemic chorus of "Devil man!" that might have made the song a suitable for release as a single, although this didn't happen.

"Real Solution #9" boasts the same riff weight but breaks periodically down to drums and effects-treated vocals reminiscent of Ministry's Al Jourgensen, with whom Zombie would often be compared in later years. "Creature of the Wheel" owes a lot to Pantera with its crushing central guitar figure, with Yseult's bass treated with a psychedelic studio effect and plenty of wailing lead guitar from Yuenger. "Electric Head Pt. 2 (The Ecstasy)," the first single, is more whimsical and less of an all-out metal assault. Well suited to commercial airplay with its catchy, descending lines and sneering chorus, the song is as commercial as *Astro-Creep* gets.

"Grease Paint and Monkey Brains" is the album's most understated song, a reclusive collage of sludge riffs that shy away from the hi-fi metal of the opening cuts. "I, Zombie" is the closest *Astro-Creep* gets to a filler track, essentially offering more of the music we've heard already. Next, however, is the album's big hit, "More Human Than Human," which reached #7 on the *Billboard* Modern Rock chart. This was due at least in part to its memorable intro, an electronic bleep followed by slide guitar that combine into a genuine earworm. The rest of the song is simple, stripped-down, and easily hummable—the characteristics of so many hits—but it's still metal, and it's funky enough to be included on the playlist at any given nu-metal club night.

After the obvious hit, White Zombie return to fun, groove-metal territory with "El Phantasmo and the Chicken-Run Blast-O-Rama," which is in essence a bolted-together drone riff with a slick drum beat anchoring it. The album concludes with "Blur the Technicolor," which features interesting clean guitar sections in between the riffs, and "Blood, Milk, and Sky," which slows down the pace and includes a cool, understated, Eastern-sounding string section that would have fitted in well anywhere on this multifaceted album. There's also a hidden track, as was the vogue in the mid-1990s: supposedly called "Where the Sidewalk Ends, the Bug Parade Begins," it's an almost orchestral piece of layered guitars (those seventy-two tracks used in full, perhaps) that slowly fades to silence in an appropriately majestic manner.

You may notice that there has been no mention of movie samples so far. That is not to say that there are none on the album: there are plenty. However, to avoid the legal hassles they had experienced after the release of *La Sexorcisto*, Rob Zombie and his band had decided to create these elements themselves rather than lift them from other copyright-holders.

The writer Marc Weidenbaum, now of *Disquiet* magazine but back in the 1990s working for *Pulse!*, enjoyed a memorable visit with Zombie at his home in Los Angeles around the time of the album's release and kindly agreed to share those memories for this book. His initial impressions of Zombie HQ were fascinating.

"Shelves rise up to the ceiling packed with figurines, those synthetic-polymer ghosts of Halloweens past," he wrote. "Aside from their class-portrait formation—tall in back, vertically challenged in front—the brigade of Toys 'R' Us backstock is as artlessly jammed against the wall as a spinster's thimble collection, treasured but neglected." Among the wild and wacky ephemera of Zombie's ostensibly modest home in the lower Hollywood Hills was "a variety of rare Draculae [that] qualifies the site for national protection as a vampire sanctuary"; numerous figurines from the Japanese cartoon *Ultraman*; a television set in the shape of an astronaut's helmet; signed photographs of the cast of the *Batman* TV series; and all manner of Zombie memorabilia, including gold and platinum albums, magazine covers, posters, and photos of Rob alongside friends and associates like Glenn Danzig. "Somewhere far beyond these walls," Weidenbaum concluded, "a lonely Webster's lexicographer is honing the definition of the word 'detritus.'"

Weidenbaum also received a preview of *Astro-Creep* during his visit, and would describe it as "a worthy successor to *La Sexorcisto*'s artful pop bombast." Citing the line "I am a jigsaw man" from "More Human Than Human," he would sum up White Zombie's music as "jumble music: a fantastic aural conglomeration of cultural and purely sonic material."

White Zombie's manager, Andy Gould, who had come on board after *La Sexorcisto*, explained to Weidenbaum that, unlike on the previous album, the samples on *Astro-Creep* were homegrown, having been assembled mostly by Rob and John Tempesta. According to Weidenbaum, *La Sexorcisto* had been delayed for close to a year as the band tried (and failed) to clear the many samples woven into the mix, and could only be released "after a time-consuming re-edit."

The homemade additions to *Astro-Creep* range from the simple, gothic chanting on "Electric Head, Part I (The Agony)" and the repeated mantra of "I'm already dead" (supposedly the last words of one of the Charles Manson murder victims in 1969) to more extravagant sounds such as the fully fledged circus soundtrack of "Grease Paint and Monkey Brains," in which a decaying pipe organ slides discordantly into sonic chaos.

◆

Faced with a million and one creative issues and supplied with the budget to solve those issues, Rob Zombie arrives now at a point in this book where he starts to flex his muscles as a true artist. With *Astro-Creep*, he wanted to be in control of the artwork in the CD booklet, for example—remember, this was the 1990s, when people still cared about artwork in large numbers. Geffen was prepared to pay for four panels of art per CD release, so who designed them all and paid for the extra twelve panels? Zombie and his band— in that order. He also designed the stage set for the forthcoming tour, managing details right down to the dimensions of the onstage production and props. T-shirts? Zombie's own designs. Patches, posters, stickers, badges? Also from the Zombie pen.

Of course, all of this came at a price. Everyone now wanted a piece of Rob Zombie. Running a band of which he was the de facto leader if not the formally appointed one, managing its aesthetics and balancing the budgets so the bills were paid, Zombie lacked the time to get everything done comfortably, although he was assisted by his management, of course.

"There does come a point where it's not much fun because it's turned into so much work," he sighed. "My phone rings all day, and it's always something, from lighting rigs, to what kind of buses, to the T-shirts that aren't going to be done on time for the tour—

we gotta get the CDs out for the Australian remixes. It's like that all day long. But how else is it gonna get done? I'm just gonna tell somebody else, 'Here, you do it'? If other people started handling everything, it would just be like any old band.

"Maybe by [directing] our videos ourselves they aren't as slick as other bands, but I don't care, because it's more real. We write the songs, make the record, make the video—and it's all one big deal. Whereas to hire the hot video guy of the month to make some big slick thing seems so—like, I've been watching MTV, and this Matt Mahurin, I mean his videos are awesome, but you could just interchange the bands, because to me each video doesn't seem particularly special to that band's personality."

Note that Zombie was fully embracing the visual aspect of White Zombie by this time. Directing or co-directing the videos— whether he was credited for that work or not—was leading into a wider aesthetic direction that would include a spinoff comic book series for Marvel Comics, home from home for anyone with a youthful superhero fetish. This inevitably meant a step into a governing role within the band.

"It's really hard sometimes," he said, when asked by Weidenbaum about managing the various creative drives in the band, including his own. "It's not like everyone can be on the same wavelength. This is a band. It is not 100 percent what I'd want to do. But I guess the reason there have been a lot of member changes is that you have to find people who are on board with where you're going. Anyone who wasn't, we had to get rid of. It gets to the point where the rest of the band has to trust me that what I'm doing is going to make sense—maybe it does, maybe it doesn't."

The music, however, was still a collaborative work, he insisted.

"When it comes to writing songs, it's a total band effort. It's not like I come in [and say], 'Here are my ideas, do them.' But what pulls it together is the sounds in my head, the way the vocals and all the crazy shit are going to make it into a White Zombie thing. . . . There are certain things there's no way to express, because I can just hear it. I can hear where the vocals are gonna fit. I can hear where all the pieces are going to go. A lot of times, what the band is playing seems to them really lame. They're like, 'This sucks, man.' But it just comes together. It's a real building process."

Zombie alluded to a difference of opinion over one of *Astro-Creep's* more successful songs, saying, "It made writing this record very difficult. 'More Human Than Human' seemed like one note over and over, and it made no sense [to anyone else] until you started layering in all the vocals and the slide guitar and stuff. Then people were like, 'Wow, you know, this really makes sense.'"

The album did make sense—to a lot of people. Embarking on a tour after its release, the members of White Zombie continued to experience an upward surge in their lifestyle as money flowed in—at last—and creature comforts became more commonplace. The pressure to maintain the band's upward trajectory never ceased, however. Reaching a wide audience was one thing; figuring out what to do to maintain that audience was quite another. But the musicians were wise enough to recognize that White Zombie still had some way to go before genuine worldwide stardom ever arrived.

For Weidenbaum, while *Astro-Creep* was ostensibly more "sample-heavy" than its predecessor, it was still very much an album of songs, with the "extra-musical" content—that is, the samples—often deployed more subtly this time around. Interestingly, this development was informed in part by Zombie's appreciation for the remixes that the band had commissioned over the years, including the versions of "Thunderkiss '65" and "Black Sunshine" featured on the 1992 *Nightcrawlers* EP and the versions of "More Human" by Nine Inch Nails alumnus Charlie Clouser, who also contributed to *Astro-Creep*, that were sent out to radio DJs alongside copies of the new album.

"It's not like they're covering your song," Zombie explained. "It's like, 'Here's how I thought your song should have sounded, but with you still singing it.' Remixes actually helped with some of the writing on this album because from the remixes on the last album, you heard your own music taken apart and put back together again. It made you think, 'Hmm, that's pretty cool. I didn't hear that the first time around.' This time, we sort of started remixing our music before it was ever finished."

Astro-Creep hit #6 on the *Billboard* 200—a huge success by anyone's standards, but especially in the 1990s, when huge numbers of albums had to sell for that to happen. Along with the tidal wave of changes that had consumed Zombie's life since the album's success transformed him into a bona-fide rock star, he embarked on a relationship with Sheri Skurkis, later Sheri Moon. The two enjoyed a first date at Toad's Place, a bar in New Haven, Connecticut, and had moved in together within a month.

Sean Yseult looked back with equanimity at this new development. She and Zombie had parted on good terms, she told me, so there was no tension when he began a new relationship—at least, not of Yseult's making. "When she wasn't around, the four of us would interact like a band, but as soon as she was back on tour, all of a sudden it was really strange again," she recalled. "Even the roadies saw it, it wasn't just me. They were very isolated. It was unfortunate, but it happens. I initiated the split, which was amicable, so I've never complained. I practically introduced them. I have no animosity toward Rob."

◆

The 1995–96 White Zombie tours rolled on, grossing high numbers and spreading the message to hundreds of thousands of fans. A mid-bill set on August 26, 1995, at the UK's Monsters of Rock festival—headlined by Metallica, who performed a snatch of "More Human Than Human"—exposed the band to their largest British audience yet. Asked about the vibe at that earth-shaking show, Yseult explained, "Look at the bands that played that day. It's crazy! At that point, I think it was the biggest crowd we had played to. Later we played in Brazil at Rock in Rio and that was like 300,000. Donington, I believe, was 80,000. It was just amazing. You get up on that stage and it's like a sea of ants, and in a way it's less intimidating than playing a club with like three people staring at you, because you can see each and every person. When it's a huge crowd like that, you can't see any faces, but you see them moving and undulating like a sea, like waves of people. And when they're responding and dancing, the energy you feel from them is just amazing."

"You know," she continued, "I can't remember what [the weather] felt like, but I just remember having sharp pains in my lungs and my ribcage because the stage was the size of a football field. It was huge. And we were used to running around, and me and Jay would always switch sides, and we're running around and headbanging and to make it from one side of the stage to the other was like, oh my God, we're panting and out of breath!"

Festival dates throughout Europe and the USA followed, with

White Zombie maximizing their opportunity to impress large numbers of people at last. Back home, reviews of *Astro-Creep* were generally approving, with the *Los Angeles Times* writing, "Rob Zombie and co. [are] Beavis and Butt-Head's favorite band . . . what seems like every emotionally challenged kid in America bought the CD. White Zombie was the great rags-to-riches story in rock. . . . *Astro-Creep* is truly fine, far more ambitious in an industrial metal-disco sort of way than the cartoony soundtrack for pre-pubescent rebellion the band could've gotten away with."

Reviewers and interviewers evidently appreciated the fact that White Zombie had paid their dues. We writers love a story arc, and although this band's arc was more of a long plateau followed by a sudden leap, it still reads great on paper. As the writer Michael Moses put it in *Foundations*, "After ten years and five releases of being looked upon as nothing more than Lower East Side mutant scum, the members of White Zombie are now hailed as brilliant psychedelic freaks. . . . Not bad—especially when you consider that it wasn't all that long ago that the band was broke and practically homeless, struggling to scrape together a few bucks just to buy guitar strings and food (in that order)."

"I'm really sick of albums that are just guitar, bass, and drums. They're so fuckin' boring," Zombie told Moses. "I wanted to bring more sounds in on this album; I wanted to experiment. These days it takes bands three or four years to make a record, and then when it finally comes out, there's not a fucking thing inside of it. And you're looking at it, saying, 'I waited four years for this?' It's ridiculous. I always try to make things that I would want to see, assuming that's what someone else wants to see. I think most bands these days don't really care—they just pump it out."

Asked if he had become wealthy, Zombie shrugged. "Well, there's not really a lot of money to be made at this point . . . unfortunately. It took a long time for the record to break and we were pretty far in debt by the time it did. There was a lot of money to pay off. People don't understand how many different people are getting paid off that same amount of money—you're paying your road crew, your managers and all these other people. But it's cool. I'm stable and that's all I ever wanted."

Hardly a flight of ecstatic bliss, is it? But then Zombie has never come across as a particularly cheerful man in interviews. He is at his most engaging when he's working, committing his talents to being productive—but he's not good at the simple pleasure of self-analysis.

"I don't really get caught up in that crap," he sighed. "I don't sit back and go 'Wow! We sold a million records!' I'm always busy working on something else. . . . I'm just not that type of person. I'm the type of person who goes, 'Fuck! I wish that show was better.' I'm always worrying about the next thing. I've never been able to sit back and enjoy the moment. Maybe I can when I'm sixty."

It seems that Rob Zombie was already sick of the flimsy sheen of fame, just a couple of years into the stardom that he and his band had worked so hard to achieve. In 1995, White Zombie were still firing on all cylinders, but the tide was turning, all right—and it seemed that radical upheaval would be on the way before too long.

FOUR

And Now The Screaming Starts!

(1996)

Heavy metal is a pretty confused world at the best of times, with multiple genres and subgenres evolving and diverging from the main genre every year or two. In 1996 the situation was more complex than ever, with nu-metal digging its claws very successfully into mainstream rock media, and the old guard positively directionless. Suddenly, metal bands weren't really considered "cool" unless they had a DJ and at least one baseball cap and a tattoo in Olde English script between them.

Fortunately, White Zombie never adopted any nu-metal tropes (leisurewear, turntable scratching, rapping, and so on) apart from Rob Zombie's slightly curious—and mildly hip-hop-indebted— hand gestures when he performed. The band were far too embedded in alternative and, let's be frank, goth culture to go in that direction. However, where the nu-metal movement benefited White Zombie was in the general openness that came with it—an idea that experimentation with unorthodox images and sounds in metal was perfectly acceptable.

This was the perfect era for White Zombie. In the '80s, people would have laughed at them; in the 2000s, people would have ignored them. The fertile, vivid early- to mid-'90s were precisely the right time for this band to grow. And grow they did, raking in pots of money on their tours but also investing huge amounts in their production. Did any of them become rich overnight? It's unlikely. There was just too much expenditure going into keeping this Zombie animated and on the road.

Asked by writer Daina Darzin if the stage show, loaded with lights and pyrotechnics as it was, represented the peak of Zombie's ambition in terms of production, the singer replied, "There's always more! The problem with that is, once you start, you think of ten more things. But there was enough money to keep it going, and I'm just going to add on as we go along. The show's pretty expensive. There's so many hidden costs you forget about, like we want to add more pyro. Which means another truck. And another truck driver. And next thing you know, this one little thing ends up costing an extra $10,000 a week. It's like every time a piece of pyro goes off, it's lit another hundred-dollar bill on fire."

But Zombie had bigger things on his mind, such as the impact on his family and fans of White Zombie's huge success. As he explained, his parents had seen the show—and enjoyed it. (Zombie's brother Mike Cummings went on to significant success with a band of his own, called Powerman 5000, in which he adopted the stage name Spider One . . . and spent many years fielding questions about what it was like to be Rob Zombie's kid brother.)

White Zombie were now in the position where they could choose the bands to support them rather than be allocated an opening act by management or a promoter. This, too, could be a chore, although it was gradually becoming clear that he finds these details stressful because he wants them done right, and finds it tricky to trust others to do the job.

"It seems like every time we tour, we get a list of bands that are available, and it's always the same bands," he pondered. "And I'll be like, these guys just did the Megadeth tour, the Pantera tour, the Danzig tour, everyone has seen them. So I got bands the kids wouldn't expect to see, some variety. There's nothing worse than having four hours and four bands of the relatively same music. I like Reverend Horton Heat; I saw them at the Whisky, and I thought they were awesome. It's rockabilly, but it's high-energy enough to work. You can tell most of the kids haven't been exposed to it, but they're into it. Kyuss we met on the Danzig tour. Babes in Toyland, we used to always play with them way back, and it was cool to have a band from another scene."

If we're trying to gauge Rob Zombie's frame of mind at a pivotal career point—as we should definitely try to do if we're to paint a successful portrait of the man over the peaks and troughs of his life to date—this would be the time to do it. Give a man an opportunity and he'll show his true self, and in 1996 the opportunities for the great man to express himself were legion. He had just scored a presenting gig for the Sci-Fi Channel, hosting zombie movies, where a cemetery set was built for him, while on tour he was joined onstage by his hero, Alice Cooper. He would understandably describe the experience as a dream come true.

The age-old nightmare of touring fatigue was wearing him down, however. Handicapped by a fear of flying (useless for any touring musician) and the terrible backstage food (doubly inconvenient for a vegetarian), it was little wonder that Zombie was not at his best when interviewed at White Zombie shows. As for the catering, he simply didn't eat much, causing friends at home some alarm when he returned each time several pounds lighter.

It's true that the biggest artists from the heavy metal scene were a little out of their depth in the grunge and alternative rock eras. Iron Maiden and Judas Priest were in a rut, both veteran metal acts having lost their charismatic front men at the time, and Metallica were about to end a five-year period of touring but not recording. All around those bands, new ones were springing up, causing no end of uncertainty about the future. Zombie was sanguine, however: as far as he was concerned, the same cycle had been repeating every few years since the early '80s.

Yuenger shared this view to an extent, explaining that a major change of some kind lay ahead in the world of alternative rock. "I believe that there will be a big change sooner or later," he said. "People start getting tired of all those alternative bands, they all look and sound the same. The media have also become a part of this big machine . . . this wacky alternative band comes around with this one song that's kind of funny, so it's big for a second, and then a new one comes out and then another one and it goes on and on. People are tired of this. Anyhow, that's what I believe, and time will prove who's right and who's wrong."

Yuenger was confident that metal would return to the fore at some stage, but that it would take a new form. "I think that the nature of metal is that every time a band takes it to a new extreme," he added. "Like there was Motörhead, and then Metallica, and then Venom, Slayer, Napalm Death, Deicide . . . Cannibal Corpse, Impaled Nazarene, Mayhem, the noisiest, you couldn't get any heavier. That's the reason metal is splintering to all of those things, some bands go punk, some others go industrial. When it will come back it will not be like, here's your thrash bands and here's your glam bands, it will be something new and concrete, but it will still be heavy."

Yuenger was enjoying himself, now that White Zombie had started to make a solid income and the cramped conditions of old were replaced by expensive hotels and luxury buses. "[The] first time we played in Europe, that was in 1989, we lived in squats or in our tour bus. We were given three bucks from the label to live on, three single bucks to buy food every day! Today it's way better, it's not stressful, or if it is it's as stressful as a regular job is. No complaints."

Not that everything was going perfectly smoothly. On February 4, 1996, a gig in Johnson City, Tennessee, had to be moved to a different venue after complaints from local residents about the youth-corrupting nature of White Zombie's songs. As Brad Tyer of the *Houston Press* wrote, "This is a band that likes to get along. Now, if only everyone wanted to cooperate. Johnson City, Tennessee, would have preferred to tell the band to go to hell, but that language may be too un-Christian for residents of such a God-fearing town." According to reports, a concerned citizen of Johnson City had cited "nasty and evil" White Zombie lyrics at a city commission meeting. "Then Baptist minister Don Strother mounted a crusade to have a February 4 White Zombie concert banned . . . it was, of course, terrific PR for the band."

Protest against music that is regarded as threatening or unsafe has been going on for decades, of course, and not just in the USA. As far back as 1951, Dean Martin's harmless but slightly smutty "Wham Bam, Thank You Ma'am" had been refused radio airplay; four years later, Elvis Presley was warned by the cops not to swivel his hips on stage; and songs such as "The Twist" were banned in Catholic schools for years, thanks to their supposedly maddening qualities. But the culture of intolerance and suppression only gained a serious political context in 1984, when the Prince album *Purple Rain* caused a stir across the USA thanks to its song "Darling Nikki," in which the eponymous female is said to be "masturbating with a magazine".

The reaction to Prince's album, which went all the way up to Ronald Reagan's office and back, was unprecedented. The issue was picked up by Mary "Tipper" Gore, wife of Bill Clinton's future vice president Al Gore, who recruited twenty wives of Washington politicians and businessmen to form the Parents' Music Resource Center (PMRC). The aim of this pressure group was to persuade the US recording industry to censor itself, in order to protect minors from the more extreme music of the day. As it happens, the idea of the public policing its own activities is neither new nor controversial: any society needs to regulate itself. But what was slightly sinister about the PMRC was that it presented an agenda that crushed anything and everything that was slightly off its middle-of-the-road, approved list. This included most heavy metal, of course, but it also meant that the freedom of speech of many mainstream pop and rock artists was compromised too.

"Never mind the PMRC," the nation's head-bangers said to themselves. "They'll never stop artistic expression." But they were in for a shock. Rather than telling Tipper Gore and her cronies to go back to the Washington golf clubs where they belonged, the Recording Industry Association of America (RIAA) bowed to the PMRC's demands and introduced the infamous "Parental Advisory" stickers that adorn CDs, DVDs, and books to this day.

The panic spread like wildfire. As public and performers watched aghast, the PMRC muscled its way into all sectors of the entertainment industry, beginning with TV and radio—the most potent disseminators of "undesirable" music to the masses. After being told of the PMRC's concerns over rock lyrics, Eddie Fritts—the head honcho of the National Association of Broadcasters—contacted the bosses of forty-five record labels asking that lyric sheets accompany all songs scheduled for radio airplay.

The PMRC's next move was to draw up a list of fifteen artists whose work it found offensive and circulate it to anyone who would listen—which unfortunately amounted to quite a lot of powerful people. The acts on the list, instantly labeled "The Filthy Fifteen," included AC/DC, Black Sabbath, Cyndi Lauper, Def Leppard, Judas Priest, Madonna, the Mary Jane Girls, Mercyful Fate, Mötley Crüe, Prince, Sheena Easton, Twisted Sister, Vanity, Venom, and WASP.

Notice how much heavy metal there is on there? The genre's much-loved lyrical themes—sex, the occult, and all-round debauchery—had caused Tipper and her buddies to get into a righteous froth, which is ironic in our case, as Rob Zombie prefers a nice cup of tea to a beer. As for the pop acts Mary Jane Girls, Vanity, Sheena Easton, and the rest of them, most were both harmless and obscure, but a line had been crossed. The '80s became, from that point on, the decade of censorship for rock and metal, especially if the music contained even the slightest reference to Satan or Satanism. This bias was very much still extant in 1996, when White Zombie drove into Johnson City.

The madness peaked when the big cheeses in Washington wanted to know exactly how dangerous rock music was to the youth of America, and brought in three musicians—jazz-rock legend Frank Zappa, Dee Snider of Twisted Sister, and country star John Denver—to speak in defense of popular music at a series of hearings. The choice of Snider to represent the metal cause was bewildering—if they'd wanted a lyrically extreme band, why didn't they call Slayer?—but in any case it was Zappa who was most incisive in his comments. He echoed most sane people's opinions when he said, "The PMRC proposal is an ill-conceived piece of nonsense which fails to deliver any real benefits to children, infringes the civil liberties of people who are not children and promises to keep the courts busy for years . . . the PMRC's demands are the equivalent of treating dandruff by decapitation."

In 1986, more and more cases of censorship were executed, and as always, it was Satanism and the occult that scared most people. This fear was manifested in ludicrous cases such as Frank Zappa's *Jazz from Hell*, which was awarded an "explicit lyrics" sticker even though it was completely instrumental. Then Slayer's 1986 album *Reign in Blood* appeared—grisly slasher lyrics, devilry, and all—causing Def Jam's usual distributor, Columbia, to refuse to handle it. In the end the Geffen firm—apparently less precious about the issue—distributed *Reign*, although there was a delay of several months in the album's international release as a result.

Thanks to Slayer and a few other extreme metal acts such as Possessed and Death, the idea that metal could be harmful was beginning to be a popular conception among those members of public who didn't actually listen to it. When Judas Priest were sued by the families of two teenagers who had entered a suicide pact after listening to the *Stained Class* album—in a direct echo of Ozzy Osbourne's "Suicide Solution" case—the idea that metal was positively dangerous in the wrong hands spiraled out of control.

The Priest case, which centered on the accusation that the band had inserted subliminal lyrics into their music, was highly damaging to the band's profile and—had they lost the case—would have been an enormous victory for the PMRC, establishing a legal precedent for future cases. Rock and metal as a whole could then have been blamed for all sorts of future ills: we had a lucky escape there.

The relevance of all this chin-stroking to White Zombie is clear, because an interesting social trend was emerging toward the end of the 1980s. The authorities had forgotten one simple fact, which was that the young consumers of so-called "deviant" music were not stupid, and the majority understood that this extreme art was just that: art. As ban followed ban and concerned parents filled the airwaves with their bleating, overkill inevitably followed, and the kids became impatient with being constantly forbidden to listen to what was, for them, just another album. Asking themselves and each other what was wrong with listening to lyrics that dealt with sex and death—perfectly valid themes for discussion, then as now—the teenagers began to mock, then to actively defy, the censorship which they perceived as petty and insulting.

The strength of this defiance was shown in the immense commercial boost which the banned artists received—both in marketing terms (a banned act was easy to promote as shocking, scary, evil and so on) and in hard cash: fans flocked to the shows and queued up to buy the albums, "Parental Advisory" stickers or not. Three huge-selling albums were all banned in 1987 and '88—Jane's Addiction's *Nothing's Shocking* (banned from some stores thanks to its sleeve art), Prince's *LoveSexy* (which faced distribution problems because of its cover image of a naked Prince) and Guns N' Roses' debut album, *Appetite for Destruction*.

Curiously, the end of the 1980s marked a hiatus in the endless war between metal bands and the industry, thanks largely to the rise of a scarier phenomenon: gangsta rap. Although the PMRC and the showbiz organizations in its pockets still fought hard to restrain albums by the few metal bands that had survived the grunge wave, their new targets were Ice-T, 2 Live Crew, and NWA, whose lyrics were far more aggressive and reality-based than anything the metallers had come up with. When 2 Live Crew rhymed "With my dick in my hands as you fall to your knees / You know what to do, 'cause I won't say please," it made Mötley Crüe's "Girls, Girls, Girls" sound like a feminist anthem. And when NWA rapper Ice Cube yelled, "Fuck the police, coming straight from the underground," he made Black Sabbath's pastoral croon of "Satan laughing spreads his wings" seem juvenile, inoffensive, and—worst of all—irrelevant.

Of course, the ceasefire was temporary, and once gangsta rap had matured into the more politically astute G-Funk, the PMRC's sights were firmly targeted on metal and the new wave of alternative rock once more. Ice-T, who had bridged both worlds with his metal band Body Count, was at the center of a huge furor with "Cop Killer" in 1992, and the late singer Oderus Urungus of GWAR was arrested in North Carolina, on charges of "disseminating obscenity" at a gig. Meanwhile, Nirvana were in trouble over the song "Rape Me" on their *In Utero* album—Wal-Mart and K-Mart refused to stock it, only relenting when the album topped the charts and a renamed version was manufactured: a perfect example of a) consumer buying-power being entirely indifferent to censorship and b) the hypocrisy of the industry.

Which brings us to the modern day.

Previous page: An early portrait of Rob Zombie, taken at CBGB, New York City, March 1987. (Catherine McGann/Getty Images)
Above: White Zombie backstage at L'Amour, Brooklyn, April 1990: Rob Zombie, Jay Yuenger, Ivan de Prume, and Sean Yseult. (Frank White)

Zombie at the Bond Street Cafe, New York City, May 1989. (Frank White)

Above: White Zombie at the peak of their powers, performing at the Target Center, Minneapolis, May 1993. (Jim Steinfeldt/Michael Ochs Archives/Getty Images)
Previous page, top: Jay Yuenger, Rob Zombie, and Sean Yseult onstage at a Rock for Choice show at the Hollywood Palladium, April 1993. (Jeff Kravitz/FilmMagic)
Previous page, bottom: A poster advertising the band's return visit to the Palladium in December of the same year. (Courtesy of Limited Runs, www.limitedruns.com)

Left to right: Sean Yseult, John Tempesta, Jay Yuenger, and Rob Zombie backstage at the Monsters of Rock festival at Castle Donington, England, August 1995. (Andre Csillag/Rex USA)

Rob Zombie stalks the stage of the Blockbuster-Sony Entertainment Centre, Camden, New Jersey, August 1996. (Frank White)

Sheri Moon and Rob Zombie at the New York premiere of the Howard
Stern biopic *Private Parts*, February 1997. (Matt Baron/BEImages)

In 1994, with the advent of Marilyn Manson, metal made the headlines due to Satanism once again. Marilyn Manson himself became the center of many a ban and arrest in the mid-'90s, notably after a show in Jacksonville, Florida, where he supposedly violated the Adult Entertainment Code. Manson was accused of inserting a dildo into his anus while urinating on the audience (a feat which would require admirable sphincter control, if nothing else).

The idea that heavy metal is somehow dangerous is a stupid, unnecessary one that has no reason to exist in 2015 because it was obsolete in 1980. As a society, we should have grown past all this nonsense years—decades—ago. There's no harm in listening to the stuff. It's fantasy-based escapist entertainment which makes its fans smile, unless you happen to be among the small number of people whose mental health is fragile. You could say the same about horror movies, although in fact that exact statement has been made so many times before now that I literally can't face reading it, let alone writing it, one more time.

Let's be professional and look at the other side of the argument. Two studies in California and Australia concluded in recent years that teenagers are at a greater risk of depression if they listen to a lot of metal. There is no way of assessing the efficacy of the studies, or the agendas of those who executed them, but let's say for the sake of argument that they are legitimate. What these results suggest is that cause and effect have been confused here: kids who are already depressed or depression-prone will choose metal to listen to as an escape or healing mechanism, rather than the music being the initial cause of their depression. Unless, and I'll say it again, you're referring to the small group of individuals who suffer from a genuine chemical disorder. Your average teenager with average mental health will not suddenly develop depression from listening to too much (is there even such a thing as too much?) heavy metal.

It's thirty years since the "Satanic panic" of the '80s, when Ozzy Osbourne, Judas Priest and the rest of them were earnestly told off for using naughty words in their songs. It didn't make sense then, and it doesn't make sense now. It is literally only fools who attempt to rehash the same old arguments, time after time.

Life isn't all about what the naked eye can see, of course. A lot of people think that we're all the unwitting slaves of a shadowy, unelected elite, and I'm sure that's true to an extent. But when it comes to the influence of heavy metal, it's simple: it is there to make you feel good. What a strange species we are. We hate things we don't understand and we actively create a culture of misery and repression. But those behavior patterns can change, and indeed they must change, or we'll never evolve into a mature society.

◆

Despite the troubles Zombie and his band faced, the tour dates stacked up. Everywhere—or close to everywhere—was certainly a way to describe White Zombie's touring schedule for 1996. After firing through the UK and Germany in May, they hooked up with Pantera for late June to late August in America. The "War of the Gargantuas" tour, as it was known, also featured Eyehategod and Deftones opening at certain dates—and has become somewhat legendary in heavy metal circles. This was primarily because both White Zombie and Pantera were experiencing their first major success at the time, but also because both groups—Pantera in particular— got up to some insane antics on the road.

"Dimebag" Darrell Abbott, Pantera's guitarist, was a man on

a serious (and seemingly unstoppable) mission when it came to refining backstage shenanigans, as documented by endless magazine and TV journalists. For example, he would wear a jumpsuit and a baseball hat and wander around pretending to be a member of the venue's technical staff, which gave him free rein to get up onstage and tinker with the other musicians' amps and instruments.

Pantera singer Phil Anselmo also got in on the action. Zombie had designed scary clowns on crucifixes that would lower down during the song "Grease Paint and Monkey Brains." Every night of the tour, Anselmo attempted to tape dildos to the clowns. Dimebag also came on stage dressed in a cape and an old man's mask, whipping the cape up to reveal an enormous dildo emitting liquid onto the band-members and the stage.

These anecdotes were the thin end of the wedge when it came to debauchery, as Deftones singer Chino Moreno remembered in an interview years later. "Honestly, that was probably one of the wildest and most fun tours," he recalled, laughing at how so many of the stories were simply unrepeatable. This was a time, he said, "before the new era of touring began—which I guess isn't as debauchery-ridden as it used to be. It was great to feel like we had a part in some of the final days of that."

Pantera would host high-stakes dice games in their dressing room each night. "They'd have free-for-all Taco Bell, 'Blacktooth Grins' [whiskey shots], and beers," Moreno added. From the sound of things his Deftones bandmate, guitarist Stephen Carpenter, was making more from the after-show gambling than he was for his stage work. "Dimebag was down a few grand, and Stephen was just coming in and cleaning house. It's funny because we were like the poorest band out there . . . we didn't have any money."

Later, Rob Zombie would look back with affection at the dates he played with Pantera, with whom White Zombie shared a management company, Concrete Management. They played almost 300 shows on the same bill. It wasn't all fun, of course: the rigors of touring tend to take their toll after years on the road, not to mention headbanging every night for two hours.

Yseult, for one, sustained a knee injury on the road. "I twisted my knee and got torn cartilage, and there was no time for me to get surgery so I had to perform for another year with a leg brace on. That was not fun," she said. "And I'll tell you, anyone that has to perform, whether it's somebody in music, theater, dance, or sports, and you hear about people getting hooked on painkillers and stuff, that's why. I didn't, but I could have, because I was in so much pain and rock docs, as they're called . . . show up at these big 10,000-seaters and go, 'Here, have a Vicodin.' Then all of a sudden you feel a lot better and not in total pain and can get through the show. I've seen it happen with a lot of musicians and I definitely felt a lot better when I was on those, and it did help me get through that year, but I'm really glad I didn't get hooked on them."

Busted limbs and exhausting schedules notwithstanding, there were bigger issues threatening the existence of White Zombie. Relationships between the band members—or more precisely, between Zombie and the other three—had deteriorated to the point where contact between them was minimal.

"People weren't getting along, and people weren't speaking," Zombie recalled, some time later. During the making of *Astro-Creep: 2000*, there was barely a time when the whole band was in the same room together. They were now traveling on separate tour buses, too, rarely seeing each other until showtime.

And yet there was still so much for Zombie to do, whether his band was in good shape or not. Now a successful musician and recognized as a video director of some skill, offers were coming in for many of his diverse talents. Marvel Comics had approached him to create a White Zombie comic, although this subsequently did not materialize; extra artwork options—based on his designs— had become possible through the release of music on CD-ROM, or "enhanced CDs" as they were quaintly called before widespread internet access made them obsolete; and Glenn Danzig asked him to work on text and artwork for his comic-book line, Verotik.

A remix album called *Supersexy Swingin' Sounds* appeared in August 1996 and, it must be said, hasn't aged well. Metal combined with elements of dance music seemed current in the era of the superstar DJ, but all these years later it doesn't stand up nearly as well as, say, *Astro-Creep*. Not that another studio album of *Astro-Creep*'s caliber seemed likely to appear at this point: collaborations within White Zombie were at their lowest ebb. Zombie recalled years later that the band had hit a wall, creatively speaking, and that had they continued much longer, ultimately White Zombie would have ended up making records only for the money.

By the end of 1996, White Zombie was essentially over. Zombie recalled a particular incident during the Pantera tour when he knew the end was nigh. He walked offstage, handed his microphone to a tech, drove to the airport, and flew home. Little or no discussion with his bandmates about the future followed.

A decade later, *Late Late Show* host Craig Kilborn asked Zombie if the ever-divisive creative differences had played a part in the band's divergence. "We toured for almost four years without ever speaking to each other," he replied. "Right when we couldn't stand each other any more, the money started coming in, so I was like, 'I'll do anything to hang onto this thing.'"

"I think they just hated me," he added. "I don't know what it was, I forget, but it didn't end good." There was a conference call of sorts to confirm the band's demise, and then that was it. They hadn't spoken since.

"You were the leader of the group, right?" Kilborn asked.

"I think that was where the hatred came from," Zombie replied, "because they didn't see it that way."

The host then asked if he had received a bigger share of White Zombie's income as the leader, he said: "Well, that's where the end came about. When you start a band in high school, you're like, 'Let's share this evenly. Let's even give the drummer a fourth, because he's a good guy' . . . you come to the realization after a while, like 'Why's this guy making a million dollars?'" (Note that he wasn't referring to latter-day White Zombie drummer John Tempesta, who would remain a regular collaborator for some time after the band's split.)

Looking back all these years later, White Zombie seemed to have broken up at the right time for the members' collective and individual sanity—and, more to the point, at a time when medium-sized bands could still make a lot of money out of CD sales and touring. Within five years, illegal file-sharing had begun to damage musicians' revenue; five years after that, iTunes dominated the market and income from physical sales was drastically reduced. White Zombie came and went before any of those issues arose—to their great fortune.

"I definitely feel grateful that we got big when we did," Sean Yseult told me. "We were so lucky with the timing. When we broke up in 1996, it was right when the record industry was starting to collapse. There was no downloading when we were popular, so people bought our records. It was incredible."

It later emerged that White Zombie's management had asked Yseult and Yeunger to consider continuing the band with a new singer, but the idea did not appeal to either of them. In any case, perhaps the time wasn't right to start a new band: not when the music industry was about to receive a near-terminal shock. A file-sharing service called Napster went live in June 1999, with the intention of distributing music files to its subscribers. Its core idea—that online distribution of record-company-owned material by Napster could be a workable business operation—failed to take off and in December the RIAA sued Napster for copyright infringement. The plaintiff requested damages of $100,000 each time a song was copied.

While the suit was in progress, Napster's profile escalated enormously as its reputation spread by word of mouth: in early 2000, several universities were obliged to remove it from their networks because demand by the student body for its use was too great. In the space of one year, creator Shawn Fanning had unleashed the marketing specialist's dream: a product that everybody *had* to have. A lawsuit arrived in April 2000, courtesy of Metallica, and was ultimately successful, in a legal sense—but by then the idea of file-sharing had spread, and literally millions of songs were distributed among users of Napster and other programs in the next few years, a process which continues today.

Looking back at this period, it seems that the predictions of some of those involved—who said that the technology could not be stopped—have come true, and then some: far from being a music-only phenomenon, now movies, software, and images are also the currency of exchange. Now that fast internet access is readily available, more or less any unencrypted digital file can be exchanged, which raises enormous questions about the livelihoods of copyright holders and the nature of copyright itself.

One last song came from White Zombie: a song they recorded, ironically enough, for the soundtrack of a movie based on the cartoon characters who had brought the band their first taste of major fame. The soundtrack to *Beavis and Butt-Head Do America*, a mildly amusing flick devoted to the eponymous metal-loving morons, features the song "Ratfinks, Suicide Tanks, and Cannibal Girls"—but more relevantly to our story, the film itself also includes a section animated by Rob Zombie himself.

Did this hint at his future activities? Indeed it did. Cementing his profile by legally adopting the name Rob Zombie after years of uncertainty over whether or not he should be known as "Rob Straker," our man struck out in a new direction. Restless in interviews, never finding enough time to express his multiple talents in any single day, and driven in many simultaneous directions, Rob Zombie was now much more than just a rock star.

FIVE

I, MONSTER

(1997–2002)

For White Zombie, the year 1997 started in what might be described as a split-personality manner. The band's version of KC and the Sunshine Band's "I'm Your Boogie Man," which had appeared on the soundtrack of *The Crow 2*, was nominated for a Grammy—but so was "Hands of Death (Burn Baby Burn)," a song Rob Zombie had recorded in collaboration with Alice Cooper for an album, *Songs in the Key of X*, "inspired by" the TV series *The X-Files*. Neither song won, but at least the idea of Zombie as a solo artist had been received favorably by the industry.

Zombie was also asked to write and direct the third installment in the *Crow* movie series, a franchise much beloved of goths and other alternative types since the success of the first film, a bleak 1994 thriller permanently haunted by the accidental death of its star, Brandon Lee, during production.

"The movie will be based on [Zombie's] own screenplay, which he's currently re-writing. Shooting should begin later this year,"

MTV News reported, but the project was ultimately scrapped. Talk about a painful introduction to the movie industry.

If you've read between the lines so far, it will be evident that Rob Zombie's desire to make films had become just as strong as his music-making instincts by the time that White Zombie split—and yet, video clips and the *Beavis and Butt-Head* dream sequence aside, serious projects continued to elude him. Perhaps this explains his extreme focus when it came to returning to music—and recording his first, career-defining solo album.

Hellbilly Deluxe: 13 Tales of Cadaverous Cavorting Inside the Spookshow International was released on August 25, 1998. Three million sales and platinum awards later, it's still Rob Zombie's most successful album, although not necessarily his most significant artistic creation, as we'll see in due course. Written in collaboration with Canadian producer Scott Humphrey, its thirteen songs showcased utter confidence and power on the part of Zombie. Drummer John Tempesta remained on board from the White Zombie lineup, but a new guitarist and bassist—Mike Riggs (formerly of Prong), and Rob "Blasko" Nicholson (ex-Danzig)—were recruited to the band.

Blasko in particular was a useful recruit to Rob Zombie's new band, largely because he had served his dues in many roles in his previous acts and was a no-nonsense problem solver as well as a reliable musician. As he explained in an interview with Joe Daly of *Bass Guitar* magazine, "The music business is just about doing it. Anything you want to be, you just have to do it. Music schools can only go so far. Sure, you can learn modes and scales and the importance of technique, but if you want to be one of those people who puts out records and goes on tour and lives out of a suitcase, there's nothing that M.I. [the Musicians' Institute in Los Angeles] could teach you. [Legendary jazz bassist] Jaco Pastorius didn't go to M.I., you know." More important than that, as far as Blasko was concerned, was marketing yourself and making yourself visible to other musicians. "That's how you get gigs."

Looking back at how he got into music, Blasko revealed a set of influences that were much like Zombie's. He got his start in the '80s, when bass players, as he recalled it, were "the cooler dudes . . . Gene Simmons was spitting blood and fire; he was the Demon, and that really turned me on. When I first got into KISS, I thought they were monsters or superheroes. It didn't register until later that those guys were musicians."

As he moved up in the industry, he became accustomed to making do in tight circumstances when his bands hit the road in hired vans (which they would invariably have to have their parents rent on their behalf). "Because we didn't want to pay for mileage, we'd disconnect the odometer; of course, whenever you disconnect the odometer, you also disconnect the speedometer, so we never knew how fast we were driving! It was really fun but there were no cellphones, no computers . . . you used a payphone when you could. Whenever you'd get a flat tire, you'd be there by the side of the road trying to flag people down to help. There was no AAA app in 1986!"

Asked by Daly what it takes to work for an artist as highly regarded as Rob Zombie, Blasko put his continuing musical employment down to his being easy to work with and resisting the temptation to pursue his own agendas. "Some people don't really wrap their heads around the hired gun role. They think they're an 'artist' and their value as an artist should be heard. I don't subscribe to that. Look, I'm proud to be a hired gun. I work with artists and I'm part of a grand vision that is the vision of the artist; I'm not trying to carve out my own thing. My role is to make the dude whose name is on the ticket kick ass. That's the job description."

Guests on the new album also included Danny Lohner and Charlie Clouser of Nine Inch Nails, on guitar and keyboards respectively—and, perhaps unexpectedly, drummer Tommy Lee of hair-metal pioneers Mötley Crüe. Lee had recently completed part of a 180-day sentence for spousal battery against his then-wife, actress Pamela Anderson, and had gone to stay with Scott Humphrey, the producer of Mötley Crüe's *Generation Swine*, who was now working on the Rob Zombie record. "I think I was there about a day or two and they were working on the record downstairs, and Scott and Rob were like, 'Dude, Tommy's upstairs, we should ask him to play.' And they asked me to play and I was like, 'I would love to play right now. I could really use . . . you know, just kind of check out, really do some music,' and I ended up playing like four tracks or so on the record. It was a lot of fun, I really enjoyed it, Rob's a cool guy."

The performance and production team did a precision-engineered job on *Hellbilly Deluxe*, presumably so named as a pun on country warbler Dwight Yoakam's 1987 album *Hillbilly Deluxe*. Thick, staccato guitar riffs overlay grooves of great solidity, over which Zombie bellows—in a lower tone than before—his lyrical observations on the darker side of life. Sure, it sounds a bit like Marilyn Manson, a little like Ministry, and a lot like White Zombie, but the overall aesthetic is Rob Zombie's alone, especially when summed up as a whole vision including the vintage movie references and the videos for the three singles which came from the album.

Asked about how his writing differed now compared with during the White Zombie era, Zombie explained that the main reason his previous band had split up was because the members no longer got along with each other.

"It wasn't because I had some artistic urge that I had to be by myself. It was just a necessity. I mean, the band could not be . . . so it was just a nightmare. It just ended over a bad feeling. And as far as the difference between the two [bands] . . . I don't know. There is a lot of aspects that are very similar and distinctively different. It's kind of hard for me to actually judge it truthfully. Because sometimes people will hear a song and they are like, 'Oh, that sounds so old White Zombie to me,' and I am like, 'Really? I don't hear it like that.' I'm not really a good judge of that."

The most persuasive song on the album, with the benefit of seventeen years' hindsight anyway, is "Superbeast," the first song proper after the intro, "Call of the Zombie." Issued as a promo single ahead of the album, the song is an up-tempo rock anthem based on a terrific riff straight from the Nine Inch Nails/Ministry canon, powering ahead with a catchy chorus that is clearly designed for large arena audiences. "Dragula" and "Living Dead Girl," also singles, are further examples of super-commercial 'dark rock' with kitsch elements that Alice Cooper himself, not to mention more extreme acts such as GWAR, would be proud to claim as their own.

Simple music—in the best sense of the word "simple"—is often the most powerful. Take "Superbeast," for example. There's basically one riff, that descending, slightly offbeat sequence of changes that powers the song along, interspersed with kick-drum-punctuating bass on three notes. It's not complex stuff; it's impactful, easy to remember, and as such very persuasive. This kind of music is easy to play, especially for musicians of the caliber of those in White

Zombie, but it's not easy to write, especially if you want to sound original.

"Perversion 99," a brief instrumental interlude based largely on percussion, separates the most commercially obvious first third of *Hellbilly Deluxe* from what follows: a suite of songs that reveal where Zombie was really coming from, musically speaking. "Demonoid Phenomenon" is his heaviest song yet in terms of sheer riff weight, owing much to Metallica's early-1990s "Black Album," at least in its more uncompromising sections. "Spookshow Baby" is more digestible and less derivative, opening with a sitar (or a studio-generated simulacrum of one) and moving through a simple, one-note chorus, while "How to Make a Monster" is the album's only really questionable song. There's nothing wrong with its structure or musicianship; it is simply mixed too low, whether intentionally or in error.

Hellbilly Deluxe regains its momentum with "Meet the Creeper," another eminently hummable song that has "radio" written all over it. "The Ballad of Resurrection Joe and Rosa Whore" is subtler, focusing on Zombie's laconically drawled vocal and surprising the listener with a sudden storm of guitars when its choruses arrive. "What Lurks on Channel X?" is a montage of vintage movie samples in the familiar Zombie style before an upbeat assemblage of electronically-enhanced guitar riffs, while "Return of the Phantom Stranger" winds down the album rather predictably, with a sound that could easily have come from any Marilyn Manson album of the era. A two-minute digital soundscape called "The Beginning of the End" finishes things off.

Of course, it's a very 1990s-sounding album—how could it not be? But what an opening statement it was. Debuting at #5 on the

Billboard 200 with first-week sales of 121,000—respectable then, unimaginable now—the album surpassed everyone's expectations, even those of Zombie itself, who expected it to perform averagely at best. Taking it on tour with the new band, Zombie threw everything his budget would allow at the stage show, including dancers, pyro, multi-level staging and fun touches such as a handheld dry-ice hose that could be emptied over the crowd. He also refined his onstage costume, smothering his face and hair with cobwebby flakes of corpse paint and making all-white contact lenses a trademark.

Like the album, the live show was cheesy, kitsch to the core, and highly entertaining: the over-the-top-ness of the images and sounds was meant to be savored. Not everyone liked the relentless references to vintage horror—a message that had been driven home endlessly for a decade and more at this point—but Riggs, Blasko, and Tempesta—as well as Sheri Moon—all participated in the live extravaganza with enthusiasm. The former even went so far as to have a transparent, hollow guitar manufactured, which he filled with a red, bloodlike liquid, which he regularly "drank" and spewed over audience members. "It's the best-sounding guitar in the whole world," he laughed. "That's how they're gonna make all guitars one day! Plexiglas and liquid is the best conductor for sound. I need about five more of them motherfuckers! . . . I'm not telling anybody how much ['blood'] I put in there to get the right tone. I figured it out by trial and error. The more blood I drink out of it, the more low end goes out of it, but no one notices it because I play so loud."

The massive production of the *Hellbilly* tour dates did not go unnoticed by the plethora of journalists who descended on Zombie for interviews when it became apparent that he had a future as a solo artist. In one session for *Pulse*, Zombie was interviewed in tandem with his friend and inspiration Alice Cooper, himself fond of regular onstage hangings and decapitations in the vintage horror style.

"The only person out there who's having any fun with [stage shows] is Rob Zombie," claimed Cooper—not unreasonably given the slightly flat state of the rock scene at the end of the 1990s. "And it's clear when you listen to his albums, and when you see his show, that he's having a great time. Other people look like they're just tortured souls up there, and you go, you know, 'Guys! Lighten up! The image is heavy and everything, but you don't have to really be that'. These guys are trying to live their lives the way their image is. . . . The idea behind rock 'n' roll is joy. It's joyful music. It's not a depressing thing. For a long time, all the new bands were like, 'Let's see how boring we can be. Let's see how depressed we can make the audience.' I don't know if that's what they think they're supposed to do."

Bringing back the live fun appears to have been high on Rob Zombie's agenda since day one. Remember that this is a guy who spent his childhood in the grey 1970s, entranced by the Technicolor movies and stereo sounds which emitted from his TV set, or at the local cinema. The power of the stage would have been a seriously strong force in an era when everyday life was not yet populated by endless portable entertainment devices and an invisible web of music and animations stretching from server to mobile phone and back again.

Audiences and members of the press new to Rob Zombie and his curious message soon became intensely interested in the man behind the makeup. Was he real or just a character? Zombie quickly became accustomed to answering this question, telling writer Russell

A. Trunk, "There's nothing I do that's a stage persona. Everything I do is anything I like. I looked the way I look now before I had a band and was obsessed with the same things I'm obsessed with now, way before I had a commercial purpose for it."

While most reviews of *Hellbilly Deluxe* and the ensuing live shows were generally positive, some critics dismissed Zombie's work as insignificant—or, worse, outmoded. To his credit, the man himself didn't seem to give a damn, telling Trunk, "At this stage of the game, none of it matters to me. When I was first starting, I'd read something and it would really bother me, but now it doesn't matter. It's all so meaningless and everyone forgets it. The records that we've had out up until now that have sold millions of copies, people forget that the reviews were atrocious, as were the reviews for many records that people now consider things that they love."

Zombie recalled an *Alternative Press* review of *La Sexorcisto* that effectively described his group as "the worst band ever . . . it was so over the top, I was convinced I'd done something to this guy on a personal level. It was so non-objective. It was like, 'I hate this band, I hate this band, I hate this band!' But now it just doesn't matter. Now I just expect it, and I'm more surprised when I read something good. You can't get upset with bad press and you can't get too happy with yourself over good press. You have to take it for what it is."

In fact, Zombie appeared to be having too much fun on the road and focusing on the big picture to take minor hindrances such as critics seriously. "Probably one of the best practical jokes, and this really worked good, was at the Reading Festival in England, [where] I brought this really, really realistic-looking fake human shit!" he chuckled. "It came in a spray can, so you could spray it out, and it smelled. One of the big phobias on a tour bus is that you are not supposed to poop on it, because it doesn't actually flush like pee. So, I put tons of fake shit in the toilet and all around the toilet floor and I then started everyone thinking with, 'I don't know who that was, but something [evil] just happened in there!' Everyone walked in there and was immediately gagging and nearly vomited from the smell. It went on for hours. It was so funny. It worked like a charm."

By anyone's standards, Zombie's life as a star was now entering the realm of the unusual. Groupies approached him on a regular basis, although he was steadfast in his fidelity to Sheri Moon. Everyday events such as the venerable chanteuse Barbara Streisand using "Thunder Kiss '65" at high volume to deter paparazzi from bothering her at her wedding in 1998 were so often quoted that he got fed up with talking about it. "Hopefully, the Funny Lady will use a track off my new album, *Hellbilly Deluxe*, to ward off meddling paparazzi at her divorce hearing," he sniped, plugging his album and taking a shot at Streisand in one cunning move.

Asked by *Melody Maker* writer Neil Kulkarni where Zombie's strange brew of entertainment came from, peaking as it did with the tour following *Hellbilly Deluxe*, he attributed its roots to the heady cultural diet he'd been weaned on as a kid, with rock 'n' roll just one "cool thing" alongside movies, TV, and comic books. "By the time I'd grown up on this endless diet of visceral junk, both fictional and factual, rock music had to be just as theatrical and extreme, had to compete with the luridness with all that stuff that had desensitized me so much. When your mom takes you to see *A Clockwork Orange* at age seven, you get a warped view of life. . . . I'm obsessed with all that strange, perfect, fucked-up Americana that's disappearing so fast now. That's what the sleeves and the live shows are all about.

Bringing showbiz back to the sick freaks who perfected it, not the hippies and nerds who run shit now."

Warming to his subject with typical passion, Zombie asked, "When did entertainment get so fucking unentertaining? I remember loving the movies, getting excited by TV specials, seeing and hearing something new every fucking day that you just had to tell everyone about. Now, it's like why bother seeing anything when you know it's just going to be a crock of crap anyway? . . . It's like you only have two choices now. You can either be [a] sappy, saccharine, anodyne, morally unimpeachable, tax-paying, simpering idiot and be popular, or you have to go to the other extreme, alienate the entire planet apart from your household pets, and really self-consciously set out to shock. I don't see why you can't be popular and extreme, over-the-edge, but still there to entertain all the ladies and gentlemen and boys and girls."

Likening his own work and attitude to that of P. T. Barnum and B-movie director William Castle, Zombie described himself as "a good American showman, here to entertain the folks some." He lamented the "engulfing deterioration in everything. . . . All that people care about is if something sounds cool, looks cool, fucks your head up. Everyone thinks everything's already been done, so Hollywood and the music biz are just turning into karoke: remaking and remodeling and restoring. Fuck that. Fuck remakes of *Psycho* and *Carnival of Souls* and *Carrie*. First you gotta realize everything is fucked. Then you start building."

With this aim firmly in mind, Zombie faced his future squarely. In 1998, he launched a record label, Zombie-a-Go-Go, a Geffen subsidiary, and released albums by two bands, the Ghastly Ones and the Bomboras, both essentially White Zombie clones with surf influences whose careers came and went in a few short years. "I like being able to pursue my own course and triumph or fuck up on my own terms," he told Kulkarni. "White Zombie are over forever, and that's my final word. It's not as if the world mourned our passing, we ain't the fucking Beach Boys, and who the fuck who want to hear a dozen people who don't know each other play songs they can't remember any more? I'm sick of compromise: with my new band and with the new album, I've just been indulged totally and I love it."

Of course, Zombie knew that his music and that of White Zombie were not radically different. Why would it be? "The vibe was always—I always did what I wanted to do. I was never held back by the fact that it was a band, or something. It was always, you know, what I wanted to do at the time. Musically, sometimes, it would be a push and a pull, because . . . if it's a band everyone has got their idea, everyone has got an opinion . . . you're trying to make everybody happy, which is never possible. And so you know when it became my own thing, I could do whatever I wanted. You know, I could do anything I wanted at any time, and there was no one to say shit, or complain about it."

◆

Actually, Zombie wasn't quite right about that. People still had plenty to say about his music, and sometimes not in a good way. Censorship reared its ugly head again in 1999, with White Zombie its target once more, even though the band itself was no longer a functioning entity. A student called Robert Parker wore a T-shirt to Westerly High School in Westerly, Rhode Island, that bore a picture of Rob Zombie alongside the number 666. The school rapidly suspended Parker, not once but twice, citing the shirt's demonic nature. The American Civil Liberties Union of Rhode Island reacted quickly, filing an appeal with the State Department of Education. An ACLU lawyer was quoted as saying, "Public schools cannot be in the business of approving a T-shirt about the Lord and banning a T-shirt of a rock band, even a sacrilegious one . . . [Parker] desires to wear his shirt in order to express himself, display his interest in and enthusiasm for certain music, and to exercise autonomy in his chosen clothing." In doing so, America's First Amendment—the right to freedom of speech—was invoked, and Parker was allowed to resume his studies as a result.

What a load of nonsense, you might think, although the case does require us to execute a quick reappraisal of the great "heavy metal music versus Satan" debate if we're to place White Zombie in its correct place in American culture. This goes all the way back to the era of slavery, when the worship music brought into America by African slaves evolved on the one hand into gospel ("respectable" music) and on the other to blues and jazz (the polar opposite). Before the World War II, black music was strictly an underground phenomenon, confined to the jazz and blues clubs of New Orleans and New York and kept well away from the bars frequented by white working-class Americans, let alone the haunts of the affluent middle classes.

Make no mistake: black music scared the pants off the average white family. Rumors abounded of debauched scenes in the underground blues clubs, in which crowds of people would smoke dope and indulge in an orgy of violent music and promiscuity. The atonal sounds of jazz and blues, the squeals of the instruments and the frenzy of the dancers all added up to the kind of whispered tales that made many a Boston dowager throw up her hands in horror when she heard them at the local church tea party. Makes you wish that someone had transported these people through time to a present-day Rob Zombie show, doesn't it?

It didn't help that many of the songs written by the leading black artists contained thinly veiled references to sex, Satan, and drugs, although they were often entirely missed by the censors of the day because the words were derived from Creole dialects or slang. When the doomed bluesman Robert Johnson sang about a "Hell Hound on My Trail," he wasn't talking about the family pooch. He was referring to a supposed deal with the devil—and when he gleefully moaned, "Squeeze my lemon, baby, till the juice runs down my leg," he wasn't anywhere near a fruit bowl. Meanwhile, the legendary Roy Brown song "Good Rockin' Tonight" is a simple euphemism for sex—and the number of blues and jazz singers who praised "Mary Jane" (marijuana) in their lyrics was vast.

It didn't take long for your average white family to notice that while the adults were busy tut-tutting and condemning the feared jazz and blues scenes, their teenage sons and daughters had gone all quiet and interested, ears flapping in the breeze. Of course, the kids wanted to check out the sex, drugs and scary music for themselves—who wouldn't?—but mom and pop weren't having it. The reason? Because that would have meant their beloved kids coming into contact with the black subculture—and specifically, their freshly scrubbed daughters coming into the close proximity of black men.

This fear was the dark heart of white America's mistrust of black music—a perceived threat that has stalked the white man for centuries, all the way from Shakespeare's *Othello* ("A black ram is tupping your white ewe") to Public Enemy's 1990 album *Fear of a*

Black Planet and beyond. The solution of America's churchmen and politicians (then, as now, inextricably linked) was to label black music as "devil's music." Satan stood for everything the white Christian establishment feared and despised—premarital sex; intoxication via drugs or alcohol; violent, destructive behavior; and loud, aggressive music. In their unsophisticated way, the parents, teachers, preachers, and cops who warned the kids away from "race music" assumed that calling it satanic would be enough to convince the little darlings not to dabble in it.

Of course, they couldn't have been more wrong. Still, it took Elvis Presley—a nonthreatening white man from a God-fearing country family, despite his establishment-bothering antics and greasy quiff—to legitimize the kids' interest in the forbidden sound. Discovered in 1954 in Memphis, Tennessee, by Sun studio owner Sam Phillips, Elvis cut some unremarkable country singles before a chance in-studio jam changed the face of music. Needing to kill some time before the next take, Elvis and his band started jamming on a blues tune by Arthur Crudup called "That's All Right," adding a speeded-up, jittery feel to the song and inadvertently inventing rock 'n' roll in doing so—a sound that combined black R&B with a white country and gospel approach. Phillips—who had infamously been credited with the statement, "If I could find a white man who had the Negro sound and the Negro feel, I could make a million dollars"—rolled the tape, and the rest is history.

By 1956 Elvis was on national television, playing a white, sanitized version of the so-called "devil's music," and America fell into the palm of his sweaty hand, followed over the next decade or so by the rest of the world. Initially, his detractors predicted that the rock 'n' roll fad wouldn't last. However, a huge shock to the

American establishment came when thousands upon thousands of teenage fans, many of them middle-class white girls, flocked to Elvis's concerts—and turned into a bloodthirsty mob when they got there, screaming, fainting, and gouging each other's eyes out in mass hysteria. The renowned journalist Robert Kaiser wrote that Elvis's music "hit them where they lived, deep in their emotions . . . even below their belts. Other singers had been doing this for generations, but they were black."

So what was Elvis's secret? Why did he make the girls scream when his predecessors just made them yawn? It was his hip-swiveling that did the trick, apparently—the knack he had for thrusting his crotch at the ladies in the front row, and the obvious implication therein. The standard heavy metal stance—legs apart, axe slung low—that we all know and love comes directly from Elvis, so you know who to thank next time Metallica and Slayer come to town. Elvis also shook his leg, making it quiver in a faintly ludicrous manner that looked a bit like he needed to urinate, which gave thousands of teenage girls a fair old thrill. The singer Hank Ballard once commented, "In white society, the movement of the butt, the shaking of the leg, all that was considered obscene. Now here's this white boy grinding and rolling his belly and shaking that notorious leg. I hadn't even seen the black dudes doing that."

Elvis had it made, it seemed. Nonetheless, his rise to the top wasn't unhindered: the USA's political-religious axis was a powerful enemy, and in no time the establishment lined up with itchy trigger-fingers, eager to take Elvis down like the devil-worshippin' punk he was. His show at the Mississippi–Alabama Fair in 1956—inevitably, the reddest-necked event in the known universe—was attended by no fewer than one hundred National Guardsmen (America's domestic military force) in order to prevent a horde of hysterical teenagers from destroying the place.

By 1957, all this puritanical censorship had gone away, because the massive commercial power of the Presley brand and his followers crushed all attempts to gag him. If a promoter refused to let him play, his fans jumped in a car and drove twelve hours to see him play in another venue. If mainstream radio turned up its nose at his records, kids just tuned into the new breed of rock 'n' roll stations on their new transistor radios (sales of which jumped by 5,000 percent from 1955 to '58). Then major TV and radio sponsors ploughed huge amounts of money into advertising on rock 'n' roll shows, lending serious commercial weight to the scene. And the final blow came when Hollywood woke up to the phenomenon and started knocking out crappy but successful teenybopper movies aimed directly at the kids.

It's a measure of the success of the white-boy-plays-black-songs approach that Elvis's successors (Bill Haley, Jerry Lee Lewis, Buddy Holly, and Gene Vincent in the US and Cliff Richard, Tommy Steele, Billy Fury, and some band called the Beatles in the UK) that rock 'n' roll and rockabilly were global phenomena by the early 1960s. Meanwhile, the early black artists who had provided the inspiration for it all—Fats Domino, Wynonie Harris, Big Joe Turner, Etta James, Big Mama Thornton (who first recorded Elvis's hit "Hound Dog") and others—were reduced to B-league status or forgotten entirely. In the pantheon of rock 'n' roll, the only black artists to make it to the status of true legends were Chuck Berry and Little Richard—the former because he pioneered a heavier, guitar-based approach (which inspired later musicians such as Jimi Hendrix) and the latter because, well, he scared the crap out of everybody. Once heard, no one forgot the huge-haired, screamingly gay Richard (who infamously sang about "tutti-frutti," a slang term for a homosexual) and his raw, shrieked vocal style. No wonder Little Richard's fans called him "The Real King of Rock 'n' Roll."

All this tied in with the rise of the teenager, a new demographic that had been hardly acknowledged before the war. Now that the kids had money—a result of increased affluence as America's economy got back on track—they had buying power and thus commercial significance. Suddenly there was a huge divide between what the teenagers wanted and what their parents wanted them to have, a generation gap which is the norm today—but which scared the hell out of society's moral guardians back then, adding weight to their arguments that the world was going to hell in a handcart.

The issue of censorship in the specific case of White Zombie in 1999 goes all the way back to those underground jazz and blues clubs: after all, 1950s rock 'n' roll spawned '60s rock, psychedelia, prog, and the many variants of heavy metal that you and I love so much—and if it truly was the devil's music, then we all owe the devil a note of thanks.

◆

A note about the former members of White Zombie, all of whom moved on to other things when the band's split—for the best part of two years an unannounced reality—was finally publicized in 1998.

Sean Yseult joined a surf band called the Famous Monsters, jammed with the Cramps, moved to New Orleans, and in later years became an acclaimed artist and designer.

Jay Yuenger continued his musical career with a variety of projects, including production for Fu Manchu. "There were a number of reasons for the band's breaking up," he said of White Zombie's split, "chiefly among them the fact that we never stopped working and really burnt ourselves out. Personally, relationships in the band became more and more strained until we weren't really communicating at all. And I think Rob really wanted to move away from live instruments and toward more synthetic, dancey music, and he knew that nobody else in the band was willing to go any farther in that direction than we had with *Astro-Creep*."

Some of the earlier members of White Zombie continue to make headlines at metal news portals to this day, including Tom Five and Ivan de Prume, who formed a band called Healer. De Prume also hosts a weekly internet radio show titled *Metalopolis*.

And that, for all intents and purposes, is the last we'll hear of White Zombie in this book, apart from a brief reappearance in boxed-set form in 2008.

Perhaps White Zombie's greatest legacy, much as their fans might not want to hear it, is in the continued success of the band's singer, who in 1998 was fielding offers of artistic projects at all sides. "I actually ended up being more successful than White Zombie, which I didn't know I would be," he told me a few years ago. "There's not a long track record of people having more successful solo careers after leaving bands, especially in the hard rock field. It's pretty much only Ozzy, so there wasn't a lot of people to look to. I just wanted to be happy being in a band, so I thought, 'Even if my solo career is a quarter as successful as White Zombie, I don't give a shit, it'll still be great.' But then when it went on, and was actually the same or bigger, it was awesome."

After composing scores for the video games *Gran Turismo 2* and *Twisted Metal III*, Zombie curated the 1999 release of a remix album called *American Made Music to Strip By*. This was a collection of mixes, some successful and some otherwise, of the material from *Hellbilly Deluxe*—and, like the unloved *Supersexy Swingin' Sounds* from three years previously, it is not necessarily Zombie at his best. Sure, anyone into late-1990s dance music with metallic elements will find something to love on it, but as an expression of art, it belongs to other artists than Zombie.

The remainder of 1999 was taken up with Zombie's efforts to break once more into the film-directing world. Despite his frustrating experiences with *The Crow 3*, it seems that he wasn't taking no for an answer when it came to movies, and a new script called *House of 1,000 Corpses* was now taking up large amounts of his creative energy. Without wanting to spoil the surprise for you, this movie only hit cinemas four years later, in April 2003, which indicates the amount of effort it required and the corresponding hindrances it encountered.

Initially, things looked bright for *House of 1,000 Corpses*, which we'll simply refer to as *House* and assume that you won't confuse this with the TV series of the same name. When I asked him why he wanted to do it in the first place, Zombie explained, "It was something I always wanted to do, but coming from where I came from, I had no clue how to make that dream come true. I first started directing White Zombie videos and my solo videos, and then I did them for Ozzy and Black Label Society and other bands, and over time directing videos became my crash course in filmmaking. I'd always studied movies and read about them obsessively since I was a little kid, and then I got a chance to make one, so I took it and ran with it."

Money, of course, lies squarely at the root of the film industry, simply because movies cost a lot to make and also because they can make staggering profits if they perform well. "The movie business is much more difficult than the music business, because it's about bigger money," he sighed. "If you want to operate on a big level and have your movie in lots of theaters all around the world, the amount of money it takes to get those things done is insane. Even a low-budget movie costs fifteen or twenty million dollars. If you asked someone to give you fifteen million dollars to make a record, they'd be like, 'Fuck you!'"

Nonetheless, Zombie was driven to get *House* done. He had already cut his teeth directing videos for White Zombie, notably the clips for "More Human Than Human," "Electric Head, Part 2 (the Ecstasy)," and "Super-Charger Heaven," as well as videos for Prong and his brother Mike's band Powerman 5000. These videos offered a tantalizing taster of what a full feature-length directing gig might be like, as he explained to filmmaker Mick Garris in a series called *Post Mortem*. "Every time I would be making a video, I would be like, 'Goddamn, we should be making a movie!' because videos cost a lot of money."

Zombie and his manager, Andy Gould, who took on the role of film producer for *House*, scored a deal for the movie with the giant Universal Studios after an earlier project for the company's theme parks had turned out well. "I went to Universal and they were doing their theme-park division," he recalled. "And they were going to start back up their Halloween Horror Nights, which they had stopped doing. I [designed] an attraction based on my album—it was a very Rob Zombie one."

Initially, all went smoothly at Universal. "Working at Universal, I swear to God, whatever we asked for they said, 'No problem!'" he laughed. "I was like, 'Really? You just ask for something and more money magically appears?' Now it seems with every movie you're so strapped for every little thing, but back then it was great. We were building these crazy sets and basically shooting everything on the back lot. Everything we wanted, it was there, yet nobody was really paying attention to anything we were doing."

It wasn't until the first test screening that things started to unravel. "Afterwards I went up to some of the executives and they were horrified with what we had made. Some people had seen it and they were like, 'Yay! Can't wait for the preview!' but the people who needed to see it hadn't seen it yet. I could tell by the looks on their faces that this was not going to be good. The next day we were gone."

As Zombie recalled it, timing was part of the problem. "At that point horror movies weren't real prevalent," he told Garris. "After that they were everywhere, but for that brief moment, Universal weren't making them, it was like the Flintstones movies and all that: they really didn't want to do horror. When they saw it they were like, 'This has no place in our gameplan.' Within two years they were doing *Dawn of the Dead* and they were fully on board, but at that point in time, it was as if we had made a porno movie and said, 'Here you go!'"

In an official statement from Universal Pictures, the company's then-chairman Stacey Snider explained, "When I looked at the cumulative effect of the entire film, it was clear that the best version of the movie would end up getting an NC-17 rating, and we felt that would make the marketing and distribution of the movie impossible for us."

Asked why she had authorized the production of the movie having read the script, Snider replied, "There are hundreds of choices Rob made where things played differently than they did in the script. On the page, when you see a cop killed, it reads like a convention of the genre, [but] in the movie, everything was underlined and emphasized—it was a celebration of the assassination of a character."

Perhaps it was all just too gory for the suits. "I have to admit that it would've been great if [Universal had] released the film," Zombie later said, "but it felt weird from the get-go. Here we were, making this crazy horror film, with this big corporate entity behind us. If you look at the history of horror films, the really scary ones, like *Texas Chainsaw Massacre*, were made by little independent companies, not big corporations."

If some at the studio were offended, he added, they should perhaps have had a better idea of what was coming. "I think the title *House of 1,000 Corpses* doesn't leave much to the imagination. It's not some weird art movie. It's for Middle America, for people who work at 7-Eleven and listen to Metallica and love horror movies. And whether this movie ends up on 300 screens or 3,000 screens, I bet its audience is going to find it."

Asked by Scott Tobias of the A.V. Club what Universal's expectations had been for the film, Zombie admitted he was not entirely sure. " I was really blatant when I talked to them. I didn't want to get into a situation where they thought I was making something mainstream. And I told them that I wanted to make a drive-in movie, something very gritty and nasty and weird. And they were all like, 'Okay, great, great, great. That sounds great.' Maybe they just didn't know what I meant by that." He also pointed to the recent Columbine High School shooting, which had made studio executives nervous about making films featuring much bloodletting—or, to be more accurate, nervous that the public wouldn't pay to see such movies.

◆

While looking for a home for *House of 1,000 Corpses*, Zombie took time out to write and record a new album for release in 2001. *The Sinister Urge*, named after a 1961 drama by cult director Ed Wood, was released on November 13, two months after the 9/11 attacks on New York and Washington, D.C. Asked about the attacks in a web chat around the time of the album's release, Zombie replied, "Obviously, I feel the same way as everybody. It was horrifying. And I believe that retaliating is the only thing we can do." He also admitted that he had been in some uncertainty about whether to withdraw scenes of the American flag from a forthcoming video, given the militaristic mood of the country after 9/11. "That was actually the original idea before that happened, and then I considered changing it because of that, because I thought it would look phony. But then I changed my mind and stuck with the original idea."

If anything, *The Sinister Urge* was more successful than *Hellbilly Deluxe*, even though three years had passed between the albums and a new generation of rock fans with short memories had been and gone. Its performance was undoubtedly helped out by the presence of its two major guest stars, Slayer guitarist Kerry King and Ozzy Osbourne, but as a suite of songs, it stands up extremely well a decade and more later.

It's a varying collection of songs, loaded with the expected samples from sources of greater or lesser degrees of kitsch. "Sinners Inc." is the spooky electronic intro, before "Demon Speeding"—also released as a single—introduces this album's default sound, a slick metal groove with an anthemic chorus. "Dead Girl Superstar" is faster and more urgent, reaffirming that hooky-but-aggressive metal is where Zombie's roots are. "Never Gonna Stop (the Red, Red Kroovy)" is positively funky, and much lighter in tone. Note the slightly amended reference to "krovvy" from Anthony Burgess's *A Clockwork Orange*, itself a modification of the Russian word for blood.

"Iron Head" is an unusual song in the overall evolution of Rob Zombie's sound, the presence of Ozzy Osbourne notwithstanding. It's essentially a nu-metal song, with a vocal that is close to a rap and the kind of syncopated rhythm that informed so many of the genre's biggest songs (think Slipknot's "Spit It Out" and Coal Chamber's "Loco"). As such, you'll like it if you like nu-metal and despise it if you don't.

Zombie and Osbourne had toured together in 1999, but it transpired that they had first met some years earlier. "It was very early on . . . 1995 or maybe before then, and I went over to his house—not the house that they had on the TV show [*The Osbournes*] but the house they lived in before that, next door to Pat Boone," Zombie later recalled. "My manager, Andy Gould, had been friends with Sharon Osbourne for a long time. You know, sometimes you just meet people and hang out for no reason. And it was great, you know, I'd always loved Ozzy, loved Black Sabbath, and at that point it was very funny because it was me and Ozzy in his house and he played me the entire album he had made with Mark Hudson that was very Beatles-sounding . . . it's never been released, but it was fantastic."

"(Go to) California" and "Feel So Numb" adhere more conventionally to the overall sound that Zombie had established as far back as *Astro-Creep*, albeit with more electronic elements and a slightly processed guitar tone. "Transylvanian Transmissions, Pt. 1" is an uneasy bit of instrumental jiggery-pokery, before "Bring Her Down (to Crippletown)" introduces a new direction for the *Sinister Urge* album. There's something about the twisty, stop-start nature of the riffs that makes this song stand out, along with the use of piano as a genuinely heavy instrument.

"Scum of the Earth"—also the name of the band that guitarist Mike Riggs went on to form after appearing on this album— is electronic metal to the extreme, with a synth-bass sound and sequenced, computer-generated whines behind Zombie's vocal snarls. Finally, "House of 1,000 Corpses"—which extends to a hidden track, "Unholy Three"—sets the scene perfectly for the forthcoming film, with its graphic snippets of news reports and country guitar. It's an understated way to end the album, although "Unholy Three" is a slight return to the sonic rage of the earlier material.

Zombie was assisted on *The Sinister Urge* by a minor galaxy of well-known musicians, as was the fashion in those days. These included Nine Inch Nails/Guns N' Roses drummer Josh Freese, sometime Jane's Addiction bassist Chris Chaney, Tommy Lee once more, and not one but two turntablists, Mix Master Mike of the Beastie Boys and DJ Lethal from Limp Bizkit. Managing this troupe took a lot of organization from Zombie and his co-producer Scott Humphrey, as well as a significant budget from Geffen, but the effort paid off, with a Top 10 chart entry in the US, a platinum award, and first-week sales of around 150,000—quite an achievement in 2001, when the downloading revolution (or catastrophe, depending on your point of view) was beginning to bite into CD sales.

Further ahead, in July 2002, a tussle in the law courts awaited.

In late 1999, the car manufacturer Mazda had allegedly used a portion of "Demonoid Phenomenon" (from *Hellbilly Deluxe*) in a TV ad without permission. Zombie launched a federal copyright infringement lawsuit against them, and the case was settled out of court. As he explained to Hollywood.com, his policy had always been to not allow his music to be used in advertising, "and then there's a car commercial running on television with my music. How do you explain to every kid that you didn't sell out and didn't do exactly what you said you weren't going to do? I don't want to play that song live and see the kids go, 'Hey! It's the truck song!' Corporate America doesn't understand that some people actually have values about things. Everything isn't for sale."

Meanwhile, work on *House of 1,000 Corpses* moved on apace, with Zombie having found a new home for his gruesome pet project at the venerable MGM Studios. It wasn't long before that deal fell apart too, however.

"We went to MGM," he said, "and that all seemed good for a while, till I said something that pissed everybody off by accident. I was on the set of *Daredevil*, interviewing Ben Affleck for MTV, and between takes he said, 'What's up with your movie?' and I said, 'Well, Universal dumped it because they have a conscience, they have morals, but MGM have no morals, ha ha ha!' The next day it was on the front page of *Variety*—me saying that. I was driving to the editing room and the editor called me and said, 'We just got here. Everything's locked up and they won't let us in!' We were done. They didn't even want to hear anything. They just booted us in two seconds."

Zombie refused to give up. "We were still editing on everybody else's dime," he told Mick Garris, "which was kinda funny. We never actually finished shooting the movie. I actually shot stuff in my house with a video camera. Sometimes it looks like a stylistic choice, with the film going to Super-8 or whatever. And because I was friends with all the actors, they came in and finished it for lunch. And then we shopped it to every single person we could find, and no one even remotely cared. 'We knew you two idiots would fuck it up!'—you know, meaning me and Andy Gould, my manager-slash-producer. We were the last two people attached: everyone else had run for the hills."

"MGM got wind of it and got so pissed off they shut us down the next day," Zombie told MTV. "We went into editing, and they were like, 'Get out.' They went berserk . . . they never called me or any of the producers. They had assistants call the editing room and they were like, 'Get out.' It was over in a second; we couldn't get any resolve on it. It was very strange."

Oddly, MGM then appeared to deny that a deal was ever place. "It was falsely announced in [Hollywood trade paper] *Variety* that we had the project," an unnamed executive said. "We never had a deal with Rob Zombie. We were in negotiations, let's put it that way, or we were thinking about it."

Zombie countered by insisting that MGM had been fully on board. "It kind of never really got out," he said, "but they were paying all of the bills, they were editing, it was all on their dime, they were investing. So once the studio's paying their money, you know they're into it. . . . What I think the reality of the situation is, whether it's MGM or Universal, or whatever, the movie's not anything that a major studio wants to touch. They don't want to deal with it. What we've done now is I own the film, and I just hired a company that will do the prints and the advertising. And I'm just gonna release it myself so it cuts out the middleman."

In the end, Zombie signed a distribution deal with Lionsgate. "Everyone else seemed like, 'We knew it! We knew you couldn't break out of the music business and make it happen,' and even Lionsgate turned us down . . . but then someone at Lionsgate who hadn't seen it, saw it, and said, 'Okay.'"

◆

With the light at the end of the tunnel firmly in view, Zombie handed over his film to Lionsgate and turned his attention to a more pressing matter—his impending marriage to Sheri Moon, about whom not much was publicly known until she became better known as an actor in Zombie's movies. Talking to writer Staci Layne Wilson at the charmingly titled *Girls and Corpses* magazine, she explained how, before she met Zombie, she had attended "broadcasting school" with ambitions of doing voiceover work for animation projects. "I was also sort of exploring maybe becoming a VJ or being some sort of on-camera personality," she recalled. "But then the way things evolved with our relationship, we moved in together and he was on the road and I would go on the road with him. The first thing I did with him was make music videos. The first one was 'Feed the Gods,' which was a White Zombie video. I did a couple of videos when he was still in White Zombie, then when he went solo he always wanted to have dancers on tour. So I just became involved with that and choreographed the numbers. I found the girls, and made the costumes. That was so much fun."

Life on the road with Zombie has changed over the years. "It's a lot different now from when I first met Rob," she added. "Then, he was still up and coming. Now we're able, thankfully, to stay in nice hotels and work out in the gym in the morning before we go to soundcheck. It's a nice routine. I really like the tour bus. We always get a bus where we have the back lounge as a bedroom, so we have a bed. We don't have to sleep in the bunks, the coffin bunks. We always bring Dracula, our dog, with us. The hardest thing about being on the road is getting healthy food sometimes. Everyone's a big carnivore in this country and it's a fast food nation."

For Sheri, life on the tour bus has generally proven to be a civilized affair. "I read a lot of books, I do a lot of crossword puzzles, we watch movies on the bus. On the last tour that we did this summer, everyone wanted to watch music documentaries, so we were really into watching those. We also have these big Uno championship games, we're mad for Uno on the bus."

If you're surprised that there's not more debauchery behind the scenes, don't be. Rob Zombie is, after all, a man with a vision and the energy to execute it. Drink and drugs have never been his idea of time well spent. When you have so much to do, and the opportunity to get it done, you don't sit around doing nothing. "To me, [Rob] has a different rock star personality onstage but it doesn't carry over to real life," Sheri continued. "He's very hardworking, disciplined and professional, but yet so creative, and his brain is always, you know, churning these ideas. Really, from the moment he gets up in the morning until the moment before we go to bed, he's always thinking of ideas, working, and being creative."

If you're getting sick of the endless claims that Rob Zombie is a creative machine with little room to let his hair down, however, never fear—there's some spontaneity to the man. Having originally planned to get married on November 9, 2002, the couple decided to pull the event forward a week and do it on October 31—Halloween—without any fuss.

"We were together for nine years. We both really didn't want to get married," recalled Sheri. "Then all of a sudden something happened and I was just like, 'You know what? Maybe we should. We might as well.' It was weird, but there was nothing profound about it. We planned the wedding and then we said, 'No, forget it. Let's just elope and then we'll have a party here.' So that's what we did . . . we were actually taking a walk in our neighborhood the day before. It was just a spur-of-the-moment decision. It just so happens that the next day was Halloween. We didn't do it for any spooky reasons or anything. We were not in costume. I wore a white sweater and jeans."

Now husband and wife, the Zombies—yes, Sheri took her husband's name, despite the puzzlement that would result when she bought anything from mail-order catalogues, for example—looked forward to their future in 2002. All sorts of milestones were cropping up to attest to the rising profile of Rob Zombie, such as a tribute album (unfortunately not great) called *The Electro-Industrial Tribute to Rob Zombie* and a "Zombie-n-the-Box" toy with which to terrify the kids.

Unfortunately, all was not well within the band, perhaps due to the incessant tour dates after *The Sinister Urge*. Looking back at this period, Zombie explained: "After *Sinister Urge*, where I was just burnt out, I was sick of in-fighting among bands . . . like anything in life, you do too much, you get burnt out."

"I forget what year it was," he added, "maybe 2002 or so on the *Sinister Urge* tour, the band started falling apart, and I really started losing interest in music. Every time you thought something was together, it would fall apart. That's when I really started focusing on movies . . ."

SIX

THE HOUSE THAT DRIPPED BLOOD

(2003)

Focus, indeed, was what was needed. The path to completion of *House of 1,000 Corpses* had been beset with hindrances, for sure, but the goal was close.

Getting the Lionsgate Films deal signed, after the fiascos with Universal and MGM—the second of which had been particularly nonsensical in the manner of its demise—was a crucial step for obvious reasons. As the press release ran, "Lionsgate Films has secured rights from Andy Gould of [management company] the Firm to musical superstar/filmmaker Rob Zombie's controversial horror film *House of 1,000 Corpses*, it was announced today by Tom Ortenberg, president of Lionsgate Films Releasing. The film will be released theatrically in the first quarter of 2003."

"With *House of 1,000 Corpses*, Rob Zombie has created an in-your-face, unrelenting horror film experience," said Ortenberg. "We are really looking forward to working with Rob and having a lot of fun with this campaign."

Andy Gould stepped up too, saying, "Whether it be *American Psycho*, *Dogma*, or *O*, Lionsgate has proven time and again that they are not afraid to take on risky, subversive projects, and that they are masters at marketing and distributing provocative, challenging material."

Now the fun bit: "Ortenberg, Peter Block, President of Home Entertainment, Acquisitions and New Media, and Jason Constantine, Vice President of Acquisitions, negotiated the deal on behalf of Lionsgate, with Andy Gould of the Firm, David Fox and Jeffrey Light of Myman, Abell, Fineman, Greenspan, and Light, LLP, Rick Yorn of the Firm and Jordan Schur of Geffen Records negotiating on behalf of writer/director Zombie."

That's a lot of names looking to get paid. And that's not even including the complexity of making the film in the first place. Even back at the beginning of the process, finding the right cast was hardly simple, for reasons that will become abundantly clear as we examine the plot.

"The hardest part of casting was casting the 'normal' people," said Zombie, in an interview with *DVD File*. "I had a very strong idea of who I wanted to play the other parts, or at least the type. So that was easy. But when it came to casting 'normal' people, that's when it got harder. You want them to be attractive enough so you want to look at them, but you don't want it to look like a car full of supermodels being attacked by maniacs. It was hard." Chief among Zombie's considerations was a desire for the audience to side with the villains of the piece. "Everyone's favorite characters are the bad guys. They're siding with the murderers. That's who they love. I thought that was hilarious."

At least Zombie had no trouble finding one of his major female actors, having opted to cast his wife, the newly renamed Sheri Moon Zombie. Although Mrs Z.'s acting experience was minimal, he walked her through the process, enabling her to deliver a startlingly virtuoso performance. "We enjoy working together, so he wrote the part for me," Sheri told *Fangoria*. "He had more faith in me than I did! I guess he saw something from directing me in the videos that made him think I could handle it. He knows me better than anyone, so it worked out okay. I was really nervous, but it was a lot of fun."

Asked why he had cast his wife in the film, Zombie explained that writing a script is easier if you have an actor in mind for a particular part. "Because then, immediately, the voice is in your head," he said. "I always wanted her for that part, and I always wanted Sid Haig to play Captain Spaulding. Even though I didn't know Sid, I had an idea of what I thought he would be like, so it was real easy to write the role." Bill Moseley's character, Otis, came about after Zombie met him at an unrelated event while he was still drafting the script. "I had a vague notion of the character, but it was a smaller role. Then I met him and he was perfect, so I just rewrote it."

Perhaps the most memorable character from *House of 1,000 Corpses* is Captain Spaulding, a sinister, amusingly foul-mouthed villain in a filthy clown costume played by the aforementioned Sid Haig. Sixty years old at the time of shooting and—like any great actor—proudly using his age as a form of dramatic costume, Haig was the veteran at the time of over fifty movies and a staggering three hundred TV episodes. Among these were performances that would obviously attract the attention of a '70s and '80s culture addict like Rob Zombie, including roles in *Coffy, Foxy Brown, Batman, Gunsmoke, Mission: Impossible, Charlie's Angels, Buck Rogers in the*

25th Century, The Dukes of Hazzard, MacGyver, and *The A-Team.* He had also appeared in George Lucas's cult pre–*Star Wars* movie *THX 1138* and even a James Bond film, 1971's *Diamonds Are Forever.*

It's notable that Quentin Tarantino—like Zombie a director who clearly believes in paying tribute to superannuated actors by giving them roles in his films—is also a big fan of Haig. In a move that he would live to regret, Haig turned down the role of the monstrous gangster Marsellus Wallace in Tarantino's *Pulp Fiction,* one of the most influential films of the 1990s. However, he did appear in the same director's next film, the inferior but still slick *Jackie Brown,* which also starred Pamela Grier, his colleague in *Coffy* and *Foxy Brown.*

Then there's Karen Black, like Haig a screen veteran with a mighty résumé. She'd been in *Easy Rider* with Dennis Hopper and Peter Fonda, for heaven's sake, playing a hooker out of her mind on LSD. She also did *Five Easy Pieces* with Jack Nicholson, for which she scooped an Oscar nomination; earned a Golden Globe for her role in the 1974 remake of *The Great Gatsby*; screamed down the screen in the rather more schlocky *Airport 1975*; and worked on seminal films made by great directors such as John Schlesinger, Robert Altman, and Alfred Hitchcock. Black had shared screen space with Bette Davis, Robert De Niro, Gene Hackman, Kris Kristofferson, Christopher Plummer, Robert Duvall, Gene Wilder, and Elliott Gould. It's safe to say that she knew her way around a set.

Together with lesser-known but still respected actors such as Bill Moseley (*The Texas Chainsaw Massacre 2*), Michael J. Pollard (*Bonnie and Clyde*), and Matthew McGrory (a giant who, at seven feet six inches in height, had starred in Iron Maiden and Marilyn Manson videos, plus films such as *Big Fish*), the cast was a disparate bunch but an affable one. By all accounts the atmosphere on set was amicable, despite the stresses that would unfold across the twenty-five-day shoot.

The soundtrack featured a fair amount of music from Rob Zombie—although this, he recalled, was largely for budgetary reasons. A highlight was a collaboration with Lionel Richie—an unlikely pairing that resulted in an entertaining version of "Brick House" by Richie's old band the Commodores. "When Rob called me on the phone he was so nervous," Richie recalled. "I said, 'Rob, why do you seem nervous?' He said, 'Just come over' . . . my housekeeper answered the door and said, 'Mr. Richie, there's a Mr. Zombie at the front door.' He showed up, this long hair, dark glasses, dark beard, blue jacket, ripped pants, red-toed combat boots, and I love the question my housekeeper asked: 'Where would you like me to put him?' I said, 'Let him in the living room.'"

Apart from a brief, uncredited cameo, Zombie's involvement in *House of 1,000 Directors* was largely behind the camera. "Except for Martin Scorsese, I really don't like director cameos," he later commented. "Scorsese is a good actor, and he's fun to watch, but most of the time, I feel like I'm watching a movie, and then the brakes come on and the movie comes to a grinding halt while the director stumbles through his few lines, and you're just like, 'Oh, dear God!' And I didn't want to be that guy."

Give a filmmaker seven million dollars and, if he knows what he's doing, he'll make it look like twice as much. The fact that Zombie pulled off *House of 1,000 Corpses* with a budget that would just about cover the wardrobe and makeup budget of an average Hollywood blockbuster—and indeed made it look pretty damn good—says a lot about his raw talent and his drive to make it work. Remember,

Zombie's previous experience behind the camera was limited only to the animation in *Beavis and Butt-head Do America* back in '96, plus a couple of music videos. Still, his artistic vision had never been in doubt: just look at the past decade-plus of production design for his live shows.

Essentially, *House* is a blood-soaked and filthy but still elegant feature-length movie that is to Zombie's later films what White Zombie's catalogue is to his own albums. Even the cultural references are similar: just as Zombie had paid homage to the vintage horror films that had populated his childhood with such mind-blowing luridity on those early records, so they reappeared in his first film.

Take the opening sequence, a deliberately retro montage of horror clips straight from the Lon Chaney era. It's pure Zombie. As we move through the early scenes, we encounter Sid Haig's repellent antihero Captain Spaulding, a white-faced clown with a foul mouth and a decaying face and body. Zombie zooms in close on Spaulding, highlighting—and enjoying—the character's moral and physical sickness as he stumbles and curses his way around the low-lit set. A caption on the screen tells us it's October 30, 1977—the height of the exploitation- and slasher-movie era for anyone of Zombie's age and preference. We're in for a hell of a ride—quite literally.

The setup is simple, and classic. The sacrificial lambs, so to speak, are four young folks who enter Spaulding's chaotic gas station in the middle of nowhere in search of entertainment. Is Spaulding himself the principal villain of the ensemble? We don't know yet—but we know he's up to no good when Zombie's camera follows him inside a back room, the point of view wavery and the music threatening, as per all the best vintage horror flicks. Zombie's editor, Robert K. Lambert, is no slouch, either, using jump cuts for extra tension at key moments and—as the action warms up—not shying away from scenes of gore and nudity when they appear.

Genuine autopsy footage, plus a clever point-of-view angle as one of Spaulding's victims is dispatched with a bullet to the face, provide the first shocks. Sure, there are flaws in Zombie's approach: he's new to his craft, after all, and as his later films will demonstrate, a director settling into his style at this point. For instance, he applies solarizing effects to the film in these early scenes, but the scenes themselves don't actually require them. If his characters were ingesting peyote at this point, or enduring a nightmare, a touch of solar would be appropriate, but not here. Perhaps Zombie was simply having fun, playing with the tools in the editing box.

The plot is exactly what you'd expect if you've been paying attention so far. The homages to *The Texas Chainsaw Massacre* and *The Hills Have Eyes* are abundant, at least if you know those films, both of which involve creepy rural families from God only knows where in deepest America capturing innocent passers-by and ruining their day in a variety of obscenely imaginative ways. This begins when the four road-tripping youths, one of whom is played by Rainn Wilson from *Six Feet Under* and *The Office*, are directed by Spaulding to visit a house owned by a spooky local character named Dr. Satan. En route they pick up a hitchhiker called Baby Firefly, a beautiful but sinister woman played by Sheri Moon Zombie . . .

"Baby is the angelic-looking bait to get the victims," said Moon of her character, who is frankly nuts. "She's part of this psychotic family and when I played her, I guess I took a little from Bette

Davis—because I love her—although no one's gonna see that. It may sound a little silly for me to say that, but I was thinking about her when I did the part."

When the car breaks down, the four travelers plus Baby end up at the Firefly home, a horrendously creepy, gothic building which no sane person would enter. After dinner with the Firefly family, a cheery bunch of utter psychos—including Karen Black as Mother Firefly and McGrory as the massive, deformed brother—the violence begins. One of the men is killed and his body parts used as artwork; another is scalped. The women are tied up.

Meanwhile, the police arrive, having found the abandoned car. They too are murdered. That night, the three remaining travelers are taken to a field, dressed as rabbits (bear with Zombie for a moment); one is killed, and the other two are lowered into a subterranean well. One is drowned by a load of aquatic zombies, but the sole remaining innocent, Denise, escapes into a network of underground tunnels. It's here that Zombie fully displays his directing quality for the first time: the final sequence, in which the victim seeks desperately for an exit in an apparently infinite labyrinth of surreal horror, sees him pull out all the stops. The special effects—almost all performed in camera, with little or no computer-generated imagery—are excellent and convincing.

The denouement comes when Denise meets Dr. Satan at last. When Denise enters our demonic vivisectionist's laboratory, the good doctor is separating the teenager who was scalped earlier from his various body parts. Understandably, she is keen to leave, and manages to escape to the surface—where a friendly local picks her up in his car before she passes out. Who is said local? Why, it's Captain Spaulding, of course, who delivers Denise to Dr. Satan, on whose operating table she awakes from her swoon. And that's that, presumably for Denise as well as for the film.

You'll have fun picking up the cultural references. The villains' names, for example, are plucked from old Groucho Marx films. Baby's brother, the most psychotic of the evildoers—performed by Bill Moseley—takes his name Otis B. Driftwood from the Marx Brothers' 1935 film *A Night at the Opera*. Other characters, including Captain Spaulding, Rufus T. Firefly, and Hugo Z. Hackenbush, are lifted from *Animal Crackers* (1930), *Duck Soup* (1933), and *A Day at the Races* (1937), respectively.

In fact, Moseley deserves a special mention for his performance as Otis. There's something self-contained and disciplined about his depiction of a totally homicidal madman that is convincing, and is especially impressive in the light of Zombie's later comments that Moseley is by nature a gentle, introverted character. The cast in general provides the film's backbone, propping up the occasional weak moment in the script and one or two instances where Zombie's artistic execution doesn't quite match up to his vision, presumably due to lack of budget.

Asked by writer Joe Daly what he regarded to be the most important element of a horror movie, Zombie explained that the thing that he had always been most attracted to, in others' work and now his own, is the characters. "Getting really caught up in crazy characters, more than situations. A lot of movies now are just like ghost movies where there's like a family, and they move into a house and 'Oh no, it might be haunted!' But that was never the type of stuff that I liked. I always liked the type of things that were more like *The Texas Chainsaw Massacre*, and you really get into the fucked-up family. That's the kind of stuff that I like. Or freaks, or Frankenstein.

I was always into the crazy characters more than spooky situations . . . you create some sort of iconic personality. I guess I'm a visual person, so I would always go toward that type of stuff."

What's crucial to note is that *House of 1,000 Corpses* is every inch a Rob Zombie film, despite the references to other influences. If you appreciate his music and grasp the overall artistic message that his albums convey—a kind of glammed-up celebration of dark culture—then you'll be fully immersed in his first film. His identity is stamped all over it, just as Woody Allen and Martin Scorsese infuse their work with their own personalities, although Zombie himself would probably wince at the thought of being likened to those great talents.

Let's break this down in detail. From the very first scene, the screen is packed full of Rob Zombie-isms. Skulls, corpses, voodoo dolls, scantily clad glamour girls with the occasional exposed breast and buttock—these are drawn straight from the most nostalgic of kitsch art. Every now and then, the film is solarized or otherwise treated to create a psychedelic effect: in fact, this happens a bit too often for comfort, the mark of a rookie director with newfound access to an editing suite. There's no denying its vintage feel, though, especially when you compare it to a pioneering horror film such as *Suspiria* (1977), to pick a relevant example.

Elsewhere, Zombie switches from color to black-and-white, or splits the screen into double or triple perspectives, again adding juice to the viewing experience. He doesn't waste any time before referencing Halloween—the date rather than the film series, although there are elements of that, too—with affectionate shots of pumpkins and so on. Creepy dolls, obviously fake but well-constructed corpses, carnivals, stuffed animal heads straight from the *Evil Dead* films: all the right tropes are here.

Where Zombie excels is in his choice of camera angles. When the car breaks down, for example, and is surrounded by spikes of rain that masterfully obscure all other sounds and help to create a feeling of immersion for the viewer, he compounds the effect by *shooting out* of the car. It's clever, instinctive directing, and I challenge anyone to name an equally effective shot from the horror genre that doesn't actually involve violence.

The film is also impressive in its attention to detail. The fake blood looks realistic: it's dark and viscous, and not at all like the usual raspberry juice. The Firefly house—which turns out to be the same building that was used for *The Best Little Whorehouse in Texas* (1982) and a feature of Universal Studios' tram tour—is dressed perfectly for the film. There's a fetus in a jar, an appropriate touch; an "Agatha Crispies" pun; vintage TV and VHS equipment, sourced with evident care; and when entrails, leathery skin, broken teeth, and sub-epidermal musculature are required, they're created convincingly.

There are a couple of genuinely nasty moments. The most efficient stratagem in any film, horror or otherwise, is to make the audience invest in a character, and we do this with the stricken father of one of the victims, who is slaughtered while the old ballad "I Remember You" by Slim Whitman (a sadistic choice of song, given the moment) plays and the character recalls happier times. The scalping referred to earlier is hard to watch: in fact, only some of the process is shown on screen, presumably because a cut was required. The grimmest moment of all comes when Otis holds a gun to a police officer's forehead. The camera pulls out slowly, and there's an agonizing twenty-second wait before he pulls the trigger. Until that moment, the viewer has no idea whether the victim will be executed. It's horrible, and clever.

There are less expertly conducted scenes, too, among the Sam Peckinpah–indebted slow-motion blood sprays and POV switches. For example, *The Munsters* plays on the TV in the Fireflys' living room when something more mundane like the news or a weather report would have been much less predictable. Some of the wall graffiti looks cheap. The Dr. Satan character doesn't quite work, instead coming off like an extra in a *Twilight* film. And the soundtrack hasn't aged too well: industrial metal's commercial peak came a decade ago as you read this, and *House* might have benefited from some musical subtlety. That said, this would indeed come with Rob Zombie's next film, so let's conclude that *House of 1,000 Corpses* is the filmic equivalent of, say, *La Sexorcisto*: vivid, undignified, and only partly successful, but a clear indication of better things to come.

One very clear impression left by *House* is how much physical work it must have taken to get the sets dressed and the takes wrapped. So much action is required on the part of the actors, and the shooting environment is so prop-heavy, that getting it all done on time and to budget must have been stressful to say the least. And that's without taking into account the lack of acting experience from Sheri, who carries a lot of the action. "We had a read-through before we actually started filming, and I was the only person in the room who wasn't a working actor, so I was intimidated just by that whole process," she recalled. "But I met Karen [Black] that day, and from then on, she took me under her wing. She was great and a true inspiration, almost like my mom on the set."

That said, Sheri managed to get convincingly into the spirit of her character's lust for bloodletting. "Baby participates actively," as she put it. She recalled one particularly scene, shot at 2am in the freezing cold, for which she was required to be covered in blood. "So

I was drenched, with this long gown on . . . I would find it utterly shocking if a person was not somewhat disturbed by doing a violent scene. I was really, really having some anxieties about it, particularly this one stabbing that I did, and that part was not fun for me at all. I'd hate to meet the guy who thought it was!"

The heavy workload must have made Zombie's tribulations with Universal and MGM doubly taxing. Kudos to the man for persevering; otherwise, his weird pet project would never have come out. "Even though there were times where it seemed like [the film was doomed]," he said, "I always felt that as soon as I started thinking that way, I was screwed. So I always pushed ahead like it was going to come out."

The cast and crew supported Zombie, as Sheri recalled. "All of us who worked on the movie stayed in touch and kept wanting to hear good news and to have the movie come out," she said. "It definitely was a nightmare for Rob. At one point after a year and a half, I just got sick of hearing about it, because there were so many highs and lows, and so many discouraging moments."

Sheri hit the nail on the head when remarking that, in the era of "torture porn" cinema, *House of 1,000 Corpses* is not, in fact, particularly extreme. "People probably overreacted," she told *Fangoria*. "It's a scary movie, and I don't think anyone will be let down, but Universal kind of pussied out." As she noted, the same studio had recently released *Hannibal*, its much-hyped sequel to *Silence of the Lambs*, which features graphic scenes of disembowelment and a widely discussed "brain-eating" sequence. "But having a star like Anthony Hopkins, which is a familiar face, made you remember you were watching a movie," Sheri added. "*House* has a lot of unknowns in it, and that possibly makes it seem more real."

Released on April 11, 2003, *House of 1,000 Corpses* earned back half its $7 million budget in its first week, eventually taking almost $17 million in total. Considering the subject matter, the understated marketing campaign, and the general antipathy to horror movies within the film industry at the time, those figures were justifiably considered to be a resounding success. As many observers would conclude at the time, Rob Zombie could hold his head high, having pulled off the near-impossible feat of succeeding in both the music and movie worlds. *House* served its cast well, scooping a "Best Supporting Actor" award for Sid Haig in that year's Annual *Fangoria* Chainsaw Awards, as well as prompting his induction into the Horror Hall of Fame.

Of Haig, now introduced to a new generation of gore-hounds by the indisputably evil but somehow charismatic Captain Spaulding character, Sheri said, "I didn't have any scenes with him, but we've become good friends ever since. He comes over to the house for dinner parties and barbecues and things like that, plus we bring him out to hockey games when we get extra tickets. One of the great experiences of working on the movie was that we remained friends with quite a few of the actors. That was nice, and I imagine it doesn't always happen on every movie."

So what does all this mean? You may or may not be a fan of horror films, although I'm assuming you are if you've got this far. If you're not, you're probably wondering why would anyone want to watch this depressing stuff. There's a simple answer, which is that *House* is good: an accomplished film made by a team of great writing and filming talent. You either respond to its content or you don't. Many people don't, which is fine, but sufficient numbers of moviegoers liked *House* to make it a respectable box-office hit. Its success is highly indicative of modern culture and the mindset of the people who populate it. The aesthetic may be unsettling, but it underpins a legitimate form of entertainment.

Not that the movie industry necessarily saw it that way. Rob Zombie had a fight on his hands when it came to the rating of *House of 1,000 Corpses.* "With all the hubbub that has been going on lately, you can't show R-rated movie previews on TV [until] after a certain hour," he told Peter M. Bracke at *DVD File.* "'Oh, it's PG-13? We can show it all afternoon! We can put it on [MTV show] *TRL.* They can play it on MTV!'" R-rated movies, on the other hand, were a different matter entirely. "We can't show it," came the networks' reply.

"It's just a quest for a larger audience," Zombie continued. "As soon as you try to make something so specific, something that appeals to everybody, you by nature take away what is special about it. I would always use the joke: 'Hey, we could appeal to more people with porno movies if we just took out all that nudity and sex out of them.' Then we could show them on TV!"

What's interesting—and essential to an understanding of Zombie's vision—is that graphic, on-screen depiction of violence is far from his goal. It is simply another tool in the box. Much more important to him was the emotional content of the film. "I'm not even that big a fan of gore," he explained. "People seem to think I am, but when I see something that's gory for the sake of being gory, I get bored by it. When it really plays into the story, it doesn't even have to be that bad. But, 'How long is the camera going to linger on the eyeball being squished in that guy's head?' What am I watching? This is stupid." As far as Zombie was concerned, the Motion Picture Association of America effectively had final cut on his (and indeed anyone else's) film, "because ultimately everything filters through them. If you had free rein to do any horror movie you wanted and could show anything you wanted, when does personal restraint come in, where you say, 'Maybe I'm just being gory for gory's sake?' How do you find the balance between being shocking and going overboard?"

As Zombie explained, he had simply wanted to show enough aggression that the conflict seemed real but not so much that it appeared gratuitous, as if it was supposed to be fun. He disliked it when violence in movies is portrayed as amusing. If there must be violence, he explained, it should seem horrible, because violence *is* horrible in real life.

Despite this commendable desire for some balance when it came to the graphic content, Zombie had evidently fought a battle to retain *House*'s R rating, as that most accurately represented his vision, even if current events were against him. The fact that he was making the movie in the shadow of the Columbine High School massacre, about which tensions remained high, made life particularly difficult. "That happened," he recalled, "and everyone got wigged out, thinking that every movie that was like this was the reason that happened. And then, the election was just firing up. I remember that [Democratic senator Joe] Lieberman was always on the cover of *The Hollywood Reporter* saying, 'Hollywood's got to clean up its act. It's got to do this and that.' And that just fed right into it. That was the kiss of death for us at that point."

Not for the first time, given his previous musical output, but certainly most pressingly at this point because of *House*'s grisly content, Zombie was asked if he thought films such as his were good for people. "I don't know if you can make the argument that they're good," he explained, "but you can certainly make the argument that they're not bad for people. I'm friends with Alice Cooper, and sometimes we talk about this, because he's gone through all kinds of bad stuff, his whole career. He's just like, 'Look, death row is not filled with murderers that murdered people because they listened to one of my records. It's just not the case.' And it's just not the case with these movies, either. It's a ridiculous argument. I think they provide an outlet for some people, not because they would then go kill someone if they didn't have that outlet, but it's entertainment. People need entertainment. If they don't have entertainment, they get bored and go crazy. As a kid, when I wasn't being entertained, the first thing I did was go out and do something destructive. That's what every kid does. As soon as you're bored, you're like, 'Let's go light something on fire.'"

There are more insidious dangers out there for the vulnerable youth of this world, warned Zombie, offering the kind of sensible sentiment that anyone over, say, thirty-five will appreciate. "When *House of 1,000 Corpses* was having problems, I was like, 'You know what the problem is going to be? It's going to be that [car] movie, *The Fast and the Furious*' . . . because this is going to be something that looks like, 'Man, it's so fun to drive your car fast and all the fucking hot chicks will love you.' And I was like, just watch how many accidents and deaths this causes. Whereas I don't think anybody is going to go, 'Oh, I just saw *The Shining*, I think I'm going to go axe somebody.'"

Zombie also knew exactly where his little film stood in relation to the wave of plastic, fake-horror movies that Hollywood has been making in recent years. "There was definitely a huge horror boom in the '80s, and then it seems like the bottom fell out and it never really came back," he said. "I think [horror has] become pretty stale. I'm not sure why it went that way."

Asked by Bracke what he thought of *Scream*, the 1996 film that appeared to have had a profound influence over the latest batch of over-lit, lowest-common-denominator horror flicks, Zombie declared, "I didn't really enjoy any of those movies . . . the whole vibe of the movie was, 'We're too good to be in a horror movie, so we're going to parody a horror movie.'" For Zombie, a key difficultly with much of the horror movies of the time was that the actors were simply too good-looking. "It's hard to relate to them in a sense, whereas in . . . films of the '70s, I think they were more accessible. And that ruins the vibe."

In the horror movies of the '70s, he continued, many of the actors were unknowns, which made for a level playing field where nobody was safe—anyone of their characters might get killed off during the course of the film. "Now you just know by the casting. You go, 'There's no way this person is going to die. Nothing bad is going to happen to her because she's the star of that TV show.'"

Promotional one-sheets, he added, provided a key insight into the way things had changed. "The one-sheet used to be of the villain, the monster, all about that guy. Then all these one-sheets became these glamour shots of the cast standing in descending order of importance, like it was a modeling competition. And that's a fucking horror movie?"

More than a few critics derided *House of 1,000 Corpses* when it first appeared, perhaps for the reasons outlined in the last paragraph: the film certainly had problems finding a niche. And yet it's aged well; like many a filmic curio, it has found an audience, one that will presumably grow as its maker's filmography expands. One critic whose word we can trust more than most is Mike "McBeardo" McPadden, a global authority on movies and wider culture of all levels of schlock. A published author, McPadden has written extensively about Rob Zombie's work, not least in his essential 2014 book *Heavy Metal Movies*. Asked for his opinion of *House of 1,000 Corpses*, McPadden told me, "It's my favorite of his films, which may be because it's the closest to a regular horror movie in a lot of ways. It's like a rock band's first album, because it's the one they've been working on their whole life. It's loaded with Rob Zombie-ness and it explodes off the screen. There's an energy that is captured because of its limitations."

"I think Rob did a great job of transferring the whole aesthetic of his music to another medium," he added. "His movies look and feel like his music sounds. That's a real talent: whether you like the material or not is beside the point. The word that comes to mind is 'flash.' He directs with a lot of swagger and his artistic vision is so complete. He's able to tap into that so fully. You really have to be awestruck by how perfectly he can move between media."

Once the box-office numbers were in for *House of 1,000 Corpses*, talk inevitably turned to the idea of a sequel. After all, the various fates of the Firefly family had not been irrevocably established at the end of the film, and for many observers, Captain Spaulding was just too good a character to get rid of. Fortunately for them, and for us, Zombie quickly came on board with the idea of a *House . . . Part 2*, although he insisted that the new film would not simply be a clone of its predecessor. "I don't want to keep making the same kinds of films over and over, by any means," he told Peter M. Bracke. "I'm already planning for *House of 1,000 Corpses'* sequel to be totally different, because I don't want to retread the same ground. I already did that movie. I want to make the sequel really different. Sequels can work, but they have to be approached as though you're continuing on a story as opposed to: 'Hey, let's just do the same thing again and put a *2* next to it!' That's definitely not what I have in mind."

"Look at a movie like *Spider-Man*," he went on. "It's a comic book character, and I've read nine million issues of *Spider-Man*, and each issue is a sequel, if you look at it that way. So he can have a million adventures. But if it's the Green Goblin again, doing the same thing, it becomes a stunt-casting thing rather than making a cool movie. If I couldn't think of anything to do with *House*, I wouldn't bother. I own the rights to the sequel, so it's not like they can take it away from me."

Interestingly, in the light of what followed some years later, Zombie was at this point completely against the idea of ever remaking a horror film—a trend that shows no sign of abating, all these years later. "I don't see the point," he said bluntly. "Hammer remade all those Universal films, and I love all the Hammer films, but some films are special for what they are very specifically. There's no reason to remake *The Godfather* or *Jaws* or *Star Wars*. I just don't see the point. It's just a cheap marketing ploy. And I also don't see the point when a movie is that good. If *The Texas Chainsaw Massacre* was originally a good idea, but not a good movie, sure, whatever. But it's perfect. What's the point? Come on: they remade *Psycho*. That's the most insane thing I've ever heard! Let's remake *Citizen Kane* while we're at it!"

◆

The year 2003 proved to be a highly successful one for Zombie. As well as making his big-screen debut as a movie director, he also signed a publishing deal for a book called *Rob Zombie Presents: Monsters, Maniacs, and Madmen*—although this was a collection of well-known, existing tales badged under the Zombie banner rather than authored by him. Furthermore, a comic-book series called *Spookshow International* came out in late 2003 with another, *The Nail*, set for publication in 2004.

Just after the release of *House*, the band Black Label Society released a single called "Stillborn," with Zombie directing the accompanying video. A blue-lit performance effort with some actors in spooky makeup pulling faces, it's hardly his greatest work to date but it did do the trick of pairing him up with BLS singer Zakk Wylde, who was also Ozzy Osbourne's guitar player at the time. Wylde's general philosophy of how to manage a long-time career in rock dovetailed with that of Zombie, based as it is largely on hard work and self-belief.

"Play the music you love," he told me. "That's what you should always do. If Led Zeppelin, back in the day, had decided to play like the Monkees, because they were real popular and they had their own TV show, what would have happened? Luckily, Zeppelin didn't like that shit, so they didn't go that way. They loved old blues stuff, so they took those riffs and jammed on them. Black Sabbath didn't play like the Monkees and then play what they really liked afterward: it doesn't work that way, but when I was seventeen, that was my perception of what you had to do. People were telling me to look like Bon Jovi back then because Jovi were so popular. But actually that was the antithesis of what I liked. I'm friends with Jon and they're all great guys, but it's just not that easy. You'll always be a day late and a dollar short if you follow what's popular."

All that remained to round off the year was a White Zombie

and Rob Zombie greatest hits album titled *Past, Present, and Future*, which came out in September and went platinum, following sales of more than a million copies in the USA alone. Not bad for an album largely made up of songs that fans had already heard, a bonus cover of the Ramones' "Blitzkrieg Bop," and two averagely good new tunes ("Two Lane Blacktop" and "Girl on Fire") notwithstanding.

Can you imagine a collection of old songs doing the same nowadays, when the music industry is close to death? No, you can't. It's almost as unlikely an idea as a dreadlocked heavy metal musician ever being taken seriously in the film world . . .

SEVEN

THE CRAZIES
(2004-06)

For a while in 2003 and 2004, it seriously seemed as if Rob Zombie wouldn't bother returning to making music. Why would he? *The Sinister Urge* had been a great album and, if it were to be his last, few fans would complain that he had gone out on anything but a high note. Simultaneously, the sequel to *House of 1,000 Corpses* was taking up most of his time in 2004—well, almost all of his time.

Forming a production company called Creep Entertainment International in tandem with a scriptwriter called Steve Niles, Zombie announced his intention to delve deeper into the world of comic books. He and Niles, who had worked on a *Batman* spinoff as well as the cult vampire series *30 Days of Night*, were introduced to each by the WCW wrestler Diamond Dallas Page. As Zombie explained, "It took a professional wrestler to get me on the phone and get this thing going. You can't say no to Diamond Dallas Page because he'll kick your ass."

While Zombie had done some work back in 2002 on the

Nocturnals comic-book series, published by the renowned Dark Horse imprint, he had yet to throw himself into the creation of a full-blown series of his own. This came initially with *Spookshow International*, a nine-issue run published between late 2003 and the summer of '04.

Collaborating on the series came as a relief from the rigors of working solo. "When I'm working on my own stuff, I always hit these points where my brain's fried and I can't get anything done," Zombie told MTV writer Jon Wiederhorn. "That's when I jump to one of these projects with Steve. I'll work on it for a while until I can't think of anything else to write, then I'll send it to him and he'll take over. Then he'll send it back to me. We've been cranking out a lot of scripts that way.

"The ones I've been doing on my own are more wacky," he added. "They have the vibe of *The Munsters*, but the ones I'm doing with Steve are not funny. They're like serious horror movies adapted into comics."

Spookshow International presented the funny side of Zombie's new venture. Each of the nine issues contained tales based around a small number of charismatic characters. Suzi X. was one: a voluptuous heroine in the Supergirl tradition, but with her curves and sex appeal amped up to 11. Her brother, El Superbeasto, was another, although there was little of the traditional about him. A muscled slab of testosterone in a Mexican wrestler's *luchador* mask, he was concerned with nothing so much as getting laid and dishing out some supernatural violence along the way. Finally, Zombie resurrected the evil Firefly clan from *House of 1,000 Corpses*, setting them loose on the page for plenty of bloodletting.

The humor is what shines most brightly from *Spookshow*

International. No matter what you say or write about comic books, the fact that these publications' readerships consist largely of introverted males of the teenage persuasion will always lead most uninterested people to dismiss them as geek porn. The truth, however, is that these publications are often written, drawn, and published to the very highest standards of the visual and literary arts. This has definitely been the case in all of the comic books published to date under the Rob Zombie name. Whether leaping off the page in glorious Technicolor (as in the case with El Superbeasto) or skulking atmospherically in heavily shadowed murk (as in the case with the 2004 series *The Nail*), this is art that forces the reader to engage with it on a cerebral level.

Of *The Nail*, a four-part miniseries of overpoweringly dark tones, Zombie explained, "The lead character is a wrestler from an era before wrestling became glamorous. I remember going to matches when I was a kid and it just seemed so sleazy—big, nasty guys cracking each other's heads open. So this character was once popular, and now he's older and he's just trying to make ends meet, and he gets involved in all these ugly situations."

The Nail was a classic Zombie-style clash of kitsch cultures, in which Rex "The Nail" Hauser, the wrestler referred to above, bumps into a posse of devil-worshipping bikers. You can probably picture the rest of the story, which is bloody and blasphemous right down to the finest etched detail. And that was happening more or less at the same time as a third comic-book series, *Bigfoot*, which came out in early 2005 and concerns the murderous activities of the eponymous yeti.

"As a kid in the '70s, Bigfoot and the Loch Ness Monster were so freaky," Zombie explained. "I still remember seeing that grainy movie footage on the TV show *In Search of . . .* , and it just left a mark. We're trying to take something that has been really perverted into stupidity by things like *Harry and the Hendersons* [the 1987 screwball comedy starring John Lithgow and Melinda Dillon] and make it scary and cool."

Zombie was clearly having fun with these projects, which he worked on before and after the shooting of his new movie. "You can literally do anything in comics," he said. "In a movie you're limited by what's possible and what you can afford. In comics you can come up with the idea to have a spaceship piloted by a giant pirate robot that fights space babes on flying motorcycles over a pterodactyl landscape, and it's no problem."

This last comment reveals much about the mind of the stressed-out filmmaker. Budgets, deadlines, equipment failures, staff problems, and even unreliable weather can make the fine art of directing movies into something of a living hell—and many of these issues would dog the production of Zombie's second film, the truly excellent *The Devil's Rejects*, which was eventually released on July 22, 2005.

Asked how long the idea of a *House of 1,000 Corpses* sequel had been brewing, Zombie explained that the moment Lionsgate had made back its budget on the first film, the company suggested he make a follow-up feature concerning the further adventures of the Firefly clan, who just about managed to survive the first film intact. In fact, he added, he had begun to formulate an actual idea for the new film the day after *House of 1,000 Corpses* came out, because Lionsgate had made back all of its money on the very first day—a huge success for any indie filmmaker.

An R-rated movie, *The Devil's Rejects* was submitted to the

MPAA no fewer than eight times, with Zombie making cuts on each occasion, before the august organization would finally grant its rating. "There were a couple of scenes in particular they just could not get over," he explained. "And, you know, I would talk to them and I'd go, 'Well, what can I cut?' There's no nudity, there's no bad language, there's no violence, there's no nothing.' They're like, 'Yeah, but the tone is too intense.' That literally is like someone watching a comedy and telling you it's too funny—make it less funny."

Asked for a teaser about the new film, Zombie made it very clear that he had upgraded his objectives this time. For starters, the location was different. "It's a totally different house in a totally different location," he explained. "The first house in the first film is kind of a cooler-looking house. This house is a much more ordinary-looking farmhouse, but the location of the other house is terrible for shooting at. There's not enough land around it, and I wanted to shoot this big scene with all these police cars coming in. I knew that the other location wouldn't work at all. So that's why I had to find a new place to shoot it."

Slip the DVD into your player, crack open a beverage, and you'll see what he means. *The Devil's Rejects* is a beautifully made yet thoroughly chilling piece of work. The three primary antiheroes from the first film—Otis Firefly (Bill Moseley), his sister Baby (Sheri Moon Zombie), and Captain Spaulding (Sid Haig)—return to the screen in fine, graphic style, with the plot resuming just a week after the events of *House of 1,000 Corpses*.

The opening scenes are a little sobering for anyone expecting more of the amusing, student-level horror japes shown in *House*. The giant Firefly brother from the first film (played once again by Matthew McGrory) is seen dragging a naked woman through a forest. There's no airbrushing here: the actress playing the corpse hits every bump on the ground, and her skin tone is grey and deathly. Her nakedness is essential rather than gratuitous, as it demonstrates the utter lack of dignity afforded her at the time of her murder. The message is clear: these people are not to be taken lightly.

Back at the Firefly ranch, the family members are asleep, or perhaps unconscious, as a posse of police cars draws up outside. With guns drawn, the cops yell their commands and the Fireflys spring into positions of self-defense. Zombie takes his time over these arrangements, using teargas effects, slow motion, and clever lighting to highlight the ensuing carnage. Although the budgets for *House of 1,000 Corpses* and *The Devil's Rejects* were roughly similar, this time Zombie was in search of class rather than glitter, with less reliance on props and more focus on textures. That said, the body-horror elements are better executed this time, too, and much more shocking for it: the severed heads that populate the Fireflys' fridge are truly nasty.

Zombie makes an excellent point in the making-of documentary that's included on the *Rejects* DVD, which is that a single inaccurate point—such as an inappropriate prop, or an implausible costume—can spoil his enjoyment of any given film because it reduces the emotional immersion. It's a crucial thing to bear in mind, and for that reason the tiniest details—everything from facial hair to the authentic 1970s sunglasses worn by the police officers—are just right. That's quite an achievement for a low- to-mid-budget film.

The music, too, is a vast improvement on that which was featured in *House of 1,000 Corpses*. There's very little overblown rock or metal here; instead, Zombie uses subtle, almost fragile melodies on guitar and keyboard to suggest menace, a wonderful touch that brings the viewer closer to the action. In the terrific opening scene, in which the

Fireflys escape their attackers and hit the road, *Natural Born Killers* style, we are reminded, not for the last time, of Zombie's love of classic western films.

Zombie would subsequently reveal that he had never particularly liked the use of heavy metal in horror movies. "It's just so obvious," he explained, "so over the top. So something like the Terry Reid songs we used in the film—they're beautiful but they're also really creepy and sad. The whole movie to me has a sad overtone to it. You know that the Firefly family are sort of doomed; you know that the sheriff is sort of doomed. So the whole thing is really sad and those songs were just so perfect for that mood. The Allman Brothers' songs—they're like sad outlaw music. Not heroic at all. It's like that really great [Charles] Manson documentary that came out in the '70s that has this sort of flute folk music running through it. That is so . . . creepy. Nice music with horrific images. A lot of people don't get it. They're like, 'Oh yeah, that's funny, it's supposed to be a funny juxtaposition.' I wasn't thinking that it would be funny. I just thought it would have a lot of emotion."

Back to the action, and an abrupt cut to Captain Spaulding's first appearance is both lighter in content and equally gritty in tone. The naked gentleman is pictured enjoying some sweaty sex with a real-life porn star, Ginger Lynn, then forty-two years of age. Both participants are portrayed mercilessly, their middle-aged physiques highlighted without embellishment or flattering lighting: again, Zombie is making no bones about the frail, flawed nature of the human body—the complete opposite of the *Scream*-influenced wave of contemporary horror films. Old, haggard, and unattractive, the two bounce away on the bed, until Spaulding is revealed to have been experiencing a dream. He gets up, goes to the toilet, and makes a coffee, the scene having provided a truly funny, if graphic, break from the staged drama of the Firefly shootout.

The movie continues apace as the Fireflys move inexorably toward their destiny. Along the way there is a memorable performance by Ken Foree (*Dawn of the Dead*) as a pimp, and another from comic actor Brian Posehn, who is slaughtered realistically during the film's most depressing scene, set in a motel. Here, Otis and Baby abuse a naked female captive, Gloria Sullivan, played with considerable courage by Priscilla Barnes. After she is raped with the barrel of Otis's gun and forced to fellate him, she dies via a knife wound to the stomach. The word "cunt" is used, too, indicating that *The Devil's Rejects* is not looking for mainstream approval—and even Captain Spaulding is pictured swearing at a small boy before assaulting his mother, which is perhaps just as well because we were starting to like him a little bit too much.

Both Bill Moseley and Priscilla Barnes deserve much respect for their handling of this brutal scene, as Zombie was quick to note in interviews after the film's release. "It was tricky because someone like Bill Moseley, who plays Otis, is just not like that. On any level," he said. "He's a nice, kind of goofy guy and he was not into it at all—it was really freaking him out. He was not having a fun time. When it became really seriously menacing after every take, he would be like, 'Oh God . . . I feel terrible.' But I think the person I have to credit most during that scene was Priscilla Barnes. Out of nowhere she got to such a real place and stayed there that she took everyone else with her. Had she not been so real, the whole film could've ended up a lot different. She stepped up her game and the others followed her. There were actually quite a few moments when different actors would step up their game and you could see other actors thinking,

'Shit, I'd better step up my game!' Danny Trejo, who plays Rondo, told me after we were done filming, 'I came into this movie thinking, 'Ah, I'll give it my C-game performance, but it soon became very apparent I had to give it my A-game performance!'"

A scene in which Otis takes two male hostages out to the desert and murders them drags on a little, but it's effective. Fluffing the execution, Otis is forced to fight them with his fists, scrabbling for his dropped gun and pistol-whipping one of his victims in a truly difficult-to-watch sequence. You're rooting for the victims to survive as you watch, meaning that Zombie has achieved every director's aim of total audience immersion.

Again, it's the realistic feel of the action that impresses the viewer most. Everyone looks hot, sweaty, and pissed off; partly as a result of the filming conditions, according to Zombie, but also because of the film's draining content. There's a lot of combat, a lot of torture, a lot of murder, and almost none of it is stylized or glossed over. The death of a female character on the road when a motor vehicle hits her at high speed is unexpected and very graphic, with blood and realistic-looking guts all over the road.

The final scene, in which the Fireflys gun their car toward a police barricade, shooting at the cops from the vehicle while Lynyrd Skynyrd's "Freebird" plays softly behind the action, offers an interesting conclusion to the film. Almost gentle in its execution, it makes the viewer wonder whether—given the choice—Zombie might not necessarily choose to make horror movies at all. It's an impression Zombie would reinforce in later interviews when he explained that he "never once" referenced another horror movie during preproduction of *The Devil's Rejects*.

"My biggest fear when I was hiring the production designer or costume designer is that they would look at horror movies, and I didn't want that look or feel," he explained. "I would leave that part to me, and I didn't want them to go and fall into the conventions of the genre." Instead, he referred his collaborators to films such as *Once Upon a Time in the West* or *Bonnie and Clyde*, as well as to "anything with desert and open road," such as *Two Lane Blacktop*.

"I wasn't just looking to specific movies, it was more about capturing that look," he continued. "Y'know, every '70s movie has that look, and we just tried to approximate that at all times. *House of 1,000 Corpses* had maybe the feel of a '70s drive-in experience but it didn't actually look like a '70s movie. Your first movie is like an explosion of all your interests and influences all at once. After that you just kind of calm down, and focus."

The Devil's Rejects more or less qualifies for inclusion in the horror genre thanks to the on-screen violence, but the torture and murder scenes are psychologically as well as visually disturbing, and Zombie delivers them with a panache that pure horror films generally lack. There's a more confident feel, with fewer tricks and less self-conscious "horror" props such as fake skulls and so on.

Zombie also made use of his people skills while working on *The Devil's Rejects*, as he revealed in the accompanying making-of documentary. One of the characters, a vengeful police officer named John Quincy Wydell, was played by William Forsythe, the veteran of many action movies, ranging from the cult (*Things to Do in Denver When You're Dead*) to the cheesy (*Extreme Prejudice*). Here, Forsythe overplays his character with sinister charisma, tearing up the screen with rage and emitting an almost psychopathic lust for violence. With a reputation for being hard to handle, he required some forceful direction.

"I really liked William. We got along great," Zombie told Carlo Cavagna at *About Film*, noting that rumors of him being difficult proved to be unfounded. "I'm a big proponent of [the idea that] whatever gets on film is what counts, because that's all anyone's going to see, except for me. I'm the one who has to deal with the hell behind the scenes. But for you, that's all that matters. If someone is like, 'Oh, I don't like Russell Crowe,' who cares? If he gives you a great performance, that's all that matters, in the average filmgoer's world."

Prior to working together on set, the two men spoke at length on the telephone. "Look, man," Zombie told Forsythe, "I want you to be Robert Shaw, Lee Marvin, Robert Mitchum. I need a strong leading man. I don't want a pretty boy. I want a really compelling [performance]."

"That was, like, everything he wanted to hear," Zombie explained to Cavagna. "I think we bonded over both having an obsession with Robert Shaw, and thinking that he was the greatest actor that ever lived. Once we both said those words—because Robert Shaw is an incredible actor, but his name doesn't come up that often—as soon as he said it, I was like, 'That's perfect. He totally, totally gets it 100 percent.' Later I realized that he grew his beard, his moustache sort of the way Robert Shaw looks in *Jaws*, a little bit."

◆

On its release, *The Devil's Rejects* was dedicated to Matthew McGrory, who had died of natural causes earlier in the summer of 2005, shortly before the film's release. It did well at the box office, closely matching its predecessor's performance by recouping its $7 million budget in its first weekend and going on to snag a total of $16 million.

Zombie subsequently revealed that his budget had almost run out by the time it came to paying for the music. "*Rejects* is not a big-budget movie," he said. "This sounds kind of pathetic, but when we were done shooting we had $50,000 left for music. So after the budget for the songs came in at $900,000, we were thinking, 'Okay, we're only $850,000 short.' Somehow we made it work; we got all the songs. I don't know how. People cutting deals, I guess."

On the plus side, Zombie had at least managed to avoid studio intrusion while making the film. "This time around it was totally different. I wish there was more of a story—it's so boring. There is no story! Lionsgate left me alone 100 percent. They never got involved . . . you never believe [that's] going to happen. They were very smart. They would come down to the set and see the dailies and they were like, 'This is great, we're gonna stay out of your way,' and they actually did. I didn't contractually have final cut, but they gave it to me. The only cuts I made were to get a rating."

Audiences and critics alike appeared to warm to the horrible Fireflys and their accomplices, despite Zombie's attempts to keep the characters unpleasant, with Sid Haig receiving the Best Actor award at the *Fangoria* Chainsaw Awards, and the Firefly family plus Captain Spaulding collectively bagging "Most Vile Villain" at the Spike TV Scream awards. Still, no one knew exactly why Zombie had made these characters so evil, and he wasn't about to tell.

"Everyone's like, 'Well, what's their motivation for being serial killers?' I'm like, 'What is anyone's motivation? They're insane, obviously.' Sometimes, people are just insane," he reasoned. "I didn't really want to get into too much back story because I just thought it might bog the movie down. A lot of times, I see movies and I think, 'Yeah, we get it. You don't have to keep explaining it to us. We get it.'"

Zombie cast his mind back to films like *Henry: Portrait of a Serial Killer*, in which no real attempt is made to explain away the "despicable" acts of the primary characters. "I like the mystery, so with *Rejects*, the movie isn't about the Fireflys in the sense of why did this happen, how could this happen, why are these people like they are? You just kind of drop in and spend a day in the life of these crazy people. It's more interesting to me without an explanation. I mean, we've all read about serial killers, we can fill in the blanks."

Explaining his decision to set his first two films in the 1970s, Zombie called the decade "my favorite time period for everything." As he told AboutFilm.com, "I didn't do it to pay homage to anything, because that seems silly. It was because I love the music from the seventies more than any other music, I love the movies of the seventies, the fashion, the look, the feel. And, I think it's probably because, at that point, I was at the right age to just be bombarded by it . . . every week, your mind was exploding. I just took that experience for granted. Now, I go to the movies and I come out feeling like, 'Oh, yeah, more of that again.' Then, it just seemed like everything was genius. Maybe I'm reliving it in my mind better than it was. But I remember thinking that every film seemed like genius."

The closest we would come to finding out what drove the on-screen maniacs was when Zombie explained that they were indirectly inspired by characters from his own background. "Not William Forsythe's character, but Otis, Baby, Spaulding . . . [they] all come from people that I grew up with and that I knew. Not that they were murderers, but just the personalities and the types."

The character of Otis, for example, was based on some kids he went to school with—three albino brothers who reminded him of the rock singer Edgar Winter. "They were bizarre. If you saw them in a movie, you'd go, 'That's unbelievable.' And then, the other characters were just based on members of my family. Growing up, the main family business was the carney business. They all worked in carnivals and they were carneys, and that's a nutty world. You run into a lot of guys who seem like Captain Spaulding."

It was interesting, too, as many interviewers would note at the time, that the utterly psychotic, revenge-seeking police sheriff John Quincy Wydell ended up being just as evil as the supposed villains; after all, he does his fair share of torture and killing on the way to avenging his slain brother.

"I just took an Old West approach because I was always obsessed with the Old West, as a kid," Zombie reasoned. "That's why Forsythe's character is a total reflection of that. I'd read books and back-stories on sheriffs and detectives from the 1890s, and that was always their thought process—total vigilante justice. Kill the bandits and hang their corpse in the street for all the town folks to look at. I was putting that in a modern setting and having that character ride that line, and then of course, cross it, at some point."

In his AboutFilm.com review of *The Devil's Rejects*, the esteemed Carlo Cavagna noted how, by comparison to the "critically reviled" *House of 1,000 Corpses*, Zombie's new film was hailed almost as a "modern American masterpiece." He kindly agreed to share his further impressions on *Rejects* for this book.

"*The Devil's Rejects*' rating (53 percent) on the Rotten Tomatoes Tomatometer may not seem all that impressive, but you wouldn't expect a low-budget, exploitative, gory hillbilly slasher movie to score anywhere near as high, not when *1,000 Corpses* scored 16 percent and more mainstream horror fare like *House of Wax* gets a 22 percent. . . . Consider *Variety*'s dismissive comments on the original ('A cobwebbed, mummified horror entry that makes obvious, cartoonishly grotesque demands for attention') and compare them to its praise for the sequel ('a brutal, punishing yet mordantly amusing work that far outpaces its predecessor in its grisly single-mindedness of vision'). Similarly, the *New York Post* called the original a 'demented dung heap' but hails *Devil's Rejects* as 'a perfect B-movie, full of wicked dread.' Roger Ebert and Richard Roeper both give *Devil's Rejects* a thumbs-up, and Peter Travers of *Rolling Stone* observes, 'Indefensible on a moral level, Rob Zombie's perversely watchable [Devil's Rejects] is loaded with filmmaking energy.'"

All this reveals a new confidence on the part of Zombie as a director. A good filmmaker has to balance the needs of his cast and crew with the limitations of the shoot, the parameters of the budget and the requirements of the producers with his or her own artistic vision—a nightmare task which, in the case of *The Devil's Rejects*, Zombie mastered with ease, despite this being only his second film.

"With *House of 1,000 Corpses*, I didn't really know enough to get what I could see in my head onto film," he admitted. "Everything seemed like a compromise; it wasn't right. Quickly I knew that the tone of that movie had become kinda goofy. I went with it, but it wasn't really what I originally set out to do. With *Rejects*, I didn't want to make *House of 1,000 Corpses Part 2*, I wanted to make this kind of postmodern, bleak Western."

Of course, the critics' first question—once *The Devil's Rejects* had become a success—was to ask if a third film in the series would now follow along in a few years' time. The answer, then as now, was no. "I don't think there'd be a point in doing it," he said. "For the most part, third movies don't work. It almost never works. I can't think of when it did. Can you? *Return of the Jedi? The Godfather 3?* [They] should have just been left alone."

"There are rare occasions when a sequel is great, or perhaps even better than the original, like *The Godfather 2* or *Bride of Frankenstein*," he added, accurately, "but those cases are pretty rare. So when it became apparent that I would be making a sequel, I approached it as though I was making a completely new film. It's a tricky thing, because I knew people were fans of the first film, but I didn't really want to do anything I had already done, except retain the characters. Once I had decided to have the Firefly family back, I set out to change the tone of the characters and the film in every way possible."

◆

As *The Devil's Rejects'* theatrical run came to a close, Zombie turned his mind at last to new music, feeling rejuvenated now by four years away from the recording studio. You will recall that his last band had splintered, sick of each other and of life on the road, after the release of *The Sinister Urge* back in 2001. "I was fed up with doing music [in the mid-2000s], not because I didn't love music any more, but because I was tired of being in bands where nobody could get along," he explained to the writer Henry Northmore of this miserable period. "And it happened to me twice, which was weird. White Zombie was a band that had personality problems all the way through and by the time the band got huge, it was just miserable. And I quit that band, started again and then the band I had with *Hellbilly* and the next album, I was like, 'Here we are again, we're playing sold-out shows and everybody hates each other.'"

Why does it have to be like this? he wondered. *Why does everything become miserable as soon as a bit of success comes along?* Zombie's response was simply to walk away from music for the time being.

"I was like, I can't do this any more," he continued. "It's just too stressful, it's too hard to have the greatest job in the world and somehow it's miserable. And that's when I went and made *Devil's Rejects* and was thinking, 'Maybe I'm just done doing music.'"

Fortunately, he then found the creative foil he needed to rediscover his passion for music. "Every lead singer needs that right-hand-man guitar player," Zombie told Northmore. And now he had found him. "It was like being a kid again and starting the whole thing over."

John 5—or John Lowery to his accountant—is a guitar player like few others. Having made his name with Marilyn Manson but also spent time working with Dave Lee Roth—now there's two radically differing guitar styles for you—John 5 was the perfect fit for Zombie's band as he was equally adept at delivering chunky groove riffs as shreddy lead solos. Joined by bassist Rob "Blasko" Nicholson from Zombie's last band and a new drummer, Tommy Clufetos—who had played with Rob's old mate Alice Cooper, among others—John 5 took part in studio sessions for Zombie's new album, which was due out in early 2006, and prepared for a stint headlining the second stage of the Ozzfest in the summer of 2005.

Speaking to Steven Rosen, Zombie hailed John 5 as a "phenomenal" guitarist. "I can demand things with him [that] I could not demand that from other guitar player, because they wouldn't have the ability to do it. So that's kind of nice to be able to reach out and branch out to people, who can play beyond the main, than perhaps the people here are in a bandwidth. And it's funny, too, because I see it in another bands, because sometimes if you are on tour with bands, I don't want to play [with] popular bands and they will come up to John. John will literally be giving the guitar player on the other band a guitar lesson."

Noting how he had witnessed many other bands come unstuck as a result of the limits of their own members' abilities, Zombie enthused about the freedom now afforded him as a solo performer. "I don't have to try to get someone to do a solo that [sounds] like Kerry King," he said. "I'll just go to Kerry King to do the solo."

With a main stage featuring Rob Zombie, Deftones, Slayer, Primus, Godsmack, and System of a Down, plus a second stage featuring Fear Factory, Static-X, Slipknot, Puya, Drain STH, Hed(pe), Apartment 26, Flashpoint, and Pushmonkey (the last three acts were virtually unknown), the touring Ozzfest debuted at Florida's West Palm Beach and worked its way through Georgia, Tennessee, North Carolina, Virginia, and New Jersey before heading back down across the southern and western states and winding up, after two long sweeps across the country, in New York in August.

Although John 5 was (on paper at least) just another in a long line of Rob Zombie guitarists, his impact on Zombie's work during the decade since has been profound. Not every rock singer needs a guitar slinger by his side to make his point, but many do—see Aerosmith and Guns N' Roses for just two of the more obvious examples—and the relief that Zombie has expressed on many occasions about John 5's presence in his band speaks volumes.

The two men had much in common, right from their first meeting. For starters, both were fans of a certain stadium-rock band. "When I was a young child, seeing KISS blew me away," the guitarist later revealed, in an interview with Steven Rosen. "And I think 99 percent of it was when people discovered KISS, it's with the makeup and the fire and the smoke and blood and everything, and it really affects someone. It's just like if Frankenstein or something like that played awesome rock music, you'd be like, 'This is incredible!' I think that's why it influences a lot of guitar players and musicians, because that's what it did for me and when you're a child it just blows you away."

In fact, what the young John 5 was drawn to initially was not so much the music but the dramatic cover art for the band's 1977 LP *Love Gun*. "I was so drawn to the cover and then hearing [guitarist] Ace [Frehley]," he continued. "I would have been a fan of Ace, because he had a lot of great things he was doing. [For] one, he was a great songwriter; I mean hands down, the guy is a phenomenal songwriter and he did some chicken-picking [guitar] too. He did that in a lot of solos, but also he was such a great inventor. I mean, he came up with the smoke coming out of the guitar and all that stuff. He was one of those epiphanies in my life; it just really changed everything for me."

It's interesting to note that, unlike Zombie, John 5 was not a huge fan of Alice Cooper, the artist who had had such a profound influence on his new boss. But that soon changed after he joined Zombie's band. "Rob loves Alice, and our bass player loves Alice, so they were always talking Alice stories, and talking about records, and I felt very left out because I didn't know anything. I knew like the 'School's Out' song, 'I'm Eighteen' the song; you know, things like that. I didn't really know much; I knew his hits."

Intrigued by his bandmates' passion, John downloaded a copy of the group's 1969 album *Pretties for You*. "And I'm tellin' ya—another epiphany! It changed my life; it's incredible: the orchestration and the writing and the parts and the styles. Oh, my God, so many different styles." He promptly worked his way through the entire Alice Cooper back catalogue. "Before, I was like, 'Yeah, Alice Cooper, he's got good songs,' but I didn't get it. But now I get it!"

With his new band in place, Zombie decided to strip down the stage show to a minimum, which it might be convenient (and maybe even correct) to regard as a continuation of the less-is-more aesthetic he had adopted as a director on the shooting of *The Devil's Rejects*. "There are no big props or otherworldly atmospheres this time," he declared. "The show has been stripped down to make it more interesting. I just wanted to do a scaled-back sort of thing. We used to have these massive stage shows where suddenly it's like [Las Vegas magicians] Siegfried and Roy. I've seen huge acts, like KISS and Alice Cooper, in a situation where there's nothing. It's ten times more interesting."

This general reluctance to embrace the over-the-top production values of the past was clearly evident in the first single from Zombie's new album, the oddly titled "Foxy, Foxy." Released on February 14, 2006—the fact of it being Valentine's Day presumably not a coincidence—the song attracted some slight criticism for its short duration and resolutely un-heavy nature.

There's nothing particularly wrong with "Foxy, Foxy," but it doesn't sound much like Zombie's previous music, which in itself is always an issue for long-standing fans. It lacks presence, perhaps, coming and going without making much of an impact. Connect this with a video that is just as stripped-down as you'd expect from Zombie's statements about the forthcoming live shows, it's understandable that some listeners felt underwhelmed. After all, in the clip he performs in a simple double-denim outfit, the creepy contact lenses and spooky production of old now completely absent.

Zombie was incensed by the suggestion that the more commercial sound of "Foxy, Foxy" was a deliberate ploy encouraged by his record company, Geffen. "Let me set the record straight. Most things don't bother me, but this does," he said. "In response to people implying that 'the record label made me write "Foxy Foxy" in order to sell more records' or whatever . . . that is total bullshit. The record label never has and never will make me do anything. If you hate the song, fine, but I am the one responsible for you hating it. Not the label. So blame me.

"It's funny how nothing ever changes," he added. "I remember the first tour for *La Sexorcisto*: fans were screaming, 'You suck!' '"Thunder Kiss '65" is gay!' 'You sold out!' Then, guess what—the same thing happened on the next record . . . '"More Human Than Human" is gay!' 'You guys suck now!' Whatever. I do what I do, same as I always have. If you don't like it, well, don't listen to it. What can I tell ya?"

"Foxy Foxy's" chorus refers to "educated horses," which was also, it subsequently emerged, the title of Zombie's new album, which came out a month later, on March 28. Almost a decade after its release, *Educated Horses* remains a slightly leftfield work in the context of Rob Zombie's overall career. After all, it appeared at a time when his interest in filmmaking far outweighed his love of music, new band or no new band. It did well commercially, reaching #5 on the *Billboard* 200 chart and selling 107,000 copies in its first week, with the usual cast, including Scott Humphrey as co-producer and guest drummers Josh Freese and Tommy Lee, on board to lend their talents.

However, *Educated Horses* sounds noticeably different to *Hellbilly Deluxe* and *The Sinister Urge*. What a strange album this

165

is, its creator's mind clearly on other things. There's no sense of urgency in the music. This time around, Zombie lets the groove do the talking—a move that occasionally works but just as often leaves the vibe feeling a touch flat.

The mellow acoustic vibes of the intro, "Sawdust in the Blood," are welcome—but they need to be followed by something more upbeat than the second track, "American Witch," if they're to deliver maximum impact to the listener. As we've already noted, "Foxy, Foxy" was a slightly unusual choice for a lead-off single; "17 Year Locust" introduces a chilled, almost desert-rock groove into the Zombie sound, together with Black Sabbath–indebted guitars and a sitar lick from John 5.

"The Scorpion Sleeps" is the real eye-opener. Beginning with a tribal glam-rock groove of the kind that has been appropriated since time immemorial by bands as disparate as Adam and the Ants and Marilyn Manson, it's pop/rock to the core, custom-built for the arena tour upon which Zombie and band were shortly to embark after the album release. The next track, "100 Ways," offers a cool two minutes of creepy atmospherics, while "Let It All Bleed Out" brings a touch of aggression at last, powering along with anthemic qualities.

"Death of It All" is a high point of the album, resting on a filigree of acoustic fingerpicking and evolving into a kind of laconic, understated rock groove, featuring soft, almost spoken-word vocals and a spine-tingling chorus melody and strings. It's the most memorable song here, laden with soundtrack-like ambience. "Ride" starts in a similarly subtle manner before stepping up a gear into a strange but listenable mélange of Tool-like textures and roars of the title. It's a resolutely uncommercial tune, but somehow attractive nonetheless.

Finally, *Educated Horses* ends with "The Devil's Rejects" and "The Lords of Salem." The former is a spooky, atmospheric strum with plenty of country picking and the memorable lines, "Hell doesn't want them, hell doesn't need them, hell doesn't love them," the doomed faces of Otis and Baby Firefly appearing in the listener's imagination as the song plays. And then we have "The Lords of Salem," a four-minute stroll through layers of heavy guitar and bass to a finale that crashes into chaos and a quick, jammed exit.

The album shines throughout with John 5's glittering contributions on guitar, of which he was immensely proud. In fact, the guitarist's generally effervescent enthusiasm for simply being in Rob Zombie's band must have made him even more welcome. As anyone who has played in a rock band will confirm, attitude is everything. Talking to Steven Rosen, the guitarist gushed, "We were in like a secret location in the middle of nowhere and it was me, Rob, Bob Marlette the producer, and the band . . . there was nothing around, and we just concentrated on music every day.

"It was really a cool way to work, because if you're in Los Angeles or New York you have so many distractions and things you have to do. 'Oh, I have to go to the post office or I've got to do this or I've got to do that.' But it wasn't like that—that's all we did . . . I didn't even see another human so it was really wild. It's amazing what you can get done when there are no other distractions."

For the guitarist, the atmosphere almost resembled that of being in "a little cult . . . we went to sleep and woke up and did it all over again. It was wild. I mean, it was a treat if we had to go to a restaurant or something. We would have to get in a car and make a plan to go to a restaurant, but it was great. It was a lot of fun!"

A thirty-three-date US tour kicked off in March 2006, with

Italian symphonic metal act Lacuna Coil and Welsh metal-core quartet Bullet for My Valentine in tow. The usual round of festival dates kept Zombie busy for the rest of the summer, after which more screen time awaited him.

Toward the end of the year, Zombie presented ten episodes of a late-night series on the Turner Classic Movies channel devoted to cult films. *TCM Underground*, as it was called, saw him introduce classic movies such as *Plan 9 from Outer Space*, *Faster, Pussycat! Kill! Kill!*, *Night of the Living Dead*, and *Freaks*. He would tell the stories behind the films' creation and discuss their fate at the box office. Check these clips out on YouTube, or when they air as reruns, and you'll see a man deeply in his element, with none of the slight nervousness or impatience that he occasionally displays in interviews concerning his music. That's the point here—he is truly in his element.

So much to do, so little time—and yet all this frenzied activity was a mere precursor to Zombie's biggest project yet. Compared to what was to come, all that had gone before was mere preparation.

EIGHT

NiGHT OF THE SORCERERS

(2007–08)

"This is the new *Halloween*," ran the announcement on Rob Zombie's MySpace page. (Remember those?) "Call it a remake, an update, a reimagining or whatever, but one thing for sure is that this is a whole new start . . . a new beginning with no connection to the other series. That is exactly why the project appeals to me. I can take it and run with it."

If you're still here after seven chapters, you're probably aware of the 1978 horror film *Halloween*, but in case you haven't seen it in a while, let's revisit the old slasher classic for a moment. Its antihero, Michael Myers, whose mask has become iconic even outside the horror world, is one of the slasher genre's most easily recognizable villains, alongside Leatherface from the *Texas Chainsaw Massacre* films, Jason Voorhees from the *Friday the 13th* franchise, and Freddy Krueger of *Nightmare on Elm Street* fame. Myers and his fondness for stabbing hapless teens with a massive kitchen knife formed the basis of several films back in the '70s and '80s, which taken as a whole collectively demonstrate how a cultural phenomenon will deteriorate if not treated properly.

The first *Halloween* was shocking, introducing the utterly murderous Myers to a frankly insatiable audience. It was directed with minimalist panache by John Carpenter, who had already made the cult movies *Dark Star* and *Assault on Precinct 13* and went on to helm *The Fog, The Thing, Escape from New York*, and *They Live*, as well as many, many other rather less impactful movies. According to some sources, Carpenter shot *Halloween* on a $325,000 budget before making $47 million back at the domestic box office—one of the greatest budget-to-profit ratios in film history. The great man then either directed, produced, or composed the music for seven *Halloween* sequels, a series which started well but soon plummeted to a level of embarrassing tedium.

This was the setup for Rob Zombie's not-quite remake, set for release in the summer blockbuster season of 2007. It would be set in the original's fictional location of Haddonfield, Illinois, and feature many of the same characters, the plot would differ from that of the original. A complex collaboration of individuals and their associated companies, the new *Halloween* was produced by Zombie's manager Andy Gould and his Vision Entertainment Group and Malek Akkad of Trancas International Films, who had created the fairly feeble *Halloween H20: 20 Years Later* in 1998. The $15 million budget came from Dimension Films and the Weinstein Company, whose co-chairman Bob Weinstein announced, "Rob Zombie is a gifted musician and performer as well as a talented filmmaker. His vision for this new *Halloween* is spectacular, and I am thrilled to be collaborating with him."

"After *Rejects*, I really didn't know what was next," Zombie remarked. "I had been briefly attached to several projects, but nothing seemed right. *Rejects* was a movie very close to my heart and I didn't want to just jump on the next project in haste."

Other forces would soon intervene, however. "One day I get a call from Bob Weinstein's office saying Bob would like to have a meeting. I figured, 'Okay, sure whatever. Another meeting.' I figured it would lead to nothing, as most of these things do.

"So Bob throws out the idea of *Halloween* at me. Now, I've always been a huge fan of the original, but not so much the sequels, and I figure that Bob means another sequel. Well, this doesn't interest me at all. In fact none of this really interested me. I figured Michael Myers had run his course and his best days were far, far behind him. So, I left the meeting, figuring I'd call back later and tell them I wasn't interested. Then I started to rethink the whole thing. I mean, Michael Myers is a great character, a horror icon, much like Frankenstein and Dracula. How could I pass this up? But a sequel? A prequel? No way. I had to start fresh and breathe new life into Michael's old bones. I thought the only way to do this is to start over. I hate to use this word, but a re-imagining was the only way to go. In the past I've hated the idea of this, but then I thought what a closed-minded way to think. I was basing my thoughts on remakes I hated, not the ones I loved—*The Thing, Scarface, Cape Fear, The Fly*, and on and on. And so began Michael's journey back."

The reaction from the horror community was instant, with fans of the *Halloween* franchise demanding details of the new film on MySpace, fan sites, and bulletin boards—pretty much the only social media available back then, in the days before Facebook and Twitter took off. To his credit, Zombie trod carefully, managing people's expectations with a series of cautious statements. One of these was the clarification that John Carpenter himself had approved the remake—a crucial step when approaching material that, for many film fans of a certain age and temperament, was as sacred as *Star Wars*.

"The original *Halloween* is hallowed ground to me," Zombie told the Hollywood bible *Variety.* "I talked to Carpenter about it and he was very supportive of what I wanted to do. He said, 'Go for it, Rob. Make it your own.' And that's exactly what I intend to do. Over twenty-five years and a lot of movies, a very scary character became something of a Halloween cliché, with Michael Myers dolls that play the Halloween music when you press their stomachs. There was little connection to the original. I take that film very seriously, and I want to make it terrifying again."

As time passed, Zombie issued tantalizing tidbits of information about the production: on the subject of Michael Myers's infamous mask, he said, "I've just seen [special effects artist] Wayne Toth's finished mask for Michael, and all I can say is, 'Holy fuck.' It looks perfect. Exactly like the original. Not since 1978 has the shape looked so good. Wayne worked this sucker to death, and boy did it pay off."

As for who would play the monster, Zombie announced that a hulking fellow called Tyler Mane would inhabit the mask. At the time, Mane was not widely known, apart from a role in the first *X-Men* film and an appearance in Zombie's own *Devil's Rejects* two years earlier, but as Zombie wrote, "Tyler is mean, lean, and ready to bring you the most psychotic Michael Myers yet." The role of Dr. Loomis, the psychiatrist assigned to the young Myers's care, would be filled by none other than Malcolm McDowell, star of *A Clockwork Orange* among other films. "As many of you know," Zombie noted, "*A Clockwork Orange* is my favorite film and I am a huge, huge fan of

Malcolm. I know Malcolm will kick ass as Dr. Loomis. He is thrilled to be part of *Halloween* and is ready to make a new classic."

"Malcolm was my first and, really, only choice," he added, "because I've found that one thing you've gotta do is not really have a backup plan. In life, I find that when you've got a backup plan, that's the one you get stuck with. I wanted Malcolm, and I didn't want anybody else. And when things were falling apart and it seemed like for a second maybe we wouldn't get Malcolm, I never gave anybody an out to go elsewhere. I went, 'No, it has to be Malcolm or nobody.'"

Zombie later revealed that his original idea had been to direct two films: one focusing on Myers's childhood and another on his later, violent actions. Weinstein didn't go for this, though, so Zombie came up with the idea of retelling the story with a detailed explanation of the childhood that turned Myers into a killing machine. "It's all about Michael and his life," he wrote. "Many have feared that by explaining him, that you make him less scary. First of all, I don't think Michael could get less scary than the way he's been treated in the last bunch of films. Seriously, do you? Besides, I don't explain it. We get great insight into Michael's life, but nothing explains why he is pure evil. Nothing could. As you will see, Dr. Loomis wasted most of his life trying to figure this out, and he couldn't. To quote the doctor himself, 'The darkest souls are not those which exist within the hell of the abyss, but those which break free of the abyss and move silently among us.'"

It's interesting—and contradictory—that Zombie had decided against exploring the Firefly family's background in *The Devil's Rejects*, deeming it unnecessary since they were, in his words, "obviously insane," but now he felt that the best way to refill Michael

Myers with the scare power of the '70s was to explore what made him a monster. "What I wanted to do was spend more time with the character as a child," he explained. He had was never been satisfied with the original script's premise that a normal boy would suddenly kill someone one day without reason, he said. The question remained, what would it take to make a little kid become a murderer?

In part, the challenge with *Halloween* was to remake it in a way that was unlike other remakes. Reworkings of older films rarely work, usually because they're done solely because modern technology allows better special effects than in previous decades, in the course of which the essence that made the original effective is lost. Anyone remotely interested in cinema can reel off a list of recent remakes that have failed, either partly or entirely, and they're usually action films, horror movies, or thrillers. There's the aforementioned 1998 remake of *Psycho*, which avoided any improvement by repeating the actual shots of the 1960 original; *The Wicker Man*; *The Fog*; *The Amityville Horror*; *Carrie*; *The Hills Have Eyes*; *Evil Dead*; *I Spit on Your Grave* . . . all have been remade in recent years, and that's just in the horror genre.

Why do these films generally fail to delight audiences? Because they're just glitzed-up versions of what went before. Zombie was well aware of this problem, and strove to avoid it with his own work.

"That movie already exists," he explained, "so to do anything like that movie seems like a completely pointless venture. I think [that] is the problem with remakes, and where they get into trouble. I want to make something that in the first ten seconds [makes] you think, 'Wow. This is a whole different movie.' I'm a particular type of person and I want to make those movies. Certain directors make movies that are very much them. When you see a Quentin Tarantino movie, it's very much him."

As we saw with *The Devil's Rejects*, the idea of making a modern, anaesthetized horror film is anathema to Zombie, steeped as he is in old-school slasher culture. As he wanted one of the major emphases of the plot to be on Michael Myers's childhood, casting the right child actor for the role was crucial. He'd already decided not to take the cheesy route by giving any of the original cast a cameo, reasoning that if Jamie Lee Curtis, for example, appeared it would "break the reality" of the new film. As such, finding the right people became a serious—and difficult—job.

Fortunately, a kid named Daeg Faerch showed up to the audition. Aged just eleven at the time of production, Faerch looked rather distinctive, with a sullen demeanor and a thousand-yard stare that's deeply unusual in a child of such tender years. Given that his scenes were to be so important to the impact of the film, he had a serious burden to carry.

The opening scenes of *Halloween* waste zero time in establishing what a miserable life the young Myers endured on his way to the nuthouse. Loved but neglected by his mother Deborah (Sheri Moon Zombie), ignored by his older sister Judith, and ridiculed by his mother's white-trash boyfriend Ronnie (another carpet-chewing performance by William Forsythe), he wears a homemade mask at every opportunity. Just listening to the abuse piled on and around the preteen Myers by the moronic Ronnie actually makes you hope that his revenge will be swift and merciless. A school bully is equally vile, and is the first to succumb to Myers's rage when he is beaten to death with a tree branch while walking in a forest. It's quite a performance from Faerch, who swings plausibly from silence to homicidal rage in a matter of seconds.

The murders come thick and fast. With Ronnie satisfactorily

dispatched and the slightly less deserving Judith and her boyfriend both given the hatchet job, only Deborah and Myers's baby sister Angel are spared. After a trial, Myers is incarcerated in Warren County Sanitarium under the watch of Malcolm McDowell's caring but egocentric Doctor Loomis. As time passes, Myers becomes obsessed with creating and wearing paper masks, much to the distress of Deborah when she visits him. Although he is apparently docile, the young psychopath manages to add a nurse to his list of kills, an act that prompts Deborah to commit suicide.

At this point we jump forward to fifteen years later. Michael, now played by the hulking Tyler Mane, has grown into a massive, longhaired bear of a man who habitually allows himself to be guided helplessly by the sanatorium staff. Until, that is, he escapes, murdering a couple more hapless victims for good measure, before heading back to the abandoned family home, where he picks up his old mask.

Now Myers is at large, and we understand what he went through to make him this way. Have Zombie's efforts at creating a backstory helped to make him more real? Indeed they have, although the sympathy that the viewer feels at his terrible background rapidly diminishes as he wades through an ever-increasing pile of victims.

Not everyone enjoyed this expansion of Myers's character. Before *Halloween* was released, a reviewer at the *Ain't It Cool* film appreciation website posted a negative review of an early version of the script. Zombie replied indirectly. "I notice that so many people get crazy when someone you don't even know posts an opinion about what they think *Halloween* will or won't be. This is crazy. Do you really go through life influenced by the thoughts of others that easily? Anyway, things change so much in a movie, from moment to moment, from second to second, that all I can say is: see it for yourself and figure out if you like it or not. Really, who gives a fuck what someone else thinks? Everybody likes different shit for different reasons. But deciding that you hate or love something that doesn't even exist yet? Well, that's a little ridiculous."

Back to the film: before long, Myers is stalking his sister, now renamed Laurie Strode and played by Scout Taylor-Compton. She doesn't realize that Myers is her brother, and when he murders some teens, evades the police and the returning Dr. Loomis, and corners her in an attempt at reconciliation, she stabs and shoots him. In the final frame, he grabs her wrist as her gun explodes in his face. We are left to assume he is dead.

Halloween is masterfully filmed, with sets well dressed and shots neatly established, while the plot moves along briskly with plenty of shocks. Mane performs well, given the limitations inherent in his role, while McDowell is on peak form and the rest of the cast do their job without requiring too much suspension-of-disbelief from the viewer. The cinematography is crisp and shadowed, with Zombie opting for a modern look as he didn't want to make a retro movie.

Audiences liked Zombie's vision, repaying the producers' efforts with a mighty $80 million at the box office, making it the best-performing *Halloween* yet in unadjusted dollars and breaking a record for the most profitable Labor Day film release to date. That's a decent performance by anybody's standards, and all because Zombie had a vision and stuck to it. Had he decided to replace more elements of the original *Halloween* with inventions of his own, the film might not have resonated with cinemagoers as profoundly as it did.

At some point, and fortunately for fans of the new *Halloween*, Zombie had clearly experienced a conversion in his attitude toward remakes. As he told Alan Sculley at *Last Word Feature*, "I used to have a more anti-remake opinion of things, and I thought it was a really kind of stupid way to look at things, because so many films that I love are remakes [and] would never would exist if everybody had that attitude. I think it only works if you feel like you have an inspiration to do it, and just not because if the project is there. Because there were several other projects that came to me before *Halloween*, and they were all remakes and I turned them all down, because I just didn't have an ounce of passion for the projects and it would have been a drag. But with this one, you know, looking at it and thinking, well you know, Michael Myers, he's a pretty clean slate. You can almost do anything with him. That's when I knew it was worth approaching."

The new *Halloween* had a bigger role than mere entertainment. Zombie's goal was to restore Michael Myers to his original position, to where he actually scared people, as he had been created to do in the first place. As he explained to the writer Henry Northmore, he had loved John Carpenter's original *Halloween*, having seen it as a teen when it first came out, and had always considered it one of his all-time favorite horror movies. "But there were, like, seven sequels to *Halloween*, and I thought with each one it got worse and worse and worse and worse, until I was like, really, they've beat *Halloween* and Michael Myers and his character so deep into the ground, that it didn't seem sacrilegious to take it on. If only John Carpenter's movie existed, then maybe it would've [been intimidating] to me, because that would be, 'You're just remaking that one classic film, what are you, crazy?' But . . . I thought maybe there's a chance to make it cool again."

Let us not forget, while we're praising its cinematic qualities,

Rob Zombie at the Spectrum Arena, Philadelphia, January 2008. (Frank White)

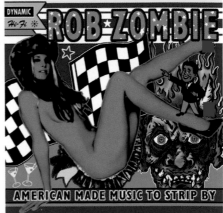
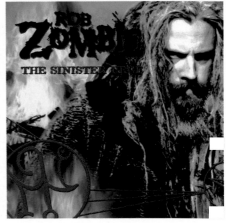

The renaissance man takes a pause,
March 2005. (Anne Cussack/Los
Angeles Times/Getty Images)

Top: Directing the action on the set of *The Devil's Rejects*. (Snap Stills/Rex USA)
Bottom: Sheri Moon Zombie, Sid Haig, and Bill Moseley in a still from the film.
(Moviestore/Rex USA)

Zombie with the young and old Michael Myers (Tyler Mane and Daeg Faerch) on the set of his 2009 remake of *Halloween*. (Snap Stills/Rex USA)

Above: Zombie on the set of his 2007 remake of *Halloween*. (Snap Stills/Rex USA)
Opposite page, top: The "ass" and "pussy" versions of remix album *Mondo Sex Head*.
Opposite page, bottom: Zombie and his right-hand man, guitarist John 5, at the Susquehanna Bank Center, Camden, New Jersey, July 2013. (Frank White)

The master at work: Rob Zombie onstage at the Susquehanna Bank Center, Camden, New Jersey, July 2013. (Frank White)

that Rob Zombie's *Halloween* is also a very violent film. The strokes of Michael Myers's knife make a sound that is unusually graphic by comparison to today's teen-friendly horror fare. On the subject of whether his films were suitable for younger viewers, Zombie remarked that the good thing about the remake craze was that younger filmgoers might want to see the older films, adding that vintage fare such as the 1975 Disney film *Escape from Witch Mountain* was essentially horror for kids.

It's an interesting point. The film to which he refers is a dark, futuristic fantasy that enthralled a generation of kids with its in-camera special effects and outlandish plot—plus it had the kind of slightly scary, Roald Dahl–esque surrealism that all children love. Actual violence, he noted, whether at the hands of Michael Myers or any other screen villain, had no place in the lives of kids.

It later emerged that very little studio pressure had been placed on Zombie when it came to the content of the film, although the title was seemingly one thing that was never up for debate. "It was always my intention to call it *Halloween*," Zombie confirmed. "In fact, I wouldn't do it if was called anything else, because I thought any other title would confuse people. Any other title would seem like a sequel, and I didn't want people thinking it was 'Part 9,' because when a movie gets to 'Part 9' it just screams 'direct-to-video piece of crap.' You can't help but think that. It's just not possible to think anything else. So I was very definitive that it had to be called *Halloween*, because I thought that anything else would devalue the project."

Further evidence that Zombie had achieved mainstream recognition in the film industry came when he was asked to direct a fake trailer to accompany the 2007 film *Grindhouse*, an homage to exploitation movies co-directed by Robert Rodriguez and Quentin Tarantino. One of four such clips filmed by various directors, Zombie's two-minute snatch of footage purported to advertise a film called *Werewolf Women of the SS*. The usual Zombie crew appears— Sheri as a sadistic nightclub singer, Bill Moseley as a random Nazi— plus Nicolas Cage, who plays Fu Manchu, the villainous Chinaman. After the serious work of *Halloween*, knocking together this little clip must have been a welcome break.

Around this time, Zombie was reported to be attached to at least two other films, the first a re-remake of *The Blob*, the 1958 thriller starring Steve McQueen that had already been remade with reasonable success in 1988. "My intention is not to have a big red blobby thing—that's the first thing I want to change," Zombie told MTV. "That gigantic Jello-looking thing might have been scary to audiences in the 1950s, but people would laugh now. I have a totally different take, one that's pretty dark."

"I'd been looking to break out of the horror genre," he added, "and this is really a science fiction movie about a thing from outer space. I intend to make it scary, and the great thing is, I have the freedom once again to take it in any crazy direction I want to. Even more than *Halloween*, where I had to deal with accepted iconic characters like Michael Myers and Laurie Strode. *The Blob* is more concept than specific storyline with characters, so I can go nuts with it."

The Blob didn't happen, for whatever reason—and nor did the second idea, based on a wrestler character similar to Rex Hauser from Zombie's comic book *The Nail*. Although a film poster emerged for the project, the movie itself is yet to appear.

◆

By now, Zombie had evolved into a creative talent who was one part musician, one part filmmaker, the rest comic-book writer, artist, and businessman. The very definition of the modern everyman, one might say. As he explained to Henry Northmore, "I love being in a band. I love playing music, there's nothing like it. I mean, I love making movies but it's the exact opposite experience, because making movies [is] very tedious and time-consuming and I'm behind the camera, I'm not in front of it, and when you're editing you're just locked away for six months in a room. I have two sides of my personality, and when I get toward the end of a film I really feel like I need to go on tour and go crazy, or I'm gonna go crazy. I think everyone who's in a rock band has that side of them [which requires] that outlet, or bad things are going to happen."

After completing the new movie, Zombie switched to the other side of his personality and began to focus on music once more. Among the issues requiring his attention was a Grammy nomination for Best Hard Rock Performance for the song "The Lords of Salem" and—more significantly—a retrospective boxed set of White Zombie recordings called *Let Sleeping Corpses Lie*. This appeared on November 25, 2008, and contained sixty-four songs, nine music videos, and ten live recordings. For a man who had spent twelve long years refusing to look back at his earlier band or even comment much on the subject, the release seemed to be an unusually retrograde move.

What's interesting, however, is that when you read between the lines of the interviews that Zombie gave to promote the boxed set, it's evident that he didn't attach too much significance to its release. "I don't know if there is importance to it," he pondered, "but I just thought it was nice to finally get all the songs out there in a good-sounding fashion, because for so many years, people have been asking, 'How do I get the old records?'" Of particular note were White Zombie's early EPs, which until now had never been issued on CD. "They were just limited edition vinyls that basically nobody has, since there were so few copies," Zombie continued. "So it's nice to have everything out there for whoever wants it."

Inevitably, interviewers wanted to know whether this meant a reanimation of sorts for White Zombie, whether as part of on ongoing reissue series, live songs being brought back into Rob Zombie's set, or even a full-blown reunion. "There is really nothing more to be done," he insisted. "I mean, they have other crappy demos and stuff they could release, but they're probably not worth listening to . . . I'd say this is probably the last thing that will come from the band, for sure. I just decided from the get-go that I would put every single thing that we recorded that was like a real recording. Every song of every vinyl record, every CD and every soundtrack, just every actual finished recording that we had."

Similarly bleak was the prospect of Zombie reviving the band's songs during his own live shows. "There is always people [saying], 'Oh, you've got to play this song, and you've got to play that song.' And then you play it, and great—that one guy is having a great time. But the other 10,000 people are looking at each other like, 'What the fuck is this stupid song?' . . . There is nothing more annoying to me than going to see a band, and they don't play the songs you want to hear. That drives me fucking crazy. [Maybe] one or two new songs, but when bands come out and they just go through like seven new songs, I want to slit my wrist."

So why release *Let Sleeping Corpses Lie* now? There were two very good reasons, it seemed. First and foremost, with the music industry sliding rapidly toward oblivion, Zombie viewed this as more or less his last chance to release such a project. "I probably already waited longer than I should have," he said. "CDs are a thing of the past: they won't be around much longer, much like vinyl and everything else. You know, maybe there will be some, but as a whole they'll be gone. But there is still something nice about putting together [a] set that you can hold in your hand."

As far as Zombie was concerned, there was very little likelihood of fans downloading the complete works of White Zombie from iTunes, for example, but they might just be tempted to buy a neatly packaged boxed set. "There is something nice about presenting things in the format that you want them to be heard, which is going away. I mean, it's the same thing is if you put movies out digitally, and everyone could edit them the way they want, it'd be kind of weird. You know, it's nice to be able to put things out, as you see that they should be presented."

Secondly, and slightly surprisingly, releasing the set made good commercial sense because White Zombie's fan base was actually growing, a decade and more after the band's demise. "I can see it, strangely enough, in just the royalty checks," Zombie revealed. "I mean, every year the band makes more money. It's weird for a band that every year has been gone longer and longer [and] seems to get more and more popular . . . there is always a new wave of kids that always gets super-jazzed on a band that's not around any more. It's just the way things go. Sometimes things just seem cooler when they get older. Luckily, we have those moments where the band hit and got really big and all that. But it was always a band that was slightly out of time and out of step with what was going on. So, sometimes things age well."

The boxed set isn't quite complete, however. The greatest

omission is a lack of decent-quality live recordings. "Unfortunately we didn't really document the band all that well," Zombie admitted. "I don't have really any live recordings that sound like anything other than somebody recording it on their Walkman."

Revisiting his old band's work had been an odd experience, it seems. "A lot of the stuff I hadn't heard in so long, I had actually forgotten," Zombie told Steven Rosen of *Ultimate Guitar*. "I mean, there were songs on those early records, that if you played me that song, if I was in a store or something and heard the song, I wouldn't even recognize it. Because I was going through the tapes and I was like, 'What the fuck is this? I don't even remember this.'"

Despite its flaws, *Let Sleeping Corpses Lie* is a solid document of both a particular era in Rob Zombie's life and a particular era of modern metal. Glitzy, vivid, and still exciting in parts despite the passage of time, these early works benefited significantly from the boxed-set treatment. There's still the issue of Zombie's yelped vocals on the early albums, of course—a considerable hurdle for anyone more keenly attuned to his modern caveman roar.

"My voice sounds so different back then that, I didn't even recognize myself when I heard it," he chuckled. "I remember everybody was complaining, 'I can't understand a fucking thing you're saying' . . . and they probably still do. I remember that was a big issue on 'Thunder Kiss.' When we were recording that, Andy Wallace, the producer, was like, 'I can't understand any of these lyrics.' So [I] went back and re-recorded 'Thunder Kiss' really clearly, and we both agreed that [it sounded] like shit. Because there was no vibe, it sounded like a guy's struggling to pronounce things too clearly."

"Thunder Kiss '65" was a hit right around the time of Nirvana's *Nevermind*, Zombie noted, "and we couldn't understand that, either.

I mean, 'Smells Like Teen Spirit'? But as far as the vocal evolution, it's kind of weird because my voice was pitched high when I first started, and I think what happened over the years was my voice kept dropping and dropping, getting lower and lower. Probably, I guess, continually damaging my vocal cords over twenty years of doing that. So I couldn't do those early songs if I had to, because I don't sound like that any more. Probably it's too many years of touring with bad monitors . . . the stage volume would be so loud, that I never ever, ever, ever could hear myself. So you're just screaming your lungs out, trying to just hear yourself and you know, I just screwed my voice doing that."

Would White Zombie ever reform? The answer appears to be a permanent no. Asked at the time of *Let Sleeping Corpses Lie*'s release whether he had been in contact with any of the other ex-members of the group, Zombie insisted that the boxed set's title should tell people all they need to know. "It's pretty self-explanatory," he said. "I didn't want everybody to think the boxed set was the beginning of something. I wanted everyone to realize it was the *end* of something."

Assembling the boxed set had nonetheless given him a renewed appreciation for his old band. "Going back and putting [it] together brought up a lot of things that I had forgotten about. Unfortunately, some of it was negative. So you know you really appreciate when you are in a good situation with a good group of musicians and a good group of guys . . . it took twenty-something years, but I feel like I finally found the three perfect people to work with."

Zombie brought 2008 to a close by donating a new song, "War Zone," to the soundtrack to *The Punisher: War Zone*. It's very much standard Zombie; if you haven't heard it, you really haven't missed much. The man himself didn't seem particularly emotionally invested in the song, explaining, "That came down like most movie songs come down. You just get a call about doing it, doing a song for a movie. Usually, there's not a lot of time, that's why, we usually ended up giving them like a remake, sort of an old song or something. But this time, there was enough time; I was already in the studio recording. I haven't seen the movie yet . . . they gave me the script, so I knew what it was about. And [we] just sort of got in there and cranked it out."

For our purposes, the song's more relevant consequence was that it gave Zombie the impetus to record a new album. "We had all those songs kind of half-finished," he mused. "And that was a good kick in the ass to actually have to finish a song. And that really became the domino effect of finishing all, starting to finish all the songs for the record actually. So it worked out good."

Around this time, Zombie was called in to meet with the Weinstein Company once again. Apparently a movie project was in the offing. But having only barely agreed to direct a remake last time around, surely he wouldn't sign up for a sequel to a remake . . . right?

NINE

VAMPIRE CIRCUS

(2009–12)

At first, Rob Zombie was reluctant to direct *Halloween II*. As he told filmmaker Mick Garris, on his *Post Mortem* show, "When I finished *Halloween*, I said to [Bob] Weinstein, 'Don't even bring it up. I'm not doing another fuckin' *Halloween*; don't even mention it.' I thought I was doing this other movie called *Tyrannosaurus Rex*—that's what I had been working on for a year. I was all excited to do that movie. I thought it was the perfect next move."

Life is never predictable in the movie business, of course, and as of 2015, *Tyrannosaurus Rex* is yet to utter its first roar. Part of the reason for this, it seems, is budgetary. "I handed in the *Tyrannosaurus Rex* script and they were like, 'Oh my God, this movie's going to cost a fortune to make. We don't want to make this.' I didn't think it would be that big of a deal, but anyway that became a problem. But I still didn't want to do *Halloween II* . . ."

Zombie soon realized, though, than a sequel would probably be made regardless, with or without his involvement. "Even if we chopped Michael Myers up and launched the pieces into space, there still would be a sequel, [because] suddenly all the pieces would reform in space and come back to Earth. So I wanted something where people felt like they got a finished movie, because nothing is more annoying than you watch a whole movie and get to the last second and you go, 'Oh come on . . .' It's the nature of the beast, but once something has become the seventh sequel, it's going to become by-the-numbers, no matter how hard you try."

For Zombie, the problem with the previous *Halloween* sequels had been that they lacked characters with whom the audience might form an emotional investment. "Michael Myers was lost in the background, a stuntman in a rubber mask. And they just introduce a bunch of new young teens, and try and come up with a wacky scenario. I don't know, it just didn't interest me."

However, Zombie soon found that ownership—emotional, fiscal, or otherwise—of any given artwork was difficult to let go. On hearing that the Weinstein Company might take his creation and hand it to another director to adapt as he or she pleased, he began to change his mind.

"I started feeling protective of it, because I started hearing what other people might be going to do with the characters," he told Garris. "I was like 'That's *my* Dr. Loomis, that's *my* Laurie Strode, I don't want anyone fucking with my world!' But then I thought the ship had sailed; I thought they were in production, and that it was a done deal, and it was too late and I blew it."

It was only some time later that Zombie ran into Rob Stein from the Weinstein Company and casually enquired as to how things were going with *Halloween II*. "He was like, 'It's not going.' I thought they were shooting [but] they didn't even have a script yet. So I said, 'I'll do it if it's still there to be done.' And I swear to God, the next day I was on the phone to Weinstein, and he was like, 'I need this thing by August!' . . . From the moment it was green-lit to theaters was seven months."

Zombie slaved over *Halloween II* from January to August 2009. The first stage—writing a script—was evidently a surprisingly stress-free process. "With the first movie, there were a lot of bizarre constraints,", he explained to the writer Hunter Stephenson. "It was a remake of someone else's film, so you're dealing with how much do you change it, how much do you leave alone? And I, like everybody else, was a big fan of [the original] *Halloween*, and that's how I originally perceived the characters, as John Carpenter had done them. So, they were stuck in my head like that too. And it wasn't until later, after I had finished that movie, that I could really see where to take all of this. Now, it's 100 percent me."

Working with original material, it seemed, proved much easier. "Nobody has any preconceived ideas. I mean, I had total freedom with *Halloween*; nobody tried to put any restraints on me, and I didn't really care what the fans were saying, because I thought, frankly, it was ridiculous. And I still do. But with this [film] I could do whatever, and nobody was going to say they thought it was going to be something in particular, or it should have been done a different way."

Asked how he approached writing the screenplay for the sequel—which is not a remake *per se* of the original *Halloween 2* from 1981, although certain scenes do overlap—Zombie explained that he had looked back at the first film and asked himself what the most probable aftermath of those events would be. Michael Myers's sister, Laurie Strode, had woken up to find that her parents and friends had been murdered by her own brother. After considering what that might do to a person, Zombie decided to make Laurie a highly damaged character.

The characters are in a dismal place, all right. With the sequel, Zombie ramps up both the graphic violence and the tension, although—with lessons learned from *The Devil's Rejects* and the first *Halloween*—the film still offers a serious attempt to get under the characters' skin and to create an environment for them that's subtle rather than blatant. Laurie Strode is the key character this time, kicking off the film with an extended dream sequence in which she revisits the climactic scenes of *Halloween*. Zombie had written a motif into the plot to explain Myers's madness: it's a white horse, accompanied by an angelic Deborah Myers (Sheri Moon Zombie) and the young Michael, played this time by a new actor, Chase Wright Vanek, Daeg Faerch having grown too tall in the interim to play the part.

Vanek does a perfectly serviceable job of playing Myers Jr., but the discontinuity between actors is slightly jarring, simply because Faerch looked so unusual in the first film. The white horse is a slightly incongruous plot device, too, but the viewer soon forgets about these things when treated to close-up shots of the trauma inflicted upon Strode's body when she is delivered to the emergency room by ambulance. Wounds are stitched in intimate detail, injured limbs look genuinely painful, and—worst of all—a broken fingernail is removed with tweezers. The mood is realistic and merciless.

Cut to the meat wagon taking what is thought to be the adult Myers's corpse to the morgue, and Zombie turns his attention to making his characters' personalities as unpleasant as the previous scene's body horror. The two morgue staff transporting the body joke humorlessly about necrophilia, making even the most sympathetic viewer rejoice when their doom comes after they hit a cow on the road in an explosion of bovine offal. Myers awakes, kicks open the rear door of the vehicle, and murders the drivers. It turns out that Strode's final bullet had failed to kill him, and now he embarks on a quest to find her, urged on by visions of his mother and younger self. Strode herself experiences the same visions as the siblings gradually grow closer and closer through the film.

As the film moves along, nameless supporting cast and extras are mercilessly dispatched. The makeup and lighting is judged perfectly; many of the incidental (and soon to be dispatched) cast are given bad teeth or hair, and made to look ugly, old or in pain. The total absence of glamour gives the violence the essential plausibility without which any horror film is doomed to failure. When Myers starts stabbing people, Zombie has him deliver unnecessarily violent blows with a high backswing of his knife hand: it's as if he wants not just to kill them but to pulverize them. The fake blood is almost black—another creepy touch—while Zombie accentuates the action with repeated snatches of the Moody Blues' 1967 hit "Nights in White Satin," an appropriately haunting tune. Additional touches such as a grumbling thunderstorm and lightning flashes, plus a soundtrack that sometimes consists only of a single, threatening piano note, add ambience.

Malcolm McDowell's ramped-up portrayal of Dr. Loomis—now a celebrity millionaire, thanks to his books on Myers—is one of the high notes of *Halloween II*. Effectively a rock star, with permanent shades and a harassed personal assistant, he barks lines such as "I'm selling sizzle not steak!" Throughout the sequel, Loomis is promoting his new book, with which he is profiting from the deaths of Myers's victims. He has, in effect, become evil himself, just like Myers, albeit through rather more subtle methods.

Anyone who has seen a few horror movies will know that few writers and directors spend any screen time analyzing the emotional impact of violence on human beings. The focus is always on bodily harm rather than mental distress. To his credit, in *Halloween II* Zombie makes an effort to portray the impact that having a mass murderer walk among us would have on our minds as well as on our physical wellbeing. Strode is shown talking tearfully with her psychiatrist; a bereaved father confronts Loomis, accusing him of being complicit in the murder of his daughter; and when Sheriff Brackett—played convincingly by the usually unsympathetic Brad Dourif—discovers his own, bloodily dispatched offspring, the numb shock on his face is revealing.

Essentially, though, the aim of *Halloween II* is not to provide penetrating psychological analysis. It is a slasher film with film noir undertones (see the scene featuring slaughtered rednecks in a field, all pools of light and tension) that is intended to make people gasp in horror. The carnage continues: a naked woman is stabbed to death against a mirror; a cop, patrolling outside the Brackett household, has his neck snapped. The bathroom scene in which a girl is murdered becomes a literal bloodbath, and there's no happy ending for anyone. Although Loomis redeems himself to an extent by dragging Myers into Sheriff Brackett's rifle's sights during the struggle in which he himself is killed, Strode is not released from her nightmare visions and ultimately winds up in a mental asylum.

◆

A lot of *Halloween* fans disliked the sequel when it was released on August 28, 2009: you only have to visit one of the many websites devoted to horror movies to see the evidence. The box office take of $40m was half that of the first film, but that in itself was nonetheless a respectable figure. Zombie revealed in a conversation with Mick Garris that Bob Weinstein had predicted that exact figure for *Halloween II*'s box-office receipts early in production, making it something of a self-fulfilling prophecy.

Criticism generally didn't bother Zombie, this many years into his career, but the constant braying of purists who regarded his treatment of the canon as "wrong" did become tiresome. "That gets to really be a bore after a while," he admitted. "People were talking about things as if they were mistakes. 'Dr. Loomis can't do that!' What are you talking about? It's not like it's a biography of a real person . . . he's a fictitious character and he can do whatever I want him to do! It's nice to not have to listen to that. 'Michael Myers can't grow a beard! Michael Myers can't be a hobo!' . . . everybody's criticism of *Halloween* [is] less about the actual movie, and more about what they thought the movie should have been, the way they saw it."

Occasionally, Zombie found it hard to believe that his films were negatively criticized in the light of the genuinely awful previous sequels, from *Halloween III: Season of the Witch* (1982) to *Halloween: Resurrection* (2002). As the series wore on, the quality of the scripts deteriorated to the point where very little of value remained for the horror fan. In comparison to its predecessors, Zombie's two *Halloweens* are masterpieces.

Stating clearly that he definitely would not direct a putative *Halloween 3*—a promise to which he has held true at the time of writing—Zombie moved through potential film projects like a shark scenting prey, for want of an analogy in keeping with the horror idiom. An animated film based on his *Spookshow International* comic books had been in development for some time, although delays to the project were interminable.

Rob and Sheri had not put their careers aside to have children, and neither were they particularly interested in extended periods of inactivity, so new projects continued to come their way—and all, as you will have noticed, without any formal training of any kind. Up until now, experience alone had been Zombie's guide.

"You really can't learn how to do any of these things," he concluded, in a teleconference conducted around this time. "You know, you can read all the books you want and take all the advice you can get, but nothing prepares you for what it's going to be, until you actually just do it. I never had a mentor, I still don't have a mentor, I wish I had a mentor. You know, that's the bummer, man . . . still, now there is tons of weird questions and situations that come up with movies, and you want to turn to somebody for advice. But I really don't have anybody. So you know, I just kind of do my thing, and look at the situations as best I can."

Zombie's animated project, named *El Superbeasto* after its principal character, was finally released on September 12, 2009, first in theaters and then, ten days later, on DVD. Zombie was the executive producer this time, pulling together the talent required to make the thing happen, although the project was not without its travails. The production company that owned *El Superbeasto* had changed hands several times since he started work on it, and as he later explained to *Slashfilm*, every time the film came near release, the company was sold and new executives came in and derailed the project.

The cast of *El Superbeasto* included a tried-and-trusted gang of former Zombie accomplices, not least his wife Sheri, plus comedian Tom Papa (whose 2012 special, *Tom Papa Live in New York City*, Zombie directed) and actors Paul Giamatti (from the cult wine movie *Sideways*) and Rosario Dawson (star of the hard-hitting teen move *Kids*). Sheri, who voiced the superheroine Suzy X., recalled how, instead of recording their voice parts separately, as is often the case with animated projects, the cast gathered together in one room at the same time. It was, she said, more natural that way. "We were able to bounce off each other. Suzy X. is the sister of the main character in [the comic strip] *The Haunted World of El Superbeasto*. She's this crime-stopping, sexy, superhero gal that everyone in the world is a big fan of. They love her and they think she's great. Her brother gets busted. He's an out-of-work wrestler who is trying to redeem himself. It's so smart and so funny, I can't wait to see the final product. It's hilarious."

The genesis of the animation went back at least four years, as Zombie told Mick Garris. "I started *El Superbeasto* when I was editing *The Devil's Rejects*. It started as a direct-to-video movie, which I was fine with, because that's what it was going to be. It was a million-dollar movie. And then people started getting excited, and pumping more money into it, and the studio got sold to someone else and new people came in. We were in a back room and no one was paying attention, so suddenly we were spending two million dollars, and three million, and four million, and five million, and another year goes by and we're still back there and no one's paying attention. Eventually they looked at it and said, 'They've spent eight million dollars, what are they doing? You've got to get it done!' But we were pretty much done. Animation was great, I'd do it again."

195

Are we going to delve deeply into *El Superbeasto*, as we've done with Zombie's other projects? No, because it isn't really worth it. The source material for *El Superbeasto* is first-class, the comic books' artwork vivid and laden with expression. However, in animated form, it simply doesn't work quite so well, instead resembling a crazed, adult *Ren and Stimpy*, although that description makes it sound better than it actually is. Whether you find the plot (such as it is) amusing is entirely subjective, but many fans will find it tricky to get through the entire film, composed largely as it is of cartoon boobs, blood splashes, and fairly weak gags.

There's a sophistication in the comic books that unfortunately didn't make it to the screen, and as a result *El Superbeasto* doesn't come close to comparing with Zombie's far more meaningful live-action films. Still, as an illustration of the bigger picture—that Rob Zombie was on a slow but steady course to break out of standard horror films and move into other areas—*El Superbeasto* did its job just fine. By now, Zombie was routinely passing on offers to direct cheesy horror films or sequels. If he was to take it on, a project had to have something special about it.

◆

This, it emerged, included the freedom to direct his musical career exactly as he wanted it. In late 2009, Zombie broke away from Geffen Records, his label since way back in the *Astro-Creep* days, and signed to Roadrunner, then as now a major-owned but independently minded label. The next album needed to be a good one, after the so-so *Educated Horses*, and when its title—*Hellbilly Deluxe 2: Noble Jackals, Penny Dreadfuls and the Systematic Dehumanization of Cool*—was announced, Zombie's fans' ears pricked up. The identification of the new record with his most successful album to date implied all sorts of cool things, such as whether he would return to the evil circus image that had so enthralled his fans back in 1998.

"The unique thing about this record," Zombie mused at the time of its release, "is [that] it's the first time since White Zombie broke up, [that] I've actually recorded with a band, in the sense that these are the guys that I tour with, that I hang out with. We are a band and we record as a band. So the record [has] a much more solid vibe, and it's going to be a much more intricate, interesting record I think, due to the fact that we have four people that are in the room all the time, contributing and working. For me it's great. My solo records have been somewhat disjointed, because it is always a changing roster [and] the people that are touring are not the people that are playing on record. Great things usually come out of situations that we have a great vibe and you can usually feel it. And that's what going on here."

He went on to describe the new record as the "capper" of his solo career to date. "For me, *Educated Horses*—I think it's a great record, I think it has a lot of great songs, but it was definitely a transitional record, because that was sort of coming out of other phase and it was [like], 'You guys were in the band, some of [you] weren't really even in the band yet . . .' But now that the band has been locked and tied for a couple of years, I feel like we're solidified it into the next real legitimate strong phase of what we're doing. And that's why it's pretty exciting."

Asked about switching to Roadrunner, Zombie explained that *Hellbilly Deluxe 2* had been in the works for some time; it was merely a case of finding the right label to release it. The titular reference to the past, meanwhile, was more than deliberate, as he explained to me shortly before the album's release.

"The first *Hellbilly Deluxe* was a great moment for me, because it was so successful and it was the start of something new. The tour for that record was the most fun tour I ever had, but then like most things do, it started to deteriorate and band members started having problems with each other. It just started falling apart, so when I started putting the music back together with a different band, I didn't want to just imitate what I'd been doing. We varied away from the *Hellbilly Deluxe* image and vibe, because I thought if I'd gotten new guys and just put them in the same suits it would have seemed really contrived and fake. The audience will always feel it if it's fake. So it was almost like we went back to the garage and restarted the band. Now it's like a new, fresh version with new people."

That was just as well, too, because the *Hellbilly Deluxe 2* tour was a monster, stretching from late 2009 all the way to mid-2012, with a few rest stops here and there. The whole affair was executed on a wholly different level to the back-breaking two-year *La Sexorcisto* tour from almost two decades earlier.

After a couple of warm-up dates in Japan in late '09, where new bassist Piggy D. (Matt Montgomery to his friends) played overseas with Zombie's band for the first time, the tour headed back to the US for shows right across the nation from late October to early December. I spoke to Piggy D.—whose faintly silly stage name masks the fact that he is a bass player of serious talent—not long after he joined Zombie's band, at which point he explained that, until then, he had primarily been a guitarist.

"Switching from guitar to bass actually wasn't that long of a learning curve," he said. "I loved the music and I loved playing with

Rob, but I hadn't realized how much I would love playing bass on stage. I'd always thought of myself as a guitarist first and a bass player second, but that's changed around now. Playing guitar onstage feels totally weird to me these days! And I feel like I'm a staple part of a mix now, because when you're playing guitar you do a solo and then you play rhythm, and it's up and down."

Casting his mind back to his formative influences, he continued, "I thought Dee Dee Ramone was the bee's knees when I was a kid, which probably has a lot to do with me playing a Fender Precision. Johnny Ramone was the reason why I picked up a guitar in the first place, and I probably do still play a bit like him. I learned how to hold an instrument from watching Johnny. When I was a kid and someone put a guitar around my neck and it was up high, I was like, 'This doesn't feel right,' and moved it down. I also loved Tommy Stinson, who was in the Replacements and is now in Guns N' Roses. Obviously I have mad respect for Cliff Burton of Metallica, too."

Prior to that, however, he had started his musical career in a quite different area. "In high school I played trumpet and tuba in marching bands—so I can read bass and treble clef. Playing tuba was really useful for me as a bass guitar player, because you learn all about locking in with the drums. After that I played guitar in a jazz band, and I really got into all the jazz players like Stu Hamm. There's such a wealth of bass solo records in jazz.

"I've been writing all kinds of music in my downtime that will affect my bass playing with Rob," he added. "We all have ideas about the parts and we're all comfortable with each other, but our guitar player John 5 will give me a riff, then leave me alone and I'll come up with the line. It's a cool band because it's so organic: it's the first time

I've been in a band where there's nobody telling me what to play!"

Hellbilly Deluxe 2 was released on February 2, 2010—three months later than planned, as a result of the label switch—prompting the band to resume touring the US, with some Canadian dates thrown in, all the way through to May. For many of those shows, the band co-headlined with Zombie's old buddy Alice Cooper.

The fun didn't stop there. The Mayhem festival followed throughout July and August, before the Cooper tour resumed. There was some time off in the fall before a slog through the US, the UK, and Australia in the early months of 2011. A raft of European festival dates followed in June before a final swing through the States in the summer of that year.

In the early days of the *Hellbilly Deluxe 2* tour, Zombie was pleasantly surprised at the crowds' reaction when he slipped the odd new song into the live set. "What I'm discovering is that the songs we've been playing from the new album are connecting in an amazing way, considering that most of the audience doesn't know the songs," he told MTV News. "Sometimes you play new songs and people think, 'Maybe I'll like it later,' but people are digging it now, which is nice." They'd play even more new songs, he explained prior to the album's release, were it not for the bootleg recordings that invariably appeared on the internet. "The whole album would be online if we played any more."

So what were these new songs? *Hellbilly Deluxe 2* kicks off with "Jesus Frankenstein," an anthemic album-opener in the familiar Zombie mold but with added dynamics. John 5 is the driving force, delivering the usual staccato riffs but leavening them with acoustic interludes and liquid shredding.

"Sick Bubblegum" continues with the solid groove and barked

chorus that we've come to expect, with an apocalyptic ending that perfectly sets up the next song, "What?," which was released as a single. This fresh-sounding cut owes as much to garage-rockers such as the Hives and the White Stripes as the dense metal template of yore and features a cheesy one-finger keyboard line that is pure *Addams Family*. Catchy, upbeat, and an obvious choice of single, it segues neatly into the acoustic intro of "Mars Needs Women." Loaded with film samples and what sounds like videogame sound effects, this song is a simple, stamping assault that leads into a countrified blues stomp, "Werewolf, Baby!"

A natural pause comes with a sequence of gloomy, atmospheric church bells, before the doom-laden "Virgin Witch" bursts into play. Pitched somewhere between Metallica and Black Sabbath, the song reminds us that for all the theatrics, Zombie is, at heart, a man of metal. "Death and Destiny Inside the Dream Factory" is different again, a raw, relatively unpolished garage workout, while "Burn" is funkier, with an almost White Zombie–like feel: even the vocals are pitched higher than usual to add to that impression.

"Cease to Exist" is slow, creepy, and threatening, a song precision-engineered for stadium crowds, while "Werewolf Women of the SS" is faster, more throwaway, and essentially less remarkable than its title. Finally, "The Man Who Laughs" closes the album with a sense of epic dignity, strings ladled over the guitars before it breaks down into an orchestral fantasy halfway through.

◆

Hellbilly Deluxe 2 hit #8 on the *Billboard* 200 and sold a respectable 50,000 copies or so in its first week. Even so, many thought it would be Zombie's last ever physical release. As he wrote online at the time,

"Well, pretty soon the CD will be dead. All you will have left is digital downloads. So before we say goodbye to the almighty CD, I thought I would give it a big sendoff. I love being able to get great artists involved on my CD artwork, and this time is the best yet. Since this may be the last true CD I make, I thought I would gather three of the top artists around to contribute some killer new Zombie art for the booklet." The images—kitsch-to-the-max Zombie art of the familiar kind—came from prestigious sources: *Nocturnals* comic book creator Dan Brereton, animator David Hartman, and Alex Horley, who had worked for DC Comics.

It's interesting to note that physical releases were seemingly no longer at the top of Zombie's agenda. Pondering the subject of the dying music industry, he described it as "a never-ending question . . . probably in another year people won't even bother manufacturing CDs because it'll be like a cassette or an 8-track: no one will even want them. . . . The downloads don't match record sales, so, you know people are mostly stealing everything. There's some change that's going to happen, but nobody can figure out what it is."

Next up for Zombie was directing an episode of the popular TV series *CSI: Miami*, which was broadcast in March 2010. Simply titled "L.A.," it guest-starred Sheri Moon Zombie alongside several other veteran's of Rob's big-screen adventures.

"I am very excited to be working on a show that has such an intense and unique visual angle on the classic crime drama formula, and look forward to putting my own bizarre stamp on the world of *CSI: Miami*," he announced beforehand, which is pretty amusing in retrospect, given how much he ended up detesting the experience. As he subsequently explained on an episode of Fox's *Red Eye* show, "It was the longest three weeks of my life. By the end I was sitting on the director's chair and someone said, 'How was that [a take]?' and I said, 'I don't give a shit!' I was so beat down by the process."

Although he didn't go into much detail, Zombie hinted that some of the problems might have been caused by *CSI*'s principal star, David Caruso, who is famous for not wanting to perform certain tasks on set. Indeed, another guest star—Zombie's old buddy Malcolm McDowell—reportedly gained great pleasure from deliberately irritating Caruso.

In the autumn of 2010, a special edition of *Hellbilly Deluxe 2* was released with the addition of three extra songs, a minor detail that we might normally omit except for the fact that an amended lineup of the band was responsible for the new material. Drummer Tommy Clufetos, who had recorded the original tracks, had since been recruited for Ozzy Osbourne's band, where—coincidentally—Zombie's previous bassist Rob "Blasko" Nicholson had also taken up residence some years before. His replacement, at least for the duration of the *Hellbilly Deluxe 2* tour, was Slipknot drummer Joey Jordison, a truly phenomenal musician whose drumming skills had earned him many industry awards.

Asked by the Artisan News Service what he thought of Ozzy "poaching" personnel from his band, Zombie was forthright in his reply. "I think there's ways to do things and I think there's ways to not do things, and I think the way they've chosen to do things is not how I would do things; I think it's kind of rude. I mean, if my guys that I have wanna go play with other people, that's fine; I don't own them. But I think there's ways to do things in a respectful way and there's ways to just be shitty, and I feel that the way things have gone down lately has been pretty shitty. But whatever . . . what comes around goes around."

Later, he told me, "The thing that's weird is, when you live and work with people, you form a really tight bond. A band becomes a family. You spend so much time with people that you really grow to trust them and feel like they're your best friends in the world. When someone you think is a good friend is lying to you, to your face, and then one day they just turn around and do something . . . . It's not every member. Some members leave on good terms, some leave on bad terms, and it's fine. I never thought that people needed to stay in this band forever: people move on in their lives. It's just the way you choose to do it. There's a professional way to do things, and then there's an asshole way to do things."

Jordison's role shouldn't be underestimated, brief though his tenure might have been. Of the many musicians with whom Rob Zombie has played, Jordison is the player of the greatest international renown. In previous years, head-bangers had seen him play with a veritable who's who of heavy rock and metal, from his main bands, Slipknot and the Murderdolls, to recording and touring gigs with heavyweights such as Metallica, Korn, and Ministry. No other drummer has that kind of portfolio, in metal or any other genre.

Anyone who has followed Jordison's career will know that his style is difficult to classify. His metal playing revolves around super-tight, super-fast snare- and kick-drum patterns, with tom rolls kept taut, economical, and energetic. He's no mere "chops freak," though, and is content to sit back in a cast-iron pocket when the groove requires it. "Drums came when I was about seven years old: they spoke to me so well, that it just flew out of me—it was really weird," he told me a few years back. "To this day, sometimes I'm actually confused: I'm like, 'What just happened?' after I play a part. The songwriting aspect of what I do has also been right with me at all times, it's something that lives inside my heart. It's easy for me, and drums are easy for me, too."

Like Zombie and several of his other collaborators, Jordison first felt the pulse of rock 'n' roll emanating from a certain Detroit foursome. "When I was a kid—maybe six or seven years old, in 1981 or thereabouts—I saw KISS on TV for the first time, and when you're that age you're curious about that kind of thing. The first record I bought with my own money was *KISS Alive*. That started to shape what I do for a living. I started getting into heavier stuff after that. I was kind of an outcast in first grade, because I was already playing guitar and drums and not really getting involved with anybody: I was a loner. Then I heard some thrash metal, and that stuff was totally gripping at that age. I loved it. I was like, 'What is this?' That's where it started. Metallica were a huge influence on me."

◆

With tour duties pretty much locked in until 2011, Rob Zombie had to hustle to find time for extracurricular activities. Although he has always stated that he is uncomfortable doing other things while he is on the road because touring demands so much from him, he still managed to fit in several other projects. The first of these was a comic-book series called *Whatever Happened to Baron Von Shock?*, about a TV host whose horror series leads him to some unexpected places, which appeared in a four-issue run in 2010. "The Baron is a local LA horror movie host in the tradition of Vampira or Zacherley," Zombie explained. "A huge celebrity within their zone. He is basically a loser who got his shot and blew it. Drugs and pussy were his only real driving passions and ultimately the reason he crashed and burned. Now he dreams of having it all back again, but at what cost?"

Rob Zombie's comic-book work is relevant here because it links directly back to the formative influences that made him who he is. Those under thirty-five years old may not remember the local TV horror hosts that the *Baron Shock* series celebrates, but because they were an intrinsic part of 1960s and '70s culture, they're dear to Zombie's heart.

Zombie's collaborators on the new project hinted obliquely that the great man was known for sticking rigidly to his way of doing things rather than anyone else's. Val Staples, a veteran editor and producer who worked on the *Baron Shock* series along with Zombie, hit a perfectly diplomatic note when he explained, "We've always tried to be very laid-back, and care primarily about putting out a great, yet timely product. We also know that when Rob wants to do a book, he wants to do it his way because he has a specific concept with which no one should tamper. So we follow his lead and let him work his magic. I credit that to why *Spookshow International* was well liked month-to-month by so many fans during its run. It was Rob's vision, not ours. Because of all of that, Rob knows he has an open door to shoot projects our way when he feels the creative comic itch, and he knows we'll deliver." Nicely put.

The projects kept coming. After taking the voice-over role of God in the film *Super* came along, Zombie turned his attention to the ABC TV show *Extreme Makeover*, which was building a "haunted house" attraction for the Oregon School for the Deaf. If that sounds like a curious installation for a school in Salem, think again: the haunted house was devised as a fundraiser for the organization, and with Zombie's name on it, horror fans queued up to get in.

"It's absolutely amazing to be able to help the school," Zombie said at the time. "To be asked to come do something to work on a haunted house and make it as scary and crazy as I could to help the school was awesome. It was a rare opportunity to put some evil to good use . . . I think what [the visitors are] liking best is it's so detailed. They seemed blown away when they went through, how detailed the sets were and the fact the walls and the characters were all animatronic and just flying off the walls everywhere."

A similar but bigger project followed in the form of Rob Zombie's *House of 1,000 Corpses* in 3D ZombieVision, a three-dimensional maze located at Universal Studios Hollywood, which Zombie designed and the good people at Universal assembled on his behalf. The attraction was open for a month or so in the run-up to Halloween, during which time Zombie was in the midst of a three-week Halloween Hootenanny tour, with Alice Cooper as his co-headliner.

Zombie ended 2010 with the release of a signature brand of coffee—a move that had proven fashionable among the heavy metal elite at this time, with members of Megadeth and Anthrax also putting their own branded beans on sale. There was no fakery here; Zombie, as you may have deduced from his relentless work ethic, has been a lifelong coffee enthusiast, so a line devoted to him makes obvious sense.

"What can I say? I fucking love coffee," he told *Noisecreep*. "I started drinking this magic drink when I was a little kid and never stopped. So that's the reason I now have my own Hellbilly brew, 24/7, cranked on black gold! Hell yeah, let's go!" (Fellow caffeine fiends will be eager to learn that French and Peruvian blends of Zombie coffee are available through his website, both of which 100 percent organic.)

Further Zombie-related activity at the end of 2010 included the publication of an excellent first book by White Zombie's Sean Yseult, the previously mentioned *I'm in the Band*. Asked what inspired her to write her memoir of these increasingly far-off days, she told me, "In 2005, Hurricane Katrina hit here in New Orleans, where I've lived since the band broke up, and my house suffered a lot of roof damage. I had a big leak going through three stories of my house, and the whole back wall and the roof had to be replaced. That made me realize that I could have lost everything: the hole was just a few feet away from where all my White Zombie stuff is stored.

"Like J. [Yuenger]," she added, "I meticulously saved everything, but unlike J. I was in the band from day one, so I had stuff that goes back to 1985. I was also the band photographer at first, so I have negatives and designs for layouts and flyers and photo albums and tons of other stuff. I wanted to scan all these things in, just to have them in one place for myself, but when people heard about it they told me I should do something for the fans. My dad was a writer, so I talked to his agent and she told me, 'This needs to happen, and I want to represent you.'"

Elsewhere, in an interview with Lina Lecaro at *LA Weekly*, Yseult explained that her book had been inspired in part by the release of *Let Sleeping Corpses Lie*, the White Zombie boxed set. The band's management had asked her for all of her Zombie video footage to add to a DVD, and so she began to dig out her boxes out of storage. She had saved all of White Zombie's old vinyl and bootleg videos, as well as tour diaries, photo albums, laminates, notebooks, her journals from booking tours—essentially everything that covered the history of the band's career. Now it was time to put it all to good use.

◆

With at least half of 2011 taken up with touring, Rob Zombie kept his mind on the road—with the exception of one major film project, which we'll come to shortly. With all this non-musical stuff going on, it's easy to forget just how demanding life on the road can be when, like Zombie, your live production is so meticulous. Before a slot at the UK's Download festival, writer Henry Northmore asked Zombie what gig-goers could expect from the live set. The answer he received demonstrates the extent to which the singer was putting his money where his mouth was when it came to performance.

Fans could expect "a huge colossal spectacle," Zombie revealed, since he intended to bring his full stage show over to the UK with him. "Financially, that's suicide," he said, "but I didn't care. Because I didn't want to stay away for twelve years and then we come over with nothing. So we are shipping the whole thing—I just hope that when it gets there it can fit on the stages. That I don't know for sure. But we're bringing everything—our giant robots and explosions and video screens and all the crap that we use all of the time, so it's a huge colossal spectacle."

The new band's lineup, meanwhile—John 5 on guitar, Piggy D. on bass, and Joey Jordison on drums—was, for Zombie's money, the best he had ever assembled. "It's just the perfect match of people," he said. "You strive for the perfect four combination and this is the best it's ever been by far . . . in every incarnation of every band I've ever had, there's always been at least one person that's the odd man out. And it's always kind of a strain on the vibe when you're trying to work.

"To have four people that can get genuinely excited about the same things all the time makes such a difference. There's never anyone in the back row going, 'Ah jeez, do we have to?' There's four people that are just totally gung-ho and because of that, everybody contributes. I never really realized it until I had four people that were on the same page how important it was. I always thought that, 'Well, okay, one person's not into it, what's the big deal?' but it really makes a difference, it really is huge."

In case you have concluded that movies have become more important to Zombie than music, consider how invested he was in 2011 in both his live show and his new album. He put plenty of thought into his set list, for starters, always bearing in mind what the punters would like to see.

"Nobody wants to hear new material when they buy a concert ticket," Zombie told Tim Louie at the *Aquarian Weekly*. "Nothing is worse than a guy saying, 'Hey! Here's some new stuff!' Testing the waters with [new songs] doesn't really make any sense because they'll change anyway, and if you played them live, I guess you would just come to the conclusion that they're terrible because no one's gonna know what they are anyway. I've never done that, so no sense in starting now."

For Zombie, the songs that are most fun to play are the ones the audience knows and likes the most, but that didn't stop him throwing in the occasional oddity. "Every once in a while it's fun to play something new and add a song into the set that we haven't played in a while," he explained, "because I've played certain songs so many times, it is almost a blur. Like, there will be times when I'm playing a song and I literally won't remember and I'm like, 'Is this the first verse or the third verse?' It just goes by in my mind like such a blur. We've been playing the song 'Pussy Liquor' off of the *House of 1,000 Corpses* soundtrack for a while, and that's always probably the most fun moment just because it was such a ridiculous, almost throwaway song that has now become so popular. Everyone used to request it, but we would never play it because I thought they were kidding. So then we started playing it and it's become a show highlight. It's pretty funny."

Surprisingly, after all these years—and despite the *Educated Horses* hiatus, during which Zombie stripped out most of the production elements to create a minimal stage show—he was still enjoying putting on the corpse paint and cobwebs every night. "I like doing the makeup," he said. "You won't feel like playing, but as soon as you get ready it's like you've transformed yourself: you're another person, and you're ready to play." Asked which songs were his favorite to play live, he shrugged. "When you make a record you do a song that you think it's the best one you've ever [written, but] then nobody likes it, so you never play it again. Then the one that took you about two seconds to write becomes the big hit, so it doesn't matter to me. Whatever the crowd likes, that makes me happy."

In August 2012, a remix album called *Mondo Sex Head* was released, featuring on its cover the exposed buttocks of Sheri Moon Zombie, although this image was subsequently changed to one of a cat following a chorus of predictable complaints from certain distributors. As Zombie later explained, instead of censoring the cover and ruining it, he simply removed the "ass" shot and replaced it with a "pussy" shot . . .

Mondo Sex Head is a reasonably interesting album, especially if you're into techno beats and bass. The remixes range from a version of "Thunder Kiss '65" that any teenager would be happy to emit at far too loud a volume from their car at a mall gathering, via a piano-heavy version of "Foxy, Foxy" that outdoes the original by some distance, to a drum 'n' bass remix of "Superbeast" that adds a serious dose of malevolence.

Zombie ended the year 2012 with three months of American dates with another co-headliner, Marilyn Manson, on what they dubbed the Twins of Evil tour. "It was similar to the Alice Cooper thing, where it seemed like a no-brainer to do a tour, but we [had never done so] for whatever reason," Zombie told writer Rick Florino. "I'm kind of glad we didn't. You run out of people to tour with. Sometimes, your album and touring cycles just don't match up. Whenever he's on tour, I'm not on tour. Whenever I'm tour, he's not on tour. That can go on for years. When you throw the movies into the mixtures, my time off the road gets really screwy. It just so happened that it finally worked."

The tour—for which Jordison, having returned to Slipknot, was replaced on drums by Ginger Fish—was not without incident. At a show in Clarkston, Michigan, on October 12, Manson was heard shouting, "I'm gonna kick [Zombie's] ass," apparently because Zombie—whose band was due on next—had reduced Manson's stage time. When he subsequently took the stage himself, Zombie made some sarcastic comments in return (now freely available to view on YouTube, if you feel so inclined), prompting the whole thing to blow up into a short-lived media storm.

The furor receded after a while, helped no doubt by the explanation Zombie posted on his Facebook page the following day. "As stupid as this all is, I feel I must clear things up," he began, before offer up his take on why "things turned ugly" at the show and backstage afterward.

"For some reason our touring partner decided to end his set by blaming me for something that I had nothing to do with and screaming he was going to 'kick Rob Zombie's ass as soon as he got offstage.' Go figure. I was backstage, hanging, watching the show thinking, 'Hey, this is gonna be a great night,' when suddenly he starts screaming threats." For Zombie, the whole thing was "ridiculous," not least because, as he noted, "I've known some of his crew for twenty fucking years and some of his crew used to work for me."

"Of course I felt the need to respond to the 'kick my ass remark,'" he continued. "Who wouldn't? Although I wish I had kept it backstage . . . co-headlining tours always go smooth because everything is cut 50/50, and I mean everything. No one fucks with anyone's show. It is even fucking Steven. I've done it co-headlining tours many times before and have had no troubles. Not with Pantera, Slayer, Alice Cooper, Korn, Megadeth, or anyone, ever. So I didn't expect any troubles on this. It seemed like a great idea at the time. But shit happens. Anyway, sorry to the fans who had to deal with the embarrassing stupidity of it all. We are all there for the same reasons to give you the best show ever . . . that's it."

You'll have noticed by now that Zombie tends to take the high road when it comes to slating his fellow artists in public; this incident aside, plus the mild rancor he displayed when two of his band members split to join Ozzy Osbourne, he tends to keep his mouth shut about such things. It's the professional way, and Rob Zombie is nothing if not professional—hence the lack of public commentary on the reasons behind White Zombie's split all the way back in 1996.

Meanwhile, in between road commitments, Zombie was directing a new film, and also—in a slight change of scenery—TV commercials for a bug-killing household product called Amdro. Why, you may ask? Well, his ad for a washing liquid called Woolite had gone down well the previous year, featuring horror-film textures and music while a garment was "tortured" on a rack of some kind, and this led directly to the Amdro gig. Check them out on YouTube:

they're beautifully done and laced with a triumphant sense of humor.

It subsequently emerged that Zombie had decided to tour with his band between shooting and editing the new movie. Bad idea. "That idea I had of doing an album and a movie at the same time was a great idea on paper, but in execution it's been insanity," he sighed. "You have no idea. I finished the movie, went on tour, came back, edited the movie, went back on tour, came back, finished the movie, and now I'm just losing my mind. I don't think I'll be doing that again. You're in the editing room and you're in that frame of mind, and then you're like, 'Okay, now I have to stop editing, go into a rehearsal space with the band, go on tour.'

"It really is like two different halves of my brain, and I have to shut one off to do the other. But that was one good thing, that sometimes there would be a problem with the movie, just like a scene that wasn't working or something, and I'd get away from it and come back to it and it would seem like the editing choice was suddenly really clear. So in some ways it worked, and in some ways it didn't."

Zombie had a clear goal in sight, however. His next film might not have had the budget of the *Halloween* films, or the sense of unhinged madness that infused *House of 1,000 Corpses*, but measured by pure artistic panache, it was unsurpassable.

TEN

THE WIZARD OF GORE

(2013–15)

"The tree-sheltered Tudor, built in 1924," the *Los Angeles Times* warbled snootily, "features wood paneling in the living room and pub rooms as well as the entry. The kitchen has been remodeled and includes a butler's pantry. There are six bedrooms and five bathrooms for a total of 6,249 square feet of interior space." Sounds nice, right? And especially so when you learn that said residence-for-sale belongs to Mr. R. and Mrs. S. Zombie, of Hancock Park, Los Angeles, and was available in early 2013 for just under four million dollars.

Adding that the Zombies also owned a residence in Woodbury, Connecticut, the newspaper noted that the Hancock Park property was last sold in 1999 for $1.799 million—a pleasing rate of appreciation for its owners, to be sure.

At the same time, Rob Zombie was beginning to feel a different kind of appreciation for his early work. As we've seen, his income from White Zombie—now defunct for almost two decades—was getting healthier every year, while his first forays into film now resided firmly in the "cult classic" category. "It's funny what ten years can do," he noted, looking back at the decidedly wacky *House of 1,000 Corpses*. "Ten years ago, people were saying, 'You guys made possibly the worst fucking film of all time,' and now it's, 'I can't believe you guys made that classic film!'"

Life was clearly progressing just fine for Zombie after all the years of struggle. His new movie, which he described as his "cinematically biggest," had been teased in trailer form as far back as May 2012 and screened at that year's Toronto Film Festival to a small number of movie critics and others. It was released to cinemas on April 19, 2013, amid much interest from his fan base. Having spent the previous couple of years re-establishing himself as a touring musician, Zombie was now reaping the rewards of that activity as the fans walked into the cinema to see his latest work, *The Lords of Salem*.

"It's a different movie for me," said Zombie. "I hate calling it a horror movie, because it's more than that. It's very much like a psychological terror film, and it's a very different style. The other films were very in-your-face violent. This is more like a total mind-fuck movie, and it's just very different, but I'm very excited about it because the fans of what I've done will love it, but it's a very different trip than I've tried before because I didn't want to just go and do the same thing again. After doing two *Halloween* films in a row, I wanted to break the mold of anything like that . . . [it's] very, very different."

It is indeed. *Lords* has a highly interesting premise, focusing on the evergreen American legend of the Salem witch trials, a series of witch-hunts and executions in colonial Massachusetts in the 1690s that resulted in the deaths of a posse of women. Sure, the legend of the Salem witches had been addressed on film before, going back as far as the 1930s, but Zombie's intention with his version of the tale was clearly to dispense with the usual quaint bonnets-and-bodices depiction of the victims and create something more contemporary and at the same time more surreal.

For the first time, Zombie was making a movie with supernatural elements. "The other ones aren't at all [about magic]," he explained to the Pulse of Radio. "*House of 1,000 Corpses* was just this crazy, bloody, *Rocky Horror Picture Show* thing, and *Devil's Rejects* was always meant to be sort of like a postmodern western, and the *Halloween* films, I tried to make them not supernatural on purpose. So this will be the first one that's sort of about supernatural things coming back to life. It's good. I'm excited. It's gonna be very different than the other films."

Zombie's plot follows a modern-day Salem woman, Heidi, played once more by his wife Sheri, who is unknowingly destined to give birth to the antichrist after being adopted by a trio of modern, *Macbeth*-indebted hags. These wrinkled old specimens are in thrall to an ancient witch who we witness delivering a squealing animatronic baby, licking blood from it and spitting the blood in its face. Charming.

Heidi, a tattooed radio DJ with dreadlocks and a penchant for vintage films and ephemera judging by the decor of her apartment, is entranced by a repeated three-note musical figure that she hears when a black metal band, the Lords of Salem, sends her an LP to play on her radio show. It's a genuinely spooky snatch of music, especially when we see and hear it played in flashback on ancient instruments by the original coven of devil-worshipping women. When the record is played on air, every female resident of Salem who hears the damn thing slips into a trance, including Heidi herself, who begins to hallucinate and slips back into a heroin habit to deal with it. A lot of unforgiving nudity follows, with Zombie's camera tracing the ageing and obese contours of several bewitched females in detail.

Enter the three witches, played with enjoyable malice by Patricia Quinn (who moviegoers will recognize as Magenta from *The Rocky Horror Picture Show*, 1975), Dee Wallace (best known as the mom in *E.T.*, 1982), and Judy Geeson (*To Sir with Love*, 1967). They murder a friendly academic who tries to alert Heidi of her destiny, take her to visit a spooky demon in what looks like a stately home and ultimately stage-manage the climactic scene. Here, at what is billed as a live performance by the Lords of Salem (although the band fail to show up), the creepy music is played again, the original medieval witches materialize, a host of female gig-goers get their kit off, and Heidi bloodily spawns a wriggling xenomorph. Finally, she transforms into a kind of demonic messiah in white contact lenses, standing proudly atop a pile of dead naked women while the witches bow before her. The credits roll and a voiceover news report informs us the bodies have been discovered in what appears to be a mass suicide, and that Heidi is missing.

Let's get a couple of flawed moments out of the way. At one point, Heidi is visited in her apartment by a wrinkled, demonic homunculus; even in partial shadow, it looks laughable. When she meets the devil in the aforementioned country mansion, he doesn't look even remotely convincing. Finally, the evil beastie to which she gives birth is just silly, a writhing mass of tentacles that doesn't even make sense, let alone cause any chills.

Those minor details aside, however, *The Lords of Salem* is wonderfully well executed. At last, Zombie is free to express his subtler side. The music, for example, is perfect, with simple, haunting melodies accompanying the slower panoramic shots, uplifting choral pieces by Bach providing the soundtrack to some of the trippier or more visually resplendent scenes, two instances of the Velvet Underground's psychedelic rock anthem "All Tomorrow's Parties," and that genuinely spooky three-chord riff that hypnotizes women into removing their outerwear.

Other high points? The many shots of a long, silent corridor with a door at the end. Of course, it's pure Stanley Kubrick—and in particular pure *The Shining*—but it's totally effective. Then there's the excellent animated sequence toward the end, which edges toward Monty Python–style burlesque but is still sufficiently creepy to do the job. Even the scene in which a row of seated devil-priests are seen masturbating works in context. So much of this could have been embarrassing or just amateurish, and in the hands of a lesser director it would have been just that. Instead, with Zombie at the helm, *The Lords of Salem* is an excellent horror thriller that actually offers something new.

Asked about his approach to *The Lords of Salem*, Zombie explained, "I always thought of it as like a little Stanley Kubrick and a little Ken Russell and a little Roman Polanski. In a blender. This film is basically the exact opposite of what I've done before; that was my goal, in a way. It's really easy to have your bag of tricks and just kind of do it every time. So I purposefully did everything different." His previous movies, he explained, had been shot using handheld camera, which gave them a "very chaotic . . . very rough" feel. "I wanted them to feel almost like documentaries, and if the focus went out of focus I didn't care, because I just wanted the spontaneity of it all. But with this movie it was very slow and precise."

This time around, the camerawork is "very locked-down. Usually I've got caught up in tight close-ups all the time, but this is very wide open, and the space is almost as important as the people. So yes, it's very different. I don't know what people are going to think. I guess some people will like it! It's a double-edged sword: when you do something, whether it be music or movies, if you do the same thing all the time, people complain, but if you change it they still complain.

"I'm always happy when people say good things," he continued, "because I'm really not used to it! Truthfully, I always expect people to say horrible things, because that seems to be the only time people talk any more, when they have something bad to say. The funny thing is, I'm so used to not caring what anyone says, good or bad, that unfortunately even when people say good things . . . I wish it made me feel good, but it doesn't. I don't believe the bad stuff and I don't believe the good stuff, so you're just sort of left with the same feeling."

Asked about his wife's performance, Zombie noted how his previous movies were ensemble pieces, but that this time there is no doubt that Sheri is the star of the show. "It's really a character piece, and the whole story goes through her. There are a lot of supporting characters around her, obviously, but she's definitely the lead. It's weird: when we work together it's always good, but she's the hardest person for me to judge . . . I know her so well, that I know when her performance is truthful, because it's exactly how she'd be in real life. All the best performances are when it doesn't feel like an actor is acting."

It was just as well that Sheri delivered the goods: Zombie had plenty of other matters to deal with during the twenty-one-day shoot. "It was the fastest movie I've ever made," he said, sounding tired rather than jubilant, "although that doesn't show in the movie, thankfully." Working so quickly, he added, is "exhausting, and it leaves absolutely no room for error. That's really why the script changed a lot too, because when you start shooting, the realities of the script versus the time you have to shoot it come into play. You say, 'Well, this script would have worked great at eighty days . . . let's forget about this stuff, I guess!'"

One major problem came about when Richard Lynch, a veteran actor who was set to play a clergyman, died early in the shoot. After recasting and reshooting Lynch's scenes, Zombie then came to realize during the edit that the scenes of a film-within-the-film he had created were in fact a hindrance to the overall flow. "A lot of things got cut," he recalled. "Things always get cut, but in particular there was like a little movie within the movie, with Udo Kier and Clint Howard, and we had to lose that. It was always just a small background thing, but it just didn't make sense as we went along . . . and there were other people who were announced as having been cast, like Billy Drago, who were never actually in the movie. Billy was going to be, but then something happened. That took a while to fix, but we figured it out."

Sheri Moon, it seemed, would be a Zombie movie regular for the forseeable future. Speaking to Staci Layne Wilson at *Girls and Corpses*, she explained, "I consider myself a California girl now. I moved out here when I was seventeen. As soon as I graduated high school I came out to California and had a couple of tries. I mean I moved back to Connecticut where I grew up, twice, and went to broadcasting school. But I moved back and forth. Seventeen is really young to move out of state and be on your own. I mean, I wanted to play and have fun and be responsibility-free, but eventually you have to buckle down and get a job. So I was a little wild child when I was younger."

"Wild child" she may have been, but some reports about her early life were greatly exaggerated. "I was never a stripper," she said, refuting claims that had been made elsewhere. "I think it got misconstrued because I am, I was, and still am, a dancer. I would choreograph the numbers, make the costumes, and dance on tour with Rob. I think people hear the word dancer and have the association 'stripper.'"

Success as an actor had not changed her. "I'm not the typical narcissistic actor," she reasoned. "I don't really feel like I want to try to sell myself or market myself to people. I don't have an agent. I don't give many interviews. . . . I don't read reviews. Good ones are great to read, but you know there's bad ones out there, too. I just don't want things like that to influence me in any way or bum me out. Because we do the work, and we're proud of it. I'll look at something occasionally if Rob's like, 'Oh, check this out, it's really cool,' because he likes to see everything that's on the web regarding the movies. But I'm just a little antsy about looking at stuff. In all honesty, I really don't know much of what's like going on there."

◆

A mere four days after the cinematic release of *The Lords of Salem* came Zombie's fifth solo album, the strangely titled *Venomous Rat Regeneration Vendor*. A single and video called "Dead City Radio and the New Gods of Supertown" had garnered some interest among the faithful, with the song's highly commercial sound coming courtesy of producer Bob Marlette, who had previously worked with Alice

Cooper, Black Sabbath, Marilyn Manson, and many others. Its chorus—containing as it does the word "radio"—was designed for maximum exposure, while the video clip—a performance montage of Zombie and band, Sheri contorting herself, and a break dancer busting moves—offered a stark, effective introduction to the new Rob Zombie sound.

"In the last ten years, as the value of videos sort of declined, and I started making movies, I got bored with making videos because it just seemed like, what's the point?" Zombie told *Rolling Stone*. "But the four of us are so jazzed about the record and the tour that we really wanted to make a great video. I thought, let's give it the old community college try. This is a conceptual video—it's bizarre. It's a freak show, man."

Infused with new energy and keen to hit the road with his new songs, Zombie seemed somewhat rejuvenated. Simple, stripped-down, and heavy on the choruses, "Teenage Nosferatu Pussy" opens the album with a clear statement of intent—the intent being to sell lots of units with a clean, radio-friendly sound. "Dead City Radio and the New Gods of Supertown" is similar, with a catchy, commercial feel that showcases the most animated vocal from Zombie in some time. "Revelation Revolution" is a groove-heavy rock song, a one-note-riff driving tune of the kind that the band had been delivering one of per album for years now, while "Theme for the Rat Vendor" is a one-minute interlude of percussion and sitars. If only we knew who the Rat Vendor was . . .

The album steps up a gear in its second half with the similarly inexplicably titled "Ging Gang Gong De Do Gong De Laga Raga," which may make little sense but sees Rob Zombie doing the perfect Tom Waits impression in the verses before returning to the usual throaty roar in the chorus. "Rock and Roll (in a Black Hole)" is different again, with a computer-generated trance intro that sounds a lot like an 8-bit videogame soundtrack from the 1990s. Although the guitars do thicken it up after the midsection, the overall feel is that of a mildly gripping rock/dance experiment.

"Behold, the Pretty Filthy Creatures!" is essentially a showcase for John 5's picking hand, while "White Trash Freaks" is another electronica-influenced chunk of metal. Both serve to highlight the quality of the surprisingly good cover of "We're an American Band," originally by Grand Funk Railroad. Their 1973 hit benefits hugely from the Zombie treatment, over-the-top as it is, in particular with the expert guitar soloing and the bellowed choruses.

"We're just an American band, so it was just so perfect," John 5 said at the time. "We were talking about covers early on, and we were like, 'My God, this is like the perfect cover for us' . . . in the original song there's a lyric that says 'up all night with Freddie King.' But if you listen to our version, it's 'up all night with Kerry King.' So, that's a little [addition] to the whole thing."

As the album draws toward a close, "Lucifer Rising" is a high point, with its fearsomely catchy guitar licks and a powerful, fast tempo; "The Girl Who Loved the Monsters" is another trance-toned collection of grooves; and "Trade In Your Guns for a Coffin" is a blast from start to finish, with layers of insolent rock 'n' roll (in the vintage sense) guitars and a suitably sweary outburst from Zombie in the choruses. If you had to sum up *Venomous Rat Generation Vendor* in a few words, you'd mention the commercial sheen that Marlette gave the songs, plus the renewed dose of energy that comes from the band. Not bad for a group of head-bangers this far down the line.

Asked by *Metal Hammer* writer Joe Daly how it felt to have the new album out, Zombie seemed suitably enthusiastic, noting that the record had received some of the best reviews of his career. "People are loving it, and people seem to know the new songs that we've been playing live, and they seem to like 'em. Which is weird, because usually when you add new songs into the set, they take a minute to fit in, but these work right out of the gate."

As far as Zombie was concerned, his entire recorded output, taken as a whole, formed "one giant crazy thing," although he had no real desire to try to bridge the gap between records. "When you set out to make a record," he told Daly, "you're just trying to make something good. That's the goal. With every record, you can have these pretentious grand plans, but at the end of the day, you're just trying to get together to write a bunch of good songs."

One of Zombie's primary aims for the new record, he continued, was to come up with a set of songs "that were memorable and catchy, but where the structure and the hooks were more unconventional. So they weren't obvious, because if anything, I felt that was a trap that we could fall into easily." After all, he noted, he'd been writing and recording music for almost thirty years; if wanted to write a "fake Rob Zombie song," he could do so with ease. "There's a formula, but then I don't want to do that because then I feel that you have to keep challenging yourself to try and do different things. You don't want to become your own cover band."

◆

Moving away from films and music but indirectly retaining elements of the aesthetic of both, in June 2013 Zombie launched a completely different venture: the Great American Nightmare, a "haunted house experience" in Pomona, Los Angeles. In the Nightmare, as we'll call it, customers paid money to be faintly terrorized by a variety of attractions, including the *Lords of Salem* Total Black Out, the *Haunted World of El Superbeasto* 3-D, and the House of 1,000 Corpses—before relaxing at a fifteen-night music festival with a bill featuring artists from across the rock and dance music worlds.

As the accompanying press release explained, the project was a collaboration between "masters of the macabre" Rob Zombie and well-known haunted house designer Steve Kopelman. The "fully immersive" experience would feature three attractions, each of them based on one of Zombie's films. "The shocking—and sometimes disturbing—fright attractions will offer a three-dimensional experience with animatronics and effects, a maze that is the ultimate definition of claustrophobia and fear, sudden chills and startling thrills, and salacious humor that will make one scream with fright and laughter."

"This is it!" Zombie himself was quoted as saying. "The ultimate badass Halloween experience! No one will walk away disappointed. I am thrilled to bring the Great American Nightmare to California and begin a reign of bloody terror!"

Could such a venture make money? Apparently so, as Zombie would go on to expand the concept by opening a second location in Chicago in 2014. In an era when the movie and music industries are in free fall, why not look outside the box?

These were the good times for Rob Zombie and his band. Free from internal dissent, with a solid album behind them and a fan base that showed no signs of shrinking, the group hit the 2013 festival circuit with a vengeance. A headline slot over Five Finger Death Punch, Mastodon, and Amon Amarth at the Mayhem festival— one of America's most successful festivals of recent years—was an immediate highlight of the year. As Zombie explained in an interview with *Rolling Stone*, the more people who attended a live event, the better. Festivals—especially in Europe—always impressed him with their gigantic size, he said, and he also enjoyed them as a way to catch up with fellow musicians.

The Mayhem festival was an opportunity for Zombie to once again exercise his creative talents to the maximum, as he explained to Joe Daly. Asked about the obstacles that accompany bringing out such a huge set, he laughed that it was "the usual nightmare" but added, "It's been great. We've only done three shows, but it's been really good."

The horror-movie backdrops that Zombie and his band performed in front of each night were comprised of things he had gradually acquired over the years. "Every single little thing that happens onstage is something I've nitpicked over," he added. "There's no company that you can go to and say, 'I need this,' and they say, 'Oh sure, we've got that for you.' You've got to create it all yourself . . . I just kind of roll from the next thing to the next thing to the next. It's amazing what you can accomplish in a day, sometimes. I don't like to waste time. People waste a lot of time in their lives, and especially as you get older, you see that time becomes more precious and you try to jam more into it."

Asked by Daly about his other concurrent projects, Zombie explained that, as ever, he was working on a number of different things. "So right now, we're on tour, but during the downtime, I'm prepping stuff for the Great American Nightmare event that I'm doing in October, which is this two week-long Halloween event, I'm working on setting up the next movie, and working on anything from new merch designs to other things. I mean, there is no free time. There's always a million things to do."

Of all of these extracurricular projects, it seemed that the Great American Nightmare was the one that was taking up the majority of Zombie's attention. "I think that, right now, people think that it's just the concert, but there's three huge haunted houses [to organize]," he said. "That's really the main attraction. And there's an outdoor pavilion that's all a haunted attraction, too, and with that, there are other events that happening at the same time; some bands, there's wrestling . . . what I wanted to do was just a giant Halloween extravaganza. You don't even have to be a fan of any of the music, and you could still go and have a kickass time.

"What's good about this is that each haunted house is based on one of the movies [that Zombie has directed], so they took the design from the movies," he added. "Like they have the Superbeasto Maze in 3-D, where you walk through a giant pair of spread legs and you go into this sort of . . . well, you know what you're going into, and that takes you through this crazy 3-D world and then that sort of goes into the *House of 1,000 Corpses* [and] *Devil's Rejects* world, which is sort of a murder ride of serial killers. It's all crazy shit like that."

◆

By now a picture has emerged of Rob Zombie as a man of serious dedication and discipline, rock star though he is. Drug free, vegetarian, in lean fighting shape, and, as far as we know, not even keen on alcohol, he devotes his time to being creative. It is often the case that successful people, no matter their field of activity, reach a point where their primary goal is maximum productivity, both because being productive is enjoyable and because it becomes clear that time is— while not exactly running out—not available in limitless quantities.

Hence Zombie's remarkable workload as he essentially carried two careers in parallel, with literally no signs of stopping.

Zombie was clearly not sitting around in the gaps between live commitments. Indeed, his sixth album was already beginning to take shape, just months after the release of *Venomous Rat Regeneration Vendor*, and by the late spring, more releases had been announced, this time his first live DVD and Blu-ray, titled *The Zombie Horror Picture Show*. This kept crowds happy throughout the summer festival season, which took in shows at some prestigious venues.

I interviewed Zombie in early 2014, just before that year's Download Festival, to which he and his the band were returning after a three-year absence. "It feels great to be coming back to Download," he mused. "I'm really looking forward to it. When we played there three years ago, it was amazing. The weather was crappy, but then it cleared up right when we played, and we had a fantastic gig. We were all super-happy afterward, so we're all thrilled to come back.

"I remember when White Zombie played with Metallica back in 1995," he continued. "I love it when festivals have a bit of history to them, like Download does. People in Europe tend to go to events because of their heritage. Appreciation for the history of these events seems to be bigger in Europe: in the United States there's more of a feeling of, 'What's the new thing?' You guys appreciate the fact that it's been around for years, and that's great—just because something is new doesn't mean it's any good."

With commendable honesty, he admitted that after all these years, some of the festival shows he'd played had begun to blur into others, but that was not the case with Download. "We do play a lot of festivals, but Download stands out because of how big it is. It always seems to be the biggest one around. But whether it's 500 people or

50,000 people, we attack the gig in the same manner. What's best is when the crowd is enthusiastic and gives energy back to you. I always say this, and all bands say this, but a band can only be as good as the audience. Some audiences are great: you can feel the energy and that just pumps you up: it's the greatest high ever. Other audiences just want to stand there like they're watching TV, and you feel like nothing's working. It's like they've forgotten to have fun. We refuse to give up, though: we just keep pounding at them! You have to remind them that they're allowed to enjoy themselves—although I know we won't have that problem at Download.

"After a certain amount of years, you have so many songs that people expect to hear. They almost fill up the whole set. At least forty-five minutes of a normal one-hour set will be songs that people totally expect you to play. That doesn't leave a lot of room to get innovative, but we haven't been over to the UK since we put out *Venomous Rat Regeneration Vendor* last year, so that's kinda cool. We'll still mix it up, though."

Asked if this meant that crowd could look forward to remixed or rearranged versions of classic Zombie tunes, he simply laughed. "I think people hate that! The truth is that every time I've seen a band and they try to update their big hits, it drives me crazy. It sucks! There's a reason why people like the songs. We'll fuck around a little bit, but we definitely won't be doing acoustic versions of the songs or anything. There's nothing worse than that! Or medleys. *Don't give me a medley of the hits. Play the fuckin' songs!*

"We treat all our shows the same," he added, "but the more people in the crowd the better, because our music translates better to large crowds. Intimate situations don't really work with what we do. The way we are on stage is better with a large stage. Sometimes when we get on a small stage and there's no room, we're like, 'What the fuck are we gonna do up here?' So Download is going to be killer."

All the best rock bands truly shine when they're playing live. Never mind if their new album is as good as the last one, at least when an artist has reached a certain number of years in the game. Rob Zombie, in his sixth decade, may or may not be making music these days that is as spellbinding as it once was; that depends entirely on your personal point of view, which in turn is often at least partly determined by your age and enthusiasm for the material. *Hellbilly Deluxe* is generally agreed to be a fine album by Rob Zombie's core fans, although those who prefer their metal a little easier on the eye or more aggressive may disagree entirely.

◆

Life had now fallen into a satisfying, creative pattern for everyone's favorite undead singer/director. At the time of writing, he and his band continue to deliver the goods around the world, barring the occasional glitch such as the fall 2014 show in Wisconsin that was cut short due to throat problems. ("I've never done this before," he told the crowd. "I can't even talk, man. There's no way I can do this show, I'm sorry. It's fucking bullshit, I know.") Zombie announced a *Devil's Rejects* comic book in late 214, with a live album called *Spookshow International Live* emerging a few months later. Of the later, he said, "It's been eight years since our last live album, so we figured it was time for another. Actually, we weren't planning on it, but we recorded a few shows and they sounded really great, so we thought, 'Fuck it! Let's get it out there.'"

As this book goes to press, a new studio album is expected in the next year or so, along with a film called *31*—which Zombie took the unusual step of financing via a crowd-funding campaign. Little is known about the film other than that it involves a group of people attempting to survive an attack by a posse of killer clowns (a classic Zombie plotline if ever we heard one), but the rewards on offer to those who helped to finance it were pretty juicy. As Zombie explained to *Rolling Stone*, people had come up to him over the years and asked how they could buy the props from the films and come to the set, leading him to realize that for someone in his position, a crowd-funding campaign does not equate to a beggar on a street corner with a hat asking for money.

After that, it seems, Zombie will be looking to take a step away from horror—or, in any case, scenes of extreme bloodletting—with a sports film called *The Broad Street Bullies*, the true-life story of the Philadelphia Flyers ice hockey team and how they won the Stanley Cup in 1974. He has described it as *Rocky* on ice: a character-driven movie about a bunch of hoodlums who decided that if they couldn't be the best hockey team, they were going to be the toughest. Building a team of tough guys that other hockey teams were afraid to play, they won that championship twice.

Which matters most to Zombie at this stage: music or movies? "It's still 50/50," he said. "Whichever one I am doing at that time is the most important thing to me. That's really the way I approach it. That's why I don't try to do them simultaneously. When I'm touring, that's what I am—that's 100 percent of what I'm about— and when I'm making a movie, that's 100 what I'm about. They're both equally important."

That said, Zombie appears to have little concept of his continuing place in the musical spectrum, or of what newer acts might be up to. "I have no idea what anyone is doing," he said, not for the first time. "This is nothing against the bands that are doing it, but I am oblivious to it. I kind of function in my own bubble most of the time. You can see it in my movies—that's the bubble that I function in. I still just drive around listening to the Allman Brothers . . . I couldn't even name a new record. Sorry."

Zombie turned fifty in 2015, a milestone significant enough that several news websites ran a story about it. Don't expect much self-analysis from the man himself, however; as ever, he is too busy taking care of the journey to pay much attention to the beginning or the end. Focused on his own vision, Zombie is—like all he most successful artists—able to set parameters about what he will or will not do, without simply being inflexible. He won't act in his or anyone else's films, for example, although he is asked to do so on a constant basis.

What else will Rob Zombie never do? Reform White Zombie. "White Zombie stopped at the height of our career—we had a triple-platinum record and we just did our huge, sold-out arena tour everywhere and then we stopped, and that's the best way to leave it." Most reunion tours, he continued, were about one thing: money. "And that's not a good reason to do it. To get back with a bunch of people that I literally haven't even spoken to in twenty years to go do a run for a bunch of money, I just think that's a big lie and I'm just not into it."

One seemingly outlandish idea that might yet come to fruition, though, is a stage musical version of *House of 1,000 Corpses*. "First, it started off almost as a joke, but then after I talked about it more, I thought it was a good idea," he admitted. "I would like to [do it]. I don't know when or how or whatever . . . one hand, it sounds ridiculous, but I think that the reality of it is that it is possible.

Because if you look at Broadway now, it's all becoming that sort of pop culture, and I think that *House of 1,000 Corpses* has very much led itself to that sort of scenario, because the whole movie plays almost like a bloody *Rocky Horror Picture Show*, anyway."

Perhaps the biggest challenge for somebody in Rob Zombie's position is trying to find new ways to keep innovating and to keep entertaining his fan base.

And there's the big question when it came to a career as long as Rob Zombie's: how do you keep it entertaining? "How do you do something that sounds fresh, without making it so different that it's not you any more?" he mused, in an interview with Steven Rosen. "That's the problem with anything that you do as time goes on, because if it's too different everybody complains, and if it's too much the same everybody complains. So we are just trying to find that sort of tight middle ground where it's your vibe and your things, but it still sounds fresh. So that's always the challenge."

Luckily, Zombie never gets bored. He's not somebody you can imagine giving it all up and going to work in a bank. "Something always comes up," he explained. "Every movie is the new challenge, and there is always a new exciting thing that goes with it. Every record is a new challenge, and that's what's great about it. Whenever you do anything that's related to art, it never gets old. It's always exciting again, the exact same process. Every movie, from the moment it starts, goes off on its own crazy path, same as every record, and you just don't know where it's going. So it never gets tired. I'm happy with that. It's not like I'm always looking for a completely new thing I have to do. I mean, all those things are still pretty exciting."

Although Zombie does occasionally stop to marvel at his good luck, it's apparent that fame and fortune for its own sake has long since failed to impress him. "I have a lot of moments like that in my life," he told Henry Northmore, "and it's very, very funny to be on tour with Alice Cooper, to be sharing the stage with [him], to be hanging out with him, to be friends, the same way it's very weird that, every time my phone rings and it's Malcolm McDowell just wanting to chitchat. I never stop loving the fact that the things that were important to me as a kid have become part of my life."

Perhaps the strangest thing now is to think that the kids in the audience at Rob Zombie shows today feel about him as he did about Alice Cooper when he was a kid himself. "It is weird, but I understand it . . . I've just come to realize that everything is important to somebody in some fashion. Because I'll meet people that are from some obscure band that hardly anyone cared about, but I loved them when I was a kid, so it's as big a deal to me to go 'Oh my God! I loved your band.' They don't have to have been a rock star, it was just a record that was significant to me thirty years ago. So I totally get it, it makes sense. That's the beauty of music and movies, you make them and shoot them out there into the world and you really just don't know what the hell they're doing. But now, with the internet you obviously get more stories from people because people have more access to find you, and tell you things, so it's pretty interesting the things you hear."

At the time of writing, Zombie's combined activities as director, producer, actor, and voiceover artist—let alone the number of soundtracks on which his music has appeared—number well into three figures. The majority tie in with his interests in cult, dark, alternative, or just amusing culture. The full list of his extra-extracurricular work is too long to include here, but highlights include voicing a zombie under his own name in a 1997 episode of the hit cartoon *Space Ghost Coast to Coast*. Later, he lent his voice to the character of Dr. Curt Connors and his alter ego, The Lizard, in a 2003 episode of *Spider-Man: The New Animated Series*. In 2006 he performed a brief voiceover as Dr. Karl in the box-office-flop horror flick *Slither*, directed by James Gunn. He also worked with the same director on 2014's surprise hit *Guardians of the Galaxy*, this time voicing the part of the Ravager Navigator.

The list goes on: Zombie has also became a regular talking head on TV shows devoted to music, movies, art, and fashion, especially of the more macabre variety. These include *Monsterama: Basil Gogos* (2004), *Dead On: The Life and Cinema of George A. Romero* (2008), and many others. There is no stopping the man. He has even received industry recognition, having received a Michael J. Hein award for Personal Achievement in Direction at the tenth annual New York City Horror Film Festival. Real acceptance will only come, though, when he wins himself an Oscar.

Rob Zombie, then, is an everyman—a creative person who can, and does, do it all, and is equally happy behind a microphone or a camera. "I love them both," he told Northmore. "If I stay away from either one for too long, I really start jonesing to get back to it. And what I'm actually trying to do now, which I don't know if this is going to be successful, is balance both at the same time. It is usually I've finished a tour, shut down the music career and jump into films for a couple of years. But what I'm trying to do this time is tour, shoot the movie, tour, come back and edit the movie, tour, release the movie, going back and forth without having to quit one for such a long period of time. I don't know if I can do this, because it may be too much for me and make me insane."

Nowadays, Zombie is beginning to show his age, with a wiry rather than powerful physique and a lifetime's worth of travel on his brow. But this is no bad thing. He is as active as any two or three other creative figures you might care to mention, and still delivers quality on every front, even in the exhausting arenas of live performance and film directing. He deserves our respect now more than ever.

And, what's more, he has never lost sight of his identity, which is so often the fate of those who enter the belly of the industry beast. To be more precise, he created his own identity and stuck to it: Rob Zombie, via Rob Cummings and Rob Straker.

"It's not like you create a persona that you want to become, it's almost like the persona is the real you," he said. "When I was younger and I had to wear nicer clothes so I could keep some crappy job, that was the fake me. Everyone's got friends and they're covered in tattoos and they put on a white shirt for their job at the bank and they have to hide everything. That's like the fake persona. What's great is I get to be the real me."

After close to three decades of writing songs and directing films about the darker side of life—from vampires, monsters, and zombies to murder, torture, and suicide—does Zombie have the right to feel proud of his recorded oeuvre? Is his work not, to take a devil's advocate stance, a little bad for people?

If you've read this far, you'll know that my answer is yes: he should take great pride in his work, and no: it isn't harmful in any way, despite the whining of the moral majority back in the good old days of the Satanic panic in the 1980s. There is no evil in Rob Zombie's work. If you're looking for an example, beating people up in order to steal their money is evil. Dropping bombs on a country just because it possesses lucrative oil supplies is evil. Invading someone else's homeland, putting six million of the residents in concentration camps and justifying it by claiming an ancient biological right to rule over them is evil. Detonating an explosive device in a packed commuter vehicle in the rush hour, no matter what your faith may tell you, is evil.

On the other hand, wearing leather, studs, theatrical makeup, and trousers that fit too snugly around the crotch area is not evil. It's not evil to throw slightly scary poses, make goat's-horns hand gestures, or do a Paddington Bear frown at the camera. It's not evil to sing "Satan laughing spreads his wings." It's not evil to sing "Shout, shout, shout, shout at the devil."

Zombie's friend Ozzy Osbourne and his band, Black Sabbath, have been mentioned a number of times in this book, so let's take a moment to analyze their role in the trajectory of heavy metal so far. Just two years into their career, they'd been asked if they were Satanists so many times that Ozzy announced to one interviewer, before the hapless journalist had even opened his mouth to speak, "You're going to ask about black magic. It's rubbish."

Like Rob Zombie in the early White Zombie days, Black Sabbath were practically homeless tramps; Ozzy couldn't even afford a pair of shoes in the early days. The only thing that separates them in cultural terms is that the former lived in a horrible pit of an apartment in New York City, while the latter did the same in Birmingham, England. Like Zombie, Sabbath were essentially harmless dudes with a penchant for horror films. (In fact, after they saw *The Exorcist* at the cinema, the members of Black Sabbath were so scared that they all slept in the same room that night.)

What happened next in heavy metal on the road to Rob

Zombie's appearance? In 1981, two legendary metal bands released their debut albums—Mötley Crüe, based in L.A., and Venom, from Newcastle. Both acts trowelled on the fake Satanism in the early days, with stories spreading like wildfire about the arcane rituals that supposedly took place in the studio, supported by the "demonic" sleeve artwork of their records. Of course, Middle America and Middle England filled their collective pants at such audacity, with parents' groups, local council committees, youth-club organizers and suchlike authoritarian fools up in arms about songs like Crüe's "Shout at the Devil" and Venom's "Witching Hour."

But what did we actually have here? Crüe were a great band back in '81, but if you dug beneath the surface a bit, it soon became clear that singer Vince Neil *et al* were basically a bunch of broke wastrels with big hair. As for Venom, with their mixture of loincloths, theatrical props, ludicrous "very metal" poses, and drummer Abaddon's Aviator sunglasses, they were ridiculous to look at. But we loved them (and we still do) because the music they made was new, fast, aggressive, raw, nasty and gripping. None of this was evil. This was funny.

By 1983, Metallica and Slayer had come out of the woodwork and were singing about the devil in laughably unsophisticated terms. The former realized that Satanism and metal was a corny combination and moved on rapidly (although "Phantom Lord" is still a classic) but Kerry King and his bunch of merry men continued along Satanic lines for the rest of the decade, making it seem worse than it actually was by including gore themes ("Piece by Piece") and Nazi references ("Angel of Death") along the way.

Okay, lyrics about bones and blood and rotten limbs aren't exactly amusing, but they were still a long way from being evil:

slasher-movie fans tuned in with glee, despite the predictable fears of society's moral guardians

Once Satan had been established as a topic for metal songwriters, he gained a secure foothold just about everywhere thanks to global-selling artists such as Zombie's heroes Alice Cooper and KISS. These people weren't remotely interested in the devil but looked a bit scary anyway, were lumped into the same pseudo-Satanic category and did rather well out of it, selling millions of records and earning huge tour revenues.

So far, so silly. Ozzy, Alice, and Paul Stanley are about as Satanic and evil as your pet hamster. Admittedly, it all got a bit more serious in the early 1990s, when a bunch of Norwegian kids got into black metal and started desecrating graves and burning down churches. This wasn't evil, but it wasn't entertaining either—it was stupid, as most of the perpetrators admitted when they grew up and got a haircut. Some of this stupidity can be attributed to the youth of the kids who applied Zippo to pew, of course—most of them were barely twenty at the time—but the finger can also be pointed at the confusing mixture of religion and philosophy that motivated them to do it. Some of the church-burners thought that destroying a Christian building was a victory for Satan; others thought it was a bonus point for Wotanism, which Christianity had replaced; and still others reasoned (in their juvenile way) that all this destruction was an expression of nihilism or anarchy, and nothing to do with the supernatural at all.

Of course, what confused the moral majority was the way the bands looked and the sound of their music. They reasoned that if something looks evil and sounds evil (and let's face it, most of the musicians smelled pretty evil too) it must *be* evil, right? Wrong. What the naysayers have always forgotten, or been too conservative to acknowledge, is that the *appearance* of evil can be thrilling, even if it's fake. We love it when Rob Zombie puts those white contact lenses in and growls "I'm the Superbeast!"; we marvel when someone is killed, eviscerated, or otherwise has their day ruined in one of his films. It's all just entertaining theater. We know this because we're not stupid.

Metal is violent music, it's true—but the violence is cathartic and intended to release tension, not to inspire more violence. Just look at the happy, exhausted crowd coming out of the mosh pit at any Rob Zombie gig: there's no evil there. As with life in general, there's an easily recognizable line in metal between spooky play-acting and actual, worrying evilness. Most of us know where that line is, despite the braying of those who watch over us. Metal is as evil as everything else—that is to say, some of it is and some of it isn't. Without their heart of darkness, the thrill of Zombie's music and films just wouldn't be the same.

Although Zombie rarely seems to look back on his catalogue in a self-congratulatory manner, he is entitled to do just that. After all, how many art students drop out, live in cockroach-infested apartments with no money, and then end up as renowned musicians or filmmakers—let alone both?

"I always knew even as a kid that I wanted to be part of everything I was a fan of," he mused, in a 2007 interview with Mike Furches. "I couldn't be satisfied by just standing on the sidelines watching. How I got from there to here is a long slow process of never giving up on anything, ever. If you really want it, you can get it. One thing is for sure, I certainly didn't achieve anything by being wasted and fucked up, as some would like to think . . . I believe in the power of one's own free will to achieve anything."

What does Zombie have left to himself, aside from all of his work in music and film? Perhaps only his painting, which is still something he does every day. "There are very few things in my life that haven't become legit," he explained to filmmaker Mick Garris with a laugh. "Once it's legit, and there's people waiting, and there's money . . . painting is the one thing I can just do and it doesn't matter. I'm afraid that once there's a show planned, then it becomes ruined! So I try to keep one thing to myself."

Much more is to come, although no one can predict what it might be. In fact, no one still knows who Rob Zombie really *is*, after he goes home to Sheri and Dracula and shuts the door on the world. As we started this book, so we'll end it.

"I don't know what people's perception of me necessarily is, but I know that it's usually wrong," he said. "Of course it is, because they don't know me any more than I know them. Who knows?"

NOTES

CHAPTER 1

2 "They were big" Reilly Capps, *Boston Globe*, August 2002

2 "I'm tired of" Reilly Capps, *Boston Globe*, August 2002

2 "It's full of" Reilly Capps, *Boston Globe*, August 2002

3 "The time period" Henry Northmore, list.co.uk, February 2011

5 "I would always" Steven Daly, *Rolling Stone*, February 1999

5 "I remember as" Sara Michelle Fetters, moviefreak.com, August 2007

5 "I love the" Carlo Cavagna, aboutfilm.com, August 2005

6 "What sets that" Scott Tobias, A.V. Club, August 2005

6 "Gory horror movies" Carlo Cavagna, aboutfilm.com, August 2005

7 "It's not the" Linda Leseman, *LA Weekly*, June 2013

8 "Everybody's pulling out" contactmusic.com, March 2006

8 "Rob and I" Steven Daly, *Rolling Stone*, February 1999

10 "I guess I" Henry Northmore, list.co.uk, February 2011

11 "I always loved" Matt Munoz, *Bakotopia*, November 2007

11 "I like music" Joe Daly, *Metal Hammer*, 2013

12 "I just thought" Steven Rosen, *Ultimate Guitar*, December 2008

13 "When I was" Henry Northmore, list.co.uk, February 2011

CHAPTER 2

15 "When I got" David A. Keeps, *Men's Health*, September 2005

16 "It's always about" Laura Hauser, *The Orion*, November 2007

20 "My main influence" Elysa Gardner, *Los Angeles Times*, June 1995

22 "I just wanted" rzr.online.fr, 1995

24 "I worked on" Mick Garris, *Post Mortem*, 2009

24 "It was a" Tom Murphy, *Westword*, September 2012

25 "We were a" Greg Kot, *Chicago Tribune*, October 1998

27 "We just got" *Creem Presents: Thrash Metal*, 1988

28 "[White Zombie's] hallmark" David Stubbs, *Melody Maker*, 1988

33 "Well, we were" Steven Rosen, 2012

33 "I didn't even" Steven Rosen, 2012

35 "I know I" Phil Freeman, *The Wire*, November 2007

36 "I was bangin'" rocknrollexperience.com, 1996

39 "We were interested" *In Your Eye*, 1996

43 "It was just" Steven Rosen, *Ultimate Guitar*, December 2008

43 "The only person" Steven Rosen, *Ultimate Guitar*, December 2008

43 "We were young" Carrie Borzillo, *Suicide Girls*, December 2008

47 "It wasn't until" *PBS on Tour*, July 2013

CHAPTER 3

53 "To say that" Matt O'Connell, *Rock Sound*, 1999

56 "In some ways" Neil Christie, gibson.com, February 2011

57 "It was kind" Daina Darzin, October 1995

58 "Our first drummer" James Greene Jr., *Crawdaddy*, March 2010

59 "Sean and I" Joe Matera, *Ultimate Guitar*, December 2008

60 "It was pretty" Joe Matera, *Ultimate Guitar*, December 2008

60 "It was a" Joe Matera, *Ultimate Guitar*, December 2008

63 "Shelves rise up" Marc Weidenbaum, *Pulse*, June 1995

65 "There does come" Marc Weidenbaum, *Pulse*, June 1995

66 "It's really hard" Marc Weidenbaum, *Pulse*, June 1995

69 "Rob Zombie and" Jonathan Gold, *Los Angeles Times*, January 1993

70 "After years" Michael Moses, *Foundations*, April 1995

70 "I'm really sick" Michael Moses, *Foundations*, April 1995

71 "I don't really" Michael Moses, *Foundations*, April 1995

CHAPTER 4

74 "There's always more" Daina Darzin, October 1995

76 "I believe that" Andreas Veneris, December 1995

77 "This is a" Brad Tyer, *Houston Press*, February 1996

85 "Honestly, that was" Rick Florino, bloody-disgusting.com, May 2010

CHAPTER 5

92 "The music business" Joe Daly, *Bass Guitar Magazine*, December 2008

93 "Because we were" Joe Daly, *Bass Guitar Magazine*, December 2008

93 "Some people don't" Joe Daly, *Bass Guitar Magazine*, December 2008

94 "I think I" MTV News, November 1998

97 "It's the best" *Fernandes Guitar*, December 2008

98 "The only person" Marc Weidenbaum, *Pulse*, June 1995

99 "There's nothing I" Russell A. Trunk, exclusivemagazine.com, 1998

99 "At this stage" Russell A. Trunk, exclusivemagazine.com, 1998

99 "Probably one of" Russell A. Trunk, exclusivemagazine.com, 1998

100 "Hopefully, the Funny" *New York Daily News*, July 1998

100 "By the time" Neil Kulkarni, *Melody Maker*, 1998

102 "I like being" Neil Kulkarni, *Melody Maker*, 1998

102 "The vibe was" Steven Rosen, *Ultimate Guitar*, December 2008

108 "There were a" Joe Matera, *Ultimate Guitar*, December 2008

111 "Every time I" Mick Garris, *Post Mortem*, 2009

111 "I went to" Mick Garris, *Post Mortem*, 2009

111 "Working at Universal" Mick Garris, *Post Mortem*, 2009

111 "Afterwards I went" Mick Garris, *Post Mortem*, 2009

113 "I was really" Scott Tobias, A.V. Club, August 2005

115 "It was very" Jane Stevenson, *Toronto Sun*, November 2007

117 "and then there's" Hollywood.com, 2002

117 "We went to" Mick Garris, *Post Mortem*, 2009

118 "MGM got wind" Jon Wiederhorn, MTV, 2002

118 "It kind of" Mick Garris, *Post Mortem*, 2009

118 "Everyone else seemed" Mick Garris, *Post Mortem*, 2009

119 "I was also" Staci Layne Wilson, *Girls and Corpses*, 2006

119 "It's a lot" Staci Layne Wilson, *Girls and Corpses*, 2006

120 "I read a" Staci Layne Wilson, *Girls and Corpses*, 2006

120 "We were together" Staci Layne Wilson, *Girls and Corpses*, 2006

121 "After *Sinister Urge*" Edward Scott Day, *Abort*, January 2009

121 "I forget what" Stephanie Ng Wan, watchmojo.com, November 2009

CHAPTER 6

124 "The hardest part" Peter M. Bracke, *DVD File*, March 2003

125 "We enjoy working" Don Kaye, *Fangoria*, December 2005

125 "Because, when I" Carlo Cavagna, aboutfilm.com, August 2005

127 "When Rob called" *Rolling Stone*, February 2003

127 "Except for Martin" Carlo Cavagna, aboutfilm.com, August 2005

129 "Baby is the" Don Kaye, *Fangoria*, December 2005

131 "Getting really caught" Joe Daly, *Metal Hammer*, 2013

134 "We had a" Don Kaye, *Fangoria*, December 2005

134 "Baby participates actively" Don Kaye, *Fangoria*, December 2005

135 "Even though there" Peter M. Bracke, *DVD File*, March 2003

135 "All of us" Don Kaye, *Fangoria*, December 2005

135 "People probably overreacted" Don Kaye, *Fangoria*, December 2005

136 "I didn't have" Don Kaye, *Fangoria*, December 2005

136 "With all the" Peter M. Bracke, *DVD File*, March 2003

136 "I'm not even" Peter M. Bracke, *DVD File*, March 2003

138 "That happened, and" Carlo Cavagna, aboutfilm.com, August 2005

138 "I don't know" Carlo Cavagna, aboutfilm.com, August 2005

139 "When *House of*" gamesradar.com, September 2007

139 "There was definitely" Peter M. Bracke, *DVD File*, March
       2003

140 "I didn't really" Peter M. Bracke, *DVD File*, March 2003

141 "I don't want" Peter M. Bracke, *DVD File*, March 2003

CHAPTER 7

145 "It took a" Jon Wiederhorn, MTV, December 2003

146 "When I'm working" Jon Wiederhorn, MTV, December 2003

147 "The lead character" Jon Wiederhorn, MTV, December 2003

148 "You can literally" Jon Wiederhorn, MTV, December 2003

149 "There were a" Launch Radio Networks, April 2005

149 "It's a totally" Obi-Swan, *Ain't It Cool News*, June 2005

151 "It's just so" David Hall, eatmybrains.com, August 2005

153 "My biggest fear" David Hall, eatmybrains.com, August 2005

155 "I really liked" Carlo Cavagna, aboutfilm.com, August 2005

156 "*Rejects* is not" David Hall, eatmybrains.com, August 2005

156 "This time around" David Hall, eatmybrains.com, August
       2005

156 "Everyone's like, 'Well'" Carlo Cavagna, aboutfilm.com, August
       2005

157 "I like the" David Hall, eatmybrains.com, August 2005

157 "Not William Forsythe's" Carlo Cavagna, aboutfilm.com,
       August 2005

158 "I just took" Carlo Cavagna, aboutfilm.com, August 2005

159 "With *House of*" Mick Garris, *Post Mortem*, 2009

159 "I don't think" The Dude, Moviesonline.ca, July 2005

160 "There are rare" David Hall, eatmybrains.com, August 2005

160 "I was fed" Henry Northmore, list.co.uk, February 2011

161 "I can demand" Steven Rosen, 2012

162 "When I was" Steven Rosen, 2012

163 "Rob loves Alice" Steven Rosen, 2012

164 "There are no" *Poughkeepsie Journal*, July 2005

165 "Let me set" Steven Rosen, 2012

CHAPTER 8

172 "The original Halloween" *Variety*, December 2006

173 "Malcolm was my" Will Harris, *Bullz-Eye*, August 2007

174 "That movie already" Amy Atkins, *Boise Weekly*, September 2006

178 "I used to have" Alan Sculley, *Last Word Feature*, November 2007

178 "But there were" Henry Northmore, list.co.uk, February 2011

180 "My intention is" Jon Wiederhorn, mtv.com, December 2003

181 "I love being" Henry Northmore, list.co.uk, February 2011

181 "I don't know" Steven Rosen, *Ultimate Guitar*, December 2008

181 "There is really" Steven Rosen, *Ultimate Guitar*, December 2008

182 "There is always" Steven Rosen, *Ultimate Guitar*, December 2008

183 "I probably waited" Steven Rosen, *Ultimate Guitar*, December 2008

183 "I can see" Steven Rosen, *Ultimate Guitar*, December 2008

185 "It's pretty self-explanatory" Steven Rosen, *Ultimate Guitar*, December 2008

186 "That came down" Edward Scott Day, *Abort*, January 2009

186 "We had all" Edward Scott Day, *Abort*, January 2009

CHAPTER 9

187 "When I finished" Mick Garris, *Post Mortem*, 2009

187 "I handed in" Mick Garris, *Post Mortem*, 2009

188 "I started feeling" Mick Garris, *Post Mortem*, 2009

189 "With the first" Hunter Stephenson, *Slashfilm*, May 2009

193 "That gets to" Owen Williams, *Empire*, 2013

194 "You really can't" Steven Rosen, *Ultimate Guitar*, December 2008

195 "We were able" Staci Layne Wilson, *Girls and Corpses*, 2006

195 "I started *El*" Mick Garris, *Post Mortem*, 2009

197 "The unique thing" Steven Rosen, 2012

200 "What I'm discovering" Kyle Anderson, MTV, December 2009

202 "a never-ending" Doug Pullen, *Flint Journal*, November 2007

203 "I think there's" Artisan News Service, July 2010

206 "We've always tried" Chris Arrant, *Newsarama*, May 2010

206 "It's absolutely amazing" KEZI.com, September 2010

206 "What can I" *Noisecreep*, December 2010

209 "a huge colossal" Henry Northmore, list.co.uk, February 2011

209 "It's just the" Henry Northmore, list.co.uk, February 2011

210 "Nobody wants to" Tim Louie, *Aquarian Weekly*, May 2012

210 "Every once in" Tim Louie, *Aquarian Weekly*, May 2012

211 "I like doing" *BANG Showbiz*, June 2011

212 "It was similar" Rick Florino, artistdirect.com, July 2012

214 "That idea I" Owen Williams, *Empire*, 2013

CHAPTER 10

215 "The tree-sheltered" Lauren Beale, *Los Angeles Times*, September 2013

216 "It's funny what" Mick Garris, *Post Mortem*, 2009

216 "It's a different" Tim Louie, *Aquarian Weekly*, May 2012

217 "The other ones" Pulse Of Radio, 2013

219 "I always thought" Owen Williams, *Empire*, 2013

220 "I'm always happy" Owen Williams, *Empire*, 2013

221 "It was the" Owen Williams, *Empire*, 2013

221 "A lot of" Owen Williams, *Empire*, 2013

221 "I consider myself" Staci Layne Wilson, *Girls and Corpses*, 2006

222 "I was never" Staci Layne Wilson, *Girls and Corpses*, 2006

222 "I'm not the" Staci Layne Wilson, *Girls and Corpses*, 2006

223 "In the last" Steve Appleford, *Rolling Stone*, March 2013

224 "We're just an" Rob Cavuoto, *Guitar International*, December 2008

225 "People are loving" Joe Daly, *Metal Hammer*, 2013

227 "The usual nightmare" Joe Daly, *Metal Hammer*, 2013

228 "I think that" Joe Daly, *Metal Hammer*, 2013

232 "It's still 50/50" Steven Rosen, 2012

233 "White Zombie stopped" Sami Jarroush, rockitoutblog.com, July 2013

233 "First, it started" Tim Louie, *Aquarian Weekly*, May 2012

234 "How do you" Steven Rosen, *Ultimate Guitar*, December 2008

234 "Something always comes" Steven Rosen, *Ultimate Guitar*, December 2008

235 "I have a" Henry Northmore, list.co.uk, February 2011

235 "It is weird" Henry Northmore, list.co.uk, February 2011

236 "I love them" Henry Northmore, list.co.uk, February 2011

237 "It's not like" Henry Northmore, list.co.uk, February 2011

241 "I always knew" Mike Furches, May 2005

242 "There are very" Mick Garris, *Post Mortem*, 2009

242 "I don't know" Steven Rosen, *Ultimate Guitar*, December 2008

DISCOGRAPHY AND FILMOGRAPHY

WHITE ZOMBIE ALBUMS AND EPS

Gods on Voodoo Moon EP (Silent Explosion, 1985)
"Gentleman Junkie" / "King of Souls" / "Tales from the Scarecrow Man" / "Cat's Eye Resurrection" / "Black Friday" / "Dead or Alive"

Pig Heaven EP (Silent Explosion, 1986)
"Pig Heaven" / "Slaughter the Grey"

Psycho-Head Blowout EP (Silent Explosion, 1987)
"Eighty Eight" / "Fast Jungle" / "Gun Crazy" / "Kick" / "Memphis" / "Magdelene" / "True Crime"

Soul-Crusher (Silent Explosion/Caroline, 1987)
"Ratmouth" / "Shake of Hate" / "Drowning the Colossus" / "Crow III" / "Die Zombie Die" / "Skin" / "Truck on Fire" / "Future Shock" / "Scum Kill" / "Diamond Ass"

Make Them Die Slowly (Caroline, 1989)
"Demonspeed" / "Disaster Blaster" / "Murderworld" / "Revenge" / "Acid Flesh" / "Power Hungry" / "Godslayer"

God of Thunder EP (Caroline, 1989)
"God of Thunder" / "Love Razor" / "Disaster Blaster"

Zombie Kiss EP (Caroline, 1990)
"God of Thunder" (live) / "Thrust!" (live)

La Sexorcisto: Devil Music, Vol. 1 (Geffen, 1992)
"Welcome to Planet Motherfucker/Psychoholic Slag" / "Knuckle Duster (Radio 1-A)" / "Thunder Kiss '65" / "Black Sunshine" / "Soul-Crusher" / "Cosmic Monsters Inc." / "Spiderbaby (Yeah-Yeah-Yeah)" / "I Am Legend" / "Knuckle Duster (Radio 2-B)" / "Thrust!" / "One Big Crunch" / "Grindhouse (A Go-Go)" / "Starface" / "Warp Asylum"

Nightcrawlers: The KMFDM Remixes EP (Geffen, 1992)
"Thunder Kiss '65 (LP Version)" / "Thunder Kiss '65 (Swinging Lovers Mix)" / "Thunder Kiss '65 (The Remix That Wouldn't Die Mix)" / "Black Sunshine (LP Version)" / "Black Sunshine (Indestructible "Sock It to Me" Psycho-Head Mix)"

Astro-Creep: 2000—Songs of Love, Destruction, and Other Synthetic Delusions of the Electric Head (Geffen, 1995)
"Electric Head Pt. 1 (The Agony)" / "Super-Charger Heaven" / "Real Solution #9" / "Creature of the Wheel" / "Electric Head Pt. 2 (The Ecstasy)" / "Grease Paint and Monkey Brains" / "I, Zombie" / "More

Human than Human" / "El Phantasmo and the Chicken-Run Blast-O-Rama" / "Blur the Technicolor" / "Blood, Milk and Sky"

Supersexy Swingin' Sounds (Geffen, 1996)
"Electric Head, Pt. 2 (Sexational After Dark Mix)" / "More Human than Human (Meet Bambi in the King's Harem Mix)" / "I, Zombie (Europe in the Raw Mix)" / "Grease Paint and Monkey Brains (Sin Centers of Suburbia Mix)" / "Blur the Technicolor (Poker from Stud to Strip Mix)" / "Super-Charger Heaven (Adults Only Mix)" / "El Phantasmo and the Chicken-Run Blast-O-Rama (Wine, Women and Song Mix)" / "Blood, Milk and Sky (Miss September Mix)" / "Real Solution #9 (Mambo Mania Mix)" / "Electric Head, Pt. 1 (Satan in High Heels Mix)" / "I'm Your Boogieman (Sex on the Rocks Mix)"

Let Sleeping Corpses Lie boxed set (Geffen, 2008)
Contains remastered versions of every White Zombie album and EP 1985–96, plus a DVD featuring music videos and live performances.

WHITE ZOMBIE SINGLES
"Thunder Kiss '65" (Geffen, 1993)
"I Am Hell" (Geffen, 1993)
"Black Sunshine" (Geffen, 1994)
"Children of the Grave" (Columbia, 1994)
"Feed the Gods" (Arista, 1994)
"Electric Head Pt. 2 (the Ecstasy)" (Geffen, 1995)
"More Human Than Human" (Geffen, 1995)
"Real Solution #9" (Geffen, 1995)
"Super-Charger Heaven" (Geffen, 1996)

"The One" (Geffen, 1996)

"I'm Your Boogieman" (Geffen, 1996)

"Ratfinks, Suicide Tanks, and Cannibal Girls" (Geffen, 1996)

ROB ZOMBIE ALBUMS

Hellbilly Deluxe (Geffen, 1998)

"Call of the Zombie" / "Superbeast" / "Dragula" / "Living Dead Girl" / "Perversion 99" / "Demonoid Phenomenon" / "Spookshow Baby" / "How to Make a Monster" / "Meet the Creeper" / "The Ballad of Resurrection Joe and Rosa Whore" / "What Lurks on Channel X?" / "Return of the Phantom Stranger" / "The Beginning of the End"

American Made Music to Strip By (Geffen, 1999)

"Dragula" ("Si Non Oscillas, Noli Tintinnare Mix" remix by Charlie Clouser) / "Superbeast" ("Porno Holocaust Mix" remix by Oliver Adams, Praga Khan) / "How to Make a Monster" ("Kitty's Purrrrformance Mix" remix by God Lives Underwater) / "Living Dead Girl" ("Subliminal Seduction Mix" remix by Charlie Clouser) / "Spookshow Baby" ("Black Leather Cat Suit Mix" remix by Rammstein) / "Demonoid Phenomenon" ("Sin Lives Mix" remix by Poly 915) / "The Ballad of Resurrection Joe and Rosa Whore" ("Ilsa She-Wolf of Hollywood Mix" remix by Philip Steir) / "What Lurks on Channel X?" ("XXX Mix" remix by Spacetruckers) / "Meet the Creeper" ("Pink Pussy Mix" remix by Steve Duda) / "Return of the Phantom Stranger" ("Tuesday Night at the Chop Shop Mix" remix by Chris Vrenna) / "Superbeast" ("Girl on a Motorcycle Mix" remix by Charlie Clouser) / "Meet the Creeper" ("Brute Man and Wonder Girl Mix" remix by DJ Lethal)

The Sinister Urge (Geffen, 2001)
"Sinners Inc." / "Demon Speeding" / "Dead Girl Superstar" / "Never Gonna Stop (The Red, Red Kroovy)" / "Iron Head (featuring Ozzy Osbourne)" / "(Go to) California" / "Feel So Numb" / "Transylvanian Transmissions, Pt. 1" / "Bring Her Down (to Crippletown)" / "Scum of the Earth" / "House of 1000 Corpses" / "Unholy Three"

Past, Present, and Future (Geffen, 2003)
"Thunder Kiss '65" / "Black Sunshine" / "Feed the Gods" / "More Human Than Human" / "Super Charger Heaven" / "The Great American Nightmare" / "Dragula" / "Living Dead Girl" / "Superbeast" / "Feel So Numb" / "Never Gonna Stop" / "Demon Speeding" / "Brick House 2003" / "Pussy Liquor" / "Blitzkreig Bop Two-Lane Blacktop" / "Girl on Fire"

Educated Horses (Geffen, 2006)
"Sawdust in the Blood" / "American Witch" / "Foxy Foxy" / "17 Year Locust" / "The Scorpion Sleeps" / "100 Ways" / "Let It All Bleed Out" / "Death of It All" / "Ride" / "The Devil's Rejects" / "The Lords of Salem"

The Best of Rob Zombie (Geffen, 2006)
"Thunder Kiss '65" / "Black Sunshine" / "More Human Than Human" / "Super-Charger Heaven" / "Dragula" / "Superbeast" / "Living Dead Girl" / "Never Gonna Stop (The Red Red Groovy)" / "House of 1000 Corpses" / "Feel So Numb" / "The Devil's Rejects" / "The Lords of Salem"

Zombie Live (Geffen, 2007)
"Sawdust in the Blood" / "American Witch" / "Demon Speeding" / "Living Dead Girl" / "More Human than Human" / "Dead Girl Superstar" / "House of 1000 Corpses" / "Let It All Bleed Out" / "Creature of the Wheel" / "Demonoid Phenomenon" / "Super-Charger Heaven" / "Never Gonna Stop (The Red, Red Kroovy)" / "Black Sunshine" / "Superbeast" / "The Devil's Rejects" / "The Lords of Salem" / "Thunder Kiss '65" / "Dragula"

Hellbilly Deluxe 2 (Roadrunner, 2010)
"Jesus Frankenstein" / "Sick Bubblegum" / "What?" / "Mars Needs Women" / "Werewolf, Baby!" / "Virgin Witch" / "Death and Destiny Inside the Dream Factory" / "Burn" / "Cease to Exist" / "Werewolf Women of the SS" / "The Man Who Laughs"

Icon (Roadrunner, 2010)
"Superbeast" / "Dragula" / "Living Dead Girl" / "Feel So Numb" / "Never Gonna Stop (The Red, Red Kroovy)" / "Scum of the Earth" / "House of 1000 Corpses" / "Foxy Foxy" / "American Witch" / "The Devil's Rejects" / "What?" / "Mars Needs Women"

Mondo Sex Head (Geffen, 2012)
"Thunder Kiss '65" (JDevil "Number of the Beast" remix) / "Living Dead Girl" (Photek remix) / "Let It All Bleed Out" (Document One remix) / "Foxy Foxy" (Ki:Theory remix) / "More Human Than Human" (Big Black Delta remix) / "Dragula" (Crosses remix) / "Pussy Liquor" (Ki:Theory remix) / "The Lords of Salem" (Das Kapital remix) / "Never Gonna Stop" (Drumcorps remix) / "Superbeast" (Kraddy remix) / "Devil's Hole Girls" (Tobias Enhus remix featuring

the Jane Antonia Cornish String Quartet) / "Burn" (The Bloody Beetroots remix) / "Mars Needs Women" (Griffin Boice remix)

Venomous Rat Regeneration Vendor (Zodiac Swan, 2013)
"Teenage Nosferatu Pussy" / "Dead City Radio and the New Gods of Supertown" / "Revelation Revolution" / "Theme for the Rat Vendor" / "Ging Gang Gong De Do Gong De Laga Raga" / "Rock and Roll (in a Black Hole)" / "Behold, the Pretty Filthy Creatures!" / "White Trash Freaks" / "We're an American Band" / "Lucifer Rising" / "The Girl Who Loved the Monsters" / "Trade in Your Guns for a Coffin"

Spookshow International: Live (T-Boy, 2015)
"Teenage Nosferatu Pussy" / "Superbeast" / "Living Dead Girl" / "Dead City Radio" / "Drum Solo" / "More Human Than Human" / "Sick Bubblegum" / "House of 1000 Corpses" / "Meet the Creeper" / "Never Gonna Stop" / "Blitzkrieg Bop" / "Thunderkiss '65" / "Jesus Frankenstein" / "We're an American Band" / "Dragula" / "Demonoid Phenomenon" / "Pussy Liqour" / "Demon Speeding" / "Ging Gang Gong De Do Gong De Laga Raga"

ROB ZOMBIE SINGLES
"Dragula" (Geffen, 1998)
"Living Dead Girl" (Geffen, 1999)
"Superbeast" (Geffen, 1999)
"Scum of the Earth" (Geffen, 2000)
"Feel So Numb" (Geffen, 2001)
"Never Gonna Stop (the Red Red Kroovy)" (Geffen, 2001)
"Demon Speeding" (Geffen, 2002)
"Two-Lane Blacktop" (Geffen, 2003)

"Foxy Foxy" (Geffen, 2006)

"American Witch" (Geffen, 2006)

"Let It All Bleed Out" (Geffen, 2006)

"What?" (Roadrunner, 2009)

"Sick Bubblegum (Roadrunner, 2010)

"Dead City Radio and the New Gods of Super Town" (Zodiac Swan, 2013)

"We're An American Band" (Zodiac Swan, 2013)

ROB ZOMBIE FILMOGRAPHY

House of 1,000 Corpses (2003)

The Devil's Rejects (2005)

Halloween (2007)

Werewolf Women of the SS (2007)

Halloween 2 (2009)

The Haunted World of El Superbeasto (2009)

CSI: Miami season 8, episode 16 (2010)

Tom Papa: Live in New York City (2012)

The Lords of Salem (2013)

The Zombie Horror Picture Show (2014)

31 (2016)

ACKNOWLEDGMENTS

Thank you to Emma, Alice, Tom, Robin and Kate, Dad, John and Jen, Chris Akin, Scott Bartlett, Peter M. Bracke, Carlo Cavagna at AboutFilm.com, Max and Gloria Cavalera, Joe Daly, Helen Donlon, John Doran, Mark Eglinton, David Ellefson, Marty Friedman, Lisa Gallagher, Mick Garris at Post Mortem, David Hall and Russell Lee at EatMyBrains.com, Matthew Hamilton, Bill Irwin, Don Kaye at Fangoria, Michelle Kerr, Tina Korhonen, Borivoj Krgin, Neil Kulkarni, Peter Landau, Tim Louie at the *Aquarian*, Joe Matera, Michael Moses, Mike "McBeardo" McPadden, Bob Nalbandian, Henry Northmore at www.list.co.uk, Patrizia Pelgrift, Martin Popoff, Steven Rosen, Ralph Santolla, Tom Seabrook, Tony Spiess, Wes Stanton, David Stubbs, Russell A. Trunk at ExclusiveMagazine.com, Andreas Veneris, Jeremy Wagner, Mick Wall, Alex Webster, Marc Weidenbaum at Disquiet, Jon Wiederhorn at MTV, Chris Williams, Owen Williams at *Empire*, Staci Layne Wilson at *Girls and Corpses*, Sean Yseult, the editorial and marketing teams at Backbeat Books, the staff of Blaze Publishing and *Bass Guitar Magazine*, and the families Alderman, Arnold, Bhardwaj, Boot-Handford, Bowles, Cadette, Carr, Edwards, Fraser, Freed, Harrington, Herbert-Jones, Hogben, Jolliffe, Knight, Lamond, Lamont, Legerton, Leim, Mathieson Spires, Mendonça, Metcalfe, Miles, Parr, Skeens, Storey, and Woollard; the many fine writers who have reviewed my books in recent years; and of course the visitors to www.joelmciver.co.uk, www.facebook.com/joelmciver, and @joelmciver.

Interviews with Rob Zombie, Sean Yseult, John 5, Piggy D., Peter Landau, Zakk Wylde, Joey Jordison, and Mike "McBeardo" McPadden (www.mcbeardo.com) were conducted by the author between 2005 and 2015, except as indicated in the endnotes. Features by Peter M. Bracke, Carlo Cavagna at AboutFilm.com, Joe Daly at *Metal Hammer* and *Bass Guitar Magazine*, Mick Garris at *Post Mortem*, David Hall and Russell Lee at EatMyBrains.com, Don Kaye at *Fangoria*, Neil Kulkarni, Tim Louie at the *Aquarian*, Joe Matera, Michael Moses, Henry Northmore at www.list.co.uk, Steven Rosen, David Stubbs, Russell A. Trunk at ExclusiveMagazine.com, Andreas Veneris, Marc Weidenbaum at *Disquiet*, Jon Wiederhorn at MTV, Owen Williams at *Empire*, and Staci Layne Wilson at *Girls and Corpses* are quoted by kind permission of the authors.

INDEX